ONE WOMAN, ONE VOTE

ONE WOMAN, ONE VOTE

THE GENDER POLITICS OF SOUTH AFRICAN ELECTIONS

EDITED BY

Glenda Fick, Sheila Meintjes, Mary Simons

EISA

The Electoral Institute of Southern Africa

Electoral Institute of Southern Africa (EISA)
2nd Floor The Atrium
41 Stanley Avenue
Auckland Park
Johannesburg

ISBN 1 919814 42 6

First published 2002

EISA is a non-partisan organisation which seeks to promote democratic principles, free and fair elections, a strong civil society and good governance at all levels of Southern African society.

Typesetting and cover design by Sue Sandrock
Printed and bound by Creda Communications

CONTENTS

ACKNOWLEDGEMENTS

The editors are grateful to EISA for its support and for the rich debates generated by the gender reference group, co-ordinated and driven by Julie Ballington.

One Woman, One Vote has had a lengthy gestation period because of the multiple roles played by the contributors, all of whom are active in a wide range of spheres. We are grateful for the generous support and patient understanding of our funders.

We acknowledge the expertise of Pat Tucker in finalising the manuscript and the early contribution of Jörgen Elklit and Stephen Rule, who introduced all of us to the intricacies and diversity of electoral systems. Vicky da Silva ably assisted with the provision of information.

EISA and the authors thank the
Royal Norwegian Embassy for its generous
financial assistance, and the
Norwegian Institute for Human Rights
for its encouragement and support of this book.

FOREWORD

Between the elections of 1994 and 1999, the Electoral Institute of South Africa (now the Electoral Institute of Southern Africa) identified gender as a crucial variable in the politics of elections. EISA's research department, feeling it was imperative to explore this issue, drew together a reference group comprising myself as EISA's Director, staff in the research department, and gender researchers, academics and gender activists to act as a think tank to guide our research and evaluations in this field.

After regular debate and discussion we wrote up the outcome of our deliberations. Some of this work has been published in local journals and in EISA's Occasional Papers series. Members of the reference group have made presentations based on their research to the Parliamentary Portfolio Joint Monitoring Committee on the Quality of Life and Status of Women and have presented their findings at two conferences. The first, organised by EISA and held in Cape Town in 1998, was attended by international electoral experts, academics, and members of the South African Parliament and of political parties. At the second conference, held at the Commission on Gender Equality in February 1999, political parties engaged in a dialogue with EISA's reference group. EISA also participated in the Women'sNet Elections initiative.

As a result of these initiatives, the reference group believed it would be valuable to refine their ideas and present them in an edited collection that could be used by electoral policy makers, political parties, and academics. This book is the result. Its contribution is to bring together two themes – the nature of the struggles of women in liberation politics and a gender analysis of electoral politics in South Africa.

Dren Nupen
Executive Director
Electoral Institute of Southern Africa.

THE CONTRIBUTORS

CATHI ALBERTYN is Professor of Law and Director of the Centre for Applied Legal Studies at the University of the Witwatersrand. She has engaged in research and advocacy on a wide range of issues relating to women, the law, and human rights. She has previously been a technical advisor to the Constitutional Assembly on gender issues and a Commissioner with the Commission on Gender Equality. She was a member of the EISA gender reference group.

JULIE BALLINGTON worked at the Electoral Institute of Southern Africa (EISA) from 1998 to 2000. She was a researcher and manager of the EISA gender and elections reference group, and has written on the participation and representation of women in South African and southern African elections. Ms Ballington joined International IDEA based in Sweden in 2001 where she is manager of the Gender and Political Participation project. She holds a Master of Arts in Political Studies from the University of the Witwatersrand where she is presently a PhD candidate.

ALICE COETZEE is a freelance journalist and consultant. She was a regional co-ordinator with the Institute for a Democratic South Africa (Idasa) Pretoria from 1991 to 1994 when she joined local government as an ANC councillor and member of the executive committee of the Greater Pretoria Metropolitan Council responsible for Gender Equity and Economic Development. While in local government she served on the executive committee of the SA Local Government Association (Salga), and as chairperson of the Salga Gender Working Group. She left local government in 1999 and her work since has included editing the 1999 *Election Bulletin*, language editing the book *Angola's War Economy: The Role of Oil and Diamonds*, published by the Institute for Security Studies in 2000; and co-editing and writing for the Idasa publication *In the Balance?* published in March 2002.

GLENDA FICK is associate professor in the School of Law, University of the Witwatersrand where she teaches Constitutional Law and Persons and Family Law. From 1997 to 2000 she was consultant to EISA where her work included a gendered analysis of constitutional and legislative provisions in South Africa and other southern African countries. She was a member of the EISA gender reference group. In 2001, as gender justice adviser to the United Nations Fund for Women (UNIFEM) in New York she worked on issues of gender equality and constitutionalism in post conflict societies under UNIFEM'S programme of Women, Peace and Security. She is an editor of the *South African Journal on Human Rights*.

AMANDA GOUWS is Professor of Political Science at the University of Stellenbosch where she is one of the co-ordinators of the Gender Studies Programme and is also the chair of the Women's Forum of the university. Her research deals with women and citizenship and she has published on the National Machinery for Women. She holds a PhD from the University of Illinois at Champaign-Urbana, USA.

SHIREEN HASSIM lectures in Political Studies in the School of Social Sciences, University of the Witwatersrand. She has been working on a political history of the women's movement in South Africa (1980-1994) for a PhD thesis. She has published widely in the area of gender politics including *South Africa: A Country Gender Analysis* (co-authored with Sally Baden and Sheila Meintjes). She was a member of the gender and elections reference group co-ordinated by EISA and a member of the editorial group of *Election Bulletin* published by Women'sNet.

SHEILA MEINTJES is a senior lecturer in the Department of Political Studies at the University of the Witwatersrand where she teaches courses in political theory, women and feminist politics and theory, and African politics. She has been appointed to the Commission on Gender Equality as a commissioner. Her research is mainly focused on women and gender politics in South Africa, including violence against women. She was a member of the EISA gender reference group.

SUBETHRI NAIDOO, a gender activist, has a Masters Degree in Public and Development Management from the University of the Witwatersrand. She was a local government councillor during the interim phase of local government (1993/1994). From 1995 to 1997 she was senior manager at the Greater Pretoria Metropolitan Council and was gender co-ordinator of Salga. She is currently local government unit leader (democracy and governance team at US Agency for International Development (USAID).

MARY SIMONS is a senior lecture in the Department of Political Studies, University of Cape Town and has been a mediator and facilitator of labour and community disputes since the mid-1980s. She was a member of the EISA gender reference group and, in 2001, was a member of an advisory committee to the Minister of Provincial and Local Government. She was the Skelton Clark Visiting Fellow in the Department of Political Studies, Queens University, Canada in the fall and winter semesters of 2001/2002 and has been appointed as the Rivers Visiting Professor and a Visiting Graduate Faculty member at East Carolina University for the fall semester 2002.

INTRODUCTION

In a country with a universal franchise; a country in which no adult citizen is prevented from going to the polls, participating in a secret ballot, or changing political allegiance at will, why should an entire book be devoted to exploring the gendered nature of electoral politics? How does gender shape the form and character of the electoral process and representative democracy in South Africa? What does 'the politics of presence' mean for the diversity of South African women in politics?

In the chapters that follow we hope to answer some of those questions and to provide an understanding of the issues involved. We explore why the presence of women in politics is important, what the representation of women as a category means, and the strategies used not only to get women into politics but also to create mechanisms of accountability in political party contexts.

Representation is shaped by the choice of electoral system and, in turn, the choice shapes the form democracy takes both in terms of who is represented and how the interests of women and men in society are reflected in the governance of the country. This requires a focus on the gendered way in which political parties, which are at the heart of the electoral process and determine who becomes a representative, constitute the political domain.

Tremblay (2000, 339) points to the difference between descriptive studies of electoral politics and gender, and a more theoretical and analytical approach, noting that there has been a gap between theoretical and empirical work by feminist and gender specialists on the subject of gender and electoral politics.

Much of the theory in this arena is based upon the experience of well-entrenched democracies of the North. Feminist critiques of western political theory have pointed to what they call the 'androcentric'[1] norms of that theory, which have determined that citizenship and the sphere of the political are not universal as much as predicated upon a male subject. Thus the empirical work that looks at participation, representation, and electoral politics falls into the trap of assuming as its basic premise that what men do is the norm. Men's political behaviour is not constructed in political theory within a gendered framework, and remains unproblematised. Thus what men do and say is not analysed but is conceived as normative.

There is a growing body of literature describing the numbers of women in Parliament and their demographic background and discussing the social and political barriers to women's effective participation, both within the electorate and within political parties. The obstacles women face in Parliament are also documented (Karam 1998). This literature provides the basis for more analytical approaches that deepen our understanding of the gendered nature of politics. Phillips categorises arguments for increasing the numbers of women in legislative bodies as 'the politics of presence' (Phillips 1989). The mere presence of women in significant numbers may bring about a practical shift in terms of working conditions, such as the hours during which legislatures sit, an increase in women's amenities, and the availability of child care. These aspects, addresssed in chapter 1, can be described as the 'demasculinisation' of a patriarchal institution.

Electoral politics is often conceived as 'the normative space' for politics. Feminist interventions confront this and show that politics exists in a wider sphere that includes a range of actions embracing lobbying, litigation, research, information dissemination, demonstration, disruption, community action, community work, grassroots social movements, and institutional political pressure groups (Minkoff 1997, 481). Feminists go further, too, to suggest that the realm of intimacy and privacy, where gender power also operates, must be seen as part of the political more widely conceived.

The political is defined and conceived in different ways both within feminism and in the South African context. Opposition to the racially exclusive nature of white democracy legitimated a concept of politics as those activities that embraced protests, rallies, boycotts, illegal strikes, and criticism of the authorities. So, to suggest in the South African context that electoral politics defines the realm of conventional politics would be to erase from our understanding the true nature of political activity in the twentieth century. This insight sharpens our understanding of authoritarian politics in colonial contexts and the way in which the politics of exclusion operates in any context.

In this book we explore whether and how gender makes a difference to the way women participate in politics. We ask whether there is a gender gap? If we take the arguments of Shireen Hassim (chapter 5) and Amanda Gouws (chapter 6) together, the answer is that there is only a gender gap when political parties are forced to take up issues which are of concern only to women as women. The way women act and respond to political parties constitutes the gap. This does not mean that all women are in agreement and act in concert. Differences between women exist at every level – political, ideological, and cultural (Gouws also points to racial differences). And once issues have been taken into political party manifestos and mainstreamed, some men can become more supportive of 'women's issues' than many women. The case of abortion in South Africa is such an example. The results of a recent survey on attitudes to abortion showed that more men than women are in favour of abortion (Helen Suzman Foundation 2000). The explanation of women's opposition may be ascribed to the deep ideological value ascribed to motherhood in many conservative cultures. Thus gender gaps can take quite surprising forms.

In democratic societies, organisational mobilisation either outside or inside the electoral arena leads to a professionalisation through which political actors become experts. This contrasts with what might be called spontaneous political action and results in interests becoming institutionalised and, in the process, legitimised. However, as Minkoff suggests, 'Successful organisational mobilisation expands the boundaries of what are defined as legitimate constituencies' (Minkoff 1997, 478). Thus what might once have been conceived as 'unconventional' is transformed into a recognised and legitimate sphere of political engagement.

In societies governed by authoritarian forms of rule, such as South Africa under apartheid, or societies which have excluded women from participation and representation in politics, the spontaneous mobilisation and organisation of political activism is such a legitimate constituency. Outside the realm of political party organisation there has also been a professionalisation of politics, especially in the highly developed democracies of the West. In South Africa the emergence of a new democratic state has created new opportunities for political lobbying. Lobby politics requires a degree of expertise, and the consequence is the proliferation of organisations specialising in particular areas, taking up particular issues and interests.

The effect of this shift is to demobilise grassroots social movement activism. Apart from professional interests such as business, commerce, or law that are embedded in the political economy, other issues define what one might call interest politics – which may or may not be linked to 'identity politics'. These interests are reflected in issues such as HIV/Aids, reproductive rights, and violence against women. Many of these activities are tied to practical needs in civil society. The outcome is the institutionalisation of interests in ways that often define women's position in welfare terms with implications for the definition of women's citizenship and women's claims to substantive rights.

The ways in which women's diverse class, race, and other interests in the political arena are secured depends on the context in which they operate. In South Africa the context of democratisation and the end of apartheid provided an opportunity for women to make a difference.

In chapter 1 Sheila Meintjes and Mary Simons explore women's participation in politics in South Africa in a context of broader understandings of democracy. They consider a number of different theoretical understandings of the processes that incorporate women into politics and which, they argue, extended to all aspects of life and presented myriad sites of struggle for women under apartheid. They focus deliberately on the electoral aspects of democracy in order to reveal its gendered elements and highlight the processes and effects of the gendered nature of electoral politics in South Africa. They concentrate on the way in which civil society has determined how political parties take up issues. They approach the subject from an historical perspective and offer a number of general observations on the masculinist nature of 'conventional' politics and how feminists challenged it both prior to and during South Africa's transition to democracy.

Julie Ballington (chapter 4) documents the mechanisms that enabled women to become representatives and the importance of a critical mass of women in Parliament. She shows clearly how the ANC's commitment to a thirty per cent quota in favour of women has enhanced South Africa's standing internationally. The danger of quotas and separate representation for women, or indeed any group, is that such mechanisms can lead to the marginalisation of those representatives and the interests they represent.

At a national level, we have nearly reached the critical mass of thirty per cent. Shireen Hassim (chapter 5) suggests that once this critical mass is reached and dilutes the dominance of the hegemonic group, whether the hegemony is based on gender, colour or culture, arguments about the differences between men and women and between women and other women fall away because the mere presence of a significant proportion of women makes their participation in representative institutions more effective. In this view, affirmative action may be of no benefit unless the critical mass is reached. Therefore, in democracies, minority group protection and special seats for women may require over-representation. This has very real implications for the ways in which democracies are run and creates some ambivalence in relation to quotas. This ambivalence is reflected to some extent by Hassim, whose views contrast with Ballington's strong call for quotas

Part of South Africa's election story is the way in which constituencies organise and mobilise outside of political parties and how issues become legitimised and institutionalised so parties are forced to take them up. In South Africa the fact that a women's agenda was one of those forces distinguishes the country from any other in the world at this point. Political mobilisation in South Africa during the 1980s drew women into a host of political arenas. This generated a double burden for them because they also mobilised around a women's agenda which became an important space and opportunity for the development of women's independent political involvement, training, networking, knowledge and leadership. The separation of civil society mobilisation and political action from the sphere of political party politics introduces what Hassim has called the 'dual politics of representation'. Hassim is concerned with bringing out the distinction between women's participation in party politics and women's organisation in civil society. The expression the 'politics of dual representation' refers to the relationship between women representatives and the constituency of women. She points to a rupture between women's organisations and women in political parties which remains unexplained in the literature. In South Africa since 1994 there has been a relative demobilisation of women's movements the outcome of which has been a conflation of building constituencies and representing them.

Hassim believes the women's sections of political parties ought to articulate the interests of women supporters of the parties and ensure that these are addressed within party manifestos and platforms. So, if women electoral representatives are to succeed within a party they must work within it and draw in new party supporters. In effect, this is how women as a constituency mobilise within a party to promote their professional careers as politicians. The challenge they face is that as they become increasingly professional the link between civil society and women in political parties diminishes.

Academic writings have shown that the presence of women as electoral candidates and in legislative bodies is not enough to ensure either their effectiveness as representatives or the advancement of a women's agenda and gender equality. Indeed, in chapter 2 Cathi Albertyn, Shireen Hassim and Sheila Meintjes subject the whole framework of participation to critical enquiry. In the South African Parliament, from 1994 onwards, the pressure from women MPs to alter the daily schedule of sittings from evenings to daytime made a significant difference to the quality of women's participation. In other areas too women's interests have benefited from the presence of women's representatives in very substantial ways.

Albertyn et al suggest that the history of women's activism provided the context within which electoral politics could be defined in the new democratic post-apartheid period. Their chapter recognises the impetus women's activism in civil society gave to increasing and guaranteeing the access of women to the representative sphere. It examines the theoretical assumptions embedded in political theory that underpin the arguments for and against group representation for women. The authors argue that the problems of representative democracy for women stem from inequalities of women in civil society.

The authors discuss the way the gendered representative institutions of masculinist politics drew women in. Drawing on the experience of democratisation in South Africa, and the theoretical debates of northern scholars like Jane Mansbridge, Anne Phillips, Iris Marion Young, and Scandinavian scholars, they show how the introduction of a women's agenda provides a new understanding of the meaning of participation and representation in terms of engendering the state and the political system.

There is, of course, a very real question about the accountability of women representatives in party political contexts. Albertyn et al argue that the dilemma resides in the gender interests of women members of political parties and the broader social interests of women generally. Hassim also raises this question in chapter 5, where she points to the 'triple burden' of gender sensitive women MPs, who operate in a space of accountability which includes more than the normal double accountability – the party and the constituency to which they have been assigned. She asserts that women MPs have the added burden of accountability to the women's section of their party. Hassim suggests that women MPs have to be engaged in their own constituency.

In chapter 3 Glenda Fick discusses extensively the criteria which enable women to be effective political participants. Fick deals with broad theoretical issues of citizenship, defining a citizen as a person who is capable of being ruled and of ruling in turn. This suggests that for a person to be an effective political agent, she or he has to have full rights to citizenship. The importance of gender equity in this debate is to construe citizenship not merely as a formal category that carries a certain right – the vote. Every citizen has this right – and in the state's view every citizen can act within those parameters. But this concept ignores the significance of context, where rights can only be exercised if one has the means to do so. For a right to have substance, then, we cannot talk about citizenship in the abstract. The status of women, issues of substantive equality, and an absence of subordination and discrimination are thus material elements in determining whether or not women are equal citizens. Fick also deals with the stages of the electoral process, and the significance of the conditions under which the vote is cast. Although the political debate about citizenship has been muted, public demands for substantive rights suggest a lively understanding of what citizenship means. Claims for social and economic rights to health services, including activism around anti-retroviral drugs for pregnant women who are HIV positive, the demand for housing, the advocacy of state intervention to protect women from domestic violence, and protests against the high levels of crime, are all examples of citizens making claims about their expectations in terms of a bundle of rights from the state.

The discussion of the electoral system by Sheila Meintjes and Mary Simons in chapter 8 suggests that the type of electoral system holds no certain outcome for women. The authors examine the argument that proportional representation (PR) systems are better for women, questioning whether a PR system, more than any other factor, in fact explains the high representation of women in those countries where it exists. Or is the explanation rather that in such countries there is a greater commitment or willingness to allow diversity in representation? It is almost impossible to answer this question with any certainty. Other factors, including open or closed lists, positive measures such as quotas and economic empowerment, have been identified in the debates about women's representation. The commitment of political parties to gender equality appears to be key to this process. However, it seems justified to argue that parties will do little or nothing to promote gender equality unless they are pushed by women either through lobbies within the parties, or organisations outside them acting as an organised, coordinated political force.

In South Africa, the evidence suggests that political parties, their ideologies, their use or not of gender quotas, and their commitment to the recruitment and representation of women are the most important factors influencing the presence of women in politics. Presence, as is consistently argued in this book, and as others have argued elsewhere (Phillips1999; Tremblay 2000, 339-43), does not translate automatically into representation of the diversity of women's interests. Rather, the outcome of presence resides in the way the detail of elections unfolds, the commitment of the political parties to women's presence and participation, and the relationship between women's organisations and the political parties.

Addressing women as political participants and the gender gap in voting behaviour (chapter 6) Amanda Gouws uses the word 'unconventional' to refer both to women's political behaviour and to mass action. The objective of feminist politics and theory has been to force political science to recognise these behaviours and actions as political. To classify illegal strikes, boycotts, and rallies as 'unconventional political activities' is to ignore the specificity of the exclusionary nature of conventional politics in South Africa.

Gouws argues interestingly, however, that where men and women vote on the same issue, there will be no gender gap in voter patterns. This does not mean that gender interests do not exist. What we see is the emergence of a new acceptance of a specific gender interest as a general norm. This is what some feminists refer to as mainstreaming. Gouws, citing Sapiro and Conover, writes that 'the election context can make a gender gap appear or disappear, because the context cues gender relevance'. The argument is that gender cues influence the voting behaviour of gender conscious voters. Gouws suggests that while women participate in elections and help to put parties in power because of their party loyalty, they do not become mainstream representatives without some enabling mechanism, in spite of the fact that they are what she calls a captive audience. There is a gap between the level at which they participate as voters and at which they become representatives and another gap between the presence of women representatives and their effective participation in policy making. There is a third gap between participation in the legislature and appointment to executive positions.

In chapter 9 Alice Coetzee and Subethrie Naidoo consider the significance to women of local government. In the Constitution local government objectives are listed as democratic and accountable government for local communities, the provision of services in a sustainable manner, the promotion of social and economic development, the promotion of a safe and healthy environment, and the involvement of communities and community organisations in the matters of local government. All these objectives need to be achieved with limited financial resources. This level of governance refers to what the Local Government White Paper calls the 'developmental arm of the state'. In South Africa, the restructuring of local government essentially follows World Bank proposals, advocating the privatisation of services. This places burdens upon the poor and especially on women.

Coetzee and Naidoo suggest that since local government is the arena of development and local delivery, women should be involved in making decisions about what delivery should take place. The same arguments made for the representation of women at the national level can be made for representation at local level. The conventional argument is that women find it easier to participate in local level politics because it is closer to their domestic responsibilities. But in South Africa, even though their numbers have approached the critical mass, women have in fact been squeezed out of decision making at local level and have gained from the interventions of organisations and lobbies at national level. The cause of this disparity is a subject for debate. It is at the local government level – the site at which the political vision and economic realities converge most starkly – that we will be able to assess the success or failure of the new democracy.

Coetzee and Naidoo highlight the struggles for recognition of the gendered nature of local government. They document the relationship between governance and women's pressures both within the South African Local Government Assocation (Salga) and outside of it.

If citizens are to be able consciously to vote for party and representative in national or local elections a comprehensive voter education programme is required. In the context of South Africa, with its high levels of illiteracy and limited experience of democratic elections, two types of voter education are vital. The South African state has a responsibility to ensure that some form of civic education is undertaken, both in civil society, through programmes of voter education between elections, and in schools, in programmes of civic education. In chapter 7 Julie Ballington examines the need to encourage women's participation through voter education.

She believes women need to be equipped with the knowledge to ensure their full engagement in democratic and electoral processes, and to appreciate the force of their vote as a means of improving their position. Capacity building for women's participation in the electoral process needs to be accompanied by awareness raising initiatives to ensure that all women are aware of their rights, are encouraged to participate in political decision making, and are informed of the importance of voting for women and political parties that advocate gender equality. Until the electorate is politically aware, intimidation, gender stereotyping, and marginalisation may continue to cloud participation in the process.

NOTE

1. Male centred and male defined

1

WOMEN AND DEMOCRACY, WOMEN IN DEMOCRACY, GENDER AND DEMOCRACY

Sheila Meintjes and Mary Simons

The struggle for representation in the governance of South Africa occurred in a multitude of complex arenas. Politics was shaped as much by the nature and multiple sites of the struggle against apartheid as it was by the ruling class. The politics and practices of apartheid repression and its structural entrenchment of racial difference were primarily a response to political action and the turbulence of popular opposition from those excluded from citizenship. As in earlier periods the entrenchment of racial difference and the character of racial capital were primarily policies and practices of domination and control to ensure exclusion of all who were not white from the spheres of power – political, economic, social, cultural and sporting.

Popular action took the form of strikes, township protests, rural uprisings, transport and consumer boycotts, and defiance of pass laws and influx control. One of its characteristics was the radical way in which black and white opponents of apartheid and/or racial capitalism made common cause. The extent of the cross-race and cross-class alliances in the opposition movements fractured the hegemony of the racial ruling class. Central to the objectives of these struggles were claims for full democratic rights for all and for social justice. One part of the story of that struggle in the twentieth century was the active mobilisation and participation of black, coloured, Indian and white women in joint organisations, together fighting the oppression of segregation and apartheid. Gender analysis is largely absent from the histories of the South African liberation struggle.

Political activists are generally represented as genderless figures but are implicitly male. The gender and class dynamics within the struggle are silenced as a consequence. If gender difference were taken into account the fractures of class, rural/urban location, education and other variables would emerge more clearly.

The contributors to this book highlight, in a variety of ways, the processes and effects of the gendered nature of electoral politics in South Africa and argue for the integration of a gender perspective into every aspect of explicating the political. In doing so, we are able to see how different procedural aspects of democratic practice determine who is elected, how they are elected, and the possible effects this has on political power and decision-making.

In a country where class, race, ethnicity, culture, religion, and gender are recognised as having political salience, the complexity of trying to find a citizenship which incorporates everyone equally is obvious. Yet equally obvious is the fact that a universal category of 'citizen' masks extremes of wealth and poverty, and the marked inequitable access to resources and political power.

HISTORICAL DIMENSIONS OF MASCULINIST POLITICAL CULTURE

The fight for democracy in South Africa was very different from the struggles for universal suffrage in the early European and American movements. In South Africa, democratic struggles began with demands for the end of white colonial oppression and for the right of all people to enjoy political rights, freedom, and equality. Embedded in this demand was the call for an end to the migrant labour system and to urban segregation, and the right to own property, as well as for formal democratic rights such as the right to vote and to participate in politics. As early as the 1860s organisations emerged in different South African colonies to claim legal equality. A national coalition of regional organisations was created in 1909, the year before white settlers formed the Union of South Africa and took over its government under British rule. The South African Native National Congress was formed in 1912, hard on the heels of Union. Women did not play a role either among the rulers or among the ruled. South African women first asserted their political right to citizenship over the suffrage (white women) and against the pass laws (black women).

African women claimed recognition as important agents of change when they were among the first to challenge the right of the new white supremacist state to dictate to the oppressed. In 1913 women in Bloemfontein refused to carry passes and generated nation-wide support for their actions. Fearing national mobilisation on the issue, the state backed down, and did not try to impose passes again for another two decades (Walker 1982; Wells1993). It was only after the Second World War that the new Afrikaner National Party government, intent on pushing through its own social engineering – 'apartheid' – dared propose once more that African women carry passes. The anti-pass struggles of the 1950s have been widely covered, and will not be detailed here save to point out that the state's policies were framed by the context of popular struggle (Walker 1982; Wells 1993). The state did not concede the case, but its response to popular opposition was to develop its repressive capacity to contain that opposition. In this way, the state was party to maintaining the relevance both of women's organisation and the liberation movements, particularly after the movements were banned in the early 1960s.

In the 1990s, new categories of rights carrying individuals were constructed, in a non-discriminatory way, in order to create a South African citizenship that embraced all. The objective was 'to count every difference as no difference, as part of the seamless whole, but also to count every potentially subversive rejection of culturally enforced norms as themselves normal, as normalizable, and as normativizable through law' (Brown 1998, 460). Once a notion of non-discrimination is set up and the differences are specified, as they are in the South African Constitution, it both opens a space for protection and regulates the categories. Wendy Brown posits that 'the language of recognition becomes the language of unfreedom', and suggests that in the context of liberal discourse, this 'becomes a vehicle of subordination through individualization, normalization, and regulation, even as it strives to produce visibility and acceptance'(Brown 1998, 461).

Women's struggles during the previous twenty years had opened the space for their accommodation within politics. The constitution-making process threatened to become a male pacting exercise, as negotiating teams and the technical committees faced one another. Party and non-party women organised to trump this effort, and challenged the all-male teams. During the Convention for a Democratic South Africa (CODESA) process, public protest by women from across the political spectrum, reminiscent of the social movements of the 1980s, extracted concessions. Thenjiwe Mtintso saw these as 'toothless', but they altered the discourse around gender, and led to the presence of women in the second round of Multi-Party Negotiations (Albertyn 1994), and probably ensured that the parties would have to take the presence of women on party lists seriously. The ANC had earlier been challenged by its own members to enunciate its position on women's emancipation (2 May Document 1991), and the organisation was firm on its stance with respect to gender equality. However, this was an ongoing struggle, as evidenced by the debates within the ANC over the quota and over the electoral list. However far we have come in South Africa in integrating gender, gender equality remains an issue of struggle. Gains are not full victories, but are an outcome of compromise.

INSTITUTIONALISING POPULAR POLITICS IN SOUTH AFRICA: MOVEMENT TO PARTY, STREETS TO PARLIAMENT

In the transition to democracy, the opposition movements, in particular the African National Congress as the movement with the largest support in the country, shifted from extra-parliamentary politics to party political engagement. The shift meant that the movements – the ANC, the PAC and AZAPO had to become political parties whose main objective was to mobilise people for the vote The ANC had to persuade its members that it remained a 'movement of the people' while simultaneously repositioning itself as a political party. Politics assumed a new professionalism. The ANC took on a bureaucratised form, adopting the routine activities of political parties, such as keeping records, running a research unit, and maintaining links with constituents in branch offices. In the period of negotiations, branches were set up in townships and in suburbs. Monthly meetings were held at branch level. More widely, public rallies were held in a bid to encourage membership. This process of adjustment has been written about elsewhere (Rantete1996), but it is pertinent here to address the implications for political organisation and mobilisation. The opening up of democratic political competition during the negotiation period and in the run up to the 1994 election created opportunities for new modes of political association.

The question of what would happen to the former United Democratic Front (UDF) organisations which, since 1983, had mobilised internal opposition to apartheid, was widely debated. The issue of how civil society would relate to the political party was part of this debate. Eventually it was agreed that organisations of youth and women in townships should be taken over by the ANC. This resulted in the loss of the culture of independent intellectual debate and autonomy that had characterised the relationship between organisations in the UDF. The ANC, with its history of internal discipline (including military discipline and an army) and its role as a 'government in waiting', was more used to centralised decision making, a factor that created conflict between the two strands of practice as the jockeying for power in the newly constituted internal ANC took place. Exile leaders found the open and critical debate on all issues disconcerting and troubling. It threatened the certainties of a somewhat authoritarian style of respect for leaders and the binding nature of decisions from above.

The disbanding of the internal women's organisations had significant consequences for those who had participated in the anti-apartheid struggles of the 1980s. Many of the leaders of these organisations were township women – women from the trade unions, as well as women from the suburbs. Although they were organised in branches that reflected the lines of segregation, debate and decision-making about strategies were both centralised and collective. It was here that real understanding and non-racial practice developed across class and racial differences (Fester 1997). These traditions were contested in the period of party making in much the same way as they were in exile politics. But in the post-election period, as the exigencies of parliamentary party politics asserted themselves a new culture began to emerge within the governing party which reflected a more top-down approach. Grass roots participation became more difficult as the routines of governing absorbed the political parties. Party politics were reconfigured from participation to support as party functionaries become more professional. The distinction between politics as a career and politics as active commitment became sharper.

The party moved from a revolutionary agenda of the overthrow of apartheid to a vehicle to contain popular aspirations. O'Donnell argues cogently that a key feature of negotiated democratic transitions is a compromise between the demands of the majority and liberal reforms. The unemployed and the working class are required to delay the satisfaction of their demands in order to secure the negotiated transition.

In the women's movement, too, separate women's organisations like the Women's National Coalition (WNC) which was launched in 1992 became less important as political intervention required new forms of association which were more issue and policy based. Political ideology, while clearly determining which parties women should join, was cross-cut by specific questions about gender equality and gendering the political process.

The WNC lost most of its leaders to the political parties. The professional and academic researchers within the organisation returned to institutions in civil society. Indeed, the issues that became the stuff of campaigns were spearheaded by new NGO coalitions, like the HIV/AIDS consortia and the anti-violence-against-women networks.

Parliamentary politics was characterised by a process of adjustment by women to an institution embedded in western norms and models of behaviour. These were based on rules of combative debate, with hours that proximate those of a 'gentleman's club'. Sheila Camerer, National Party Member of Parliament, describes Parliament under apartheid as 'a quintessential boys club', with few facilities for women, and a male-oriented culture (CGE 1999). After the first democratic elections, women challenged many of these elements, including changing the working hours to accommodate family life, providing a crèche, and building new toilets. This did not necessarily alter the debating rules, but women challenged the dominance of male 'technical experts', and asserted the right of non-professionals to participate in Parliament. New MPs without a history of career politics entered domains that were traditionally the interest zones of men, such as finance, transport, and sports committees.

It took women some time to settle down in the new institutional environment. Support for the new members came from a host of national and international organisations which provided training and empowerment. For feminist activists inside Parliament, it was not enough merely to understand the culture and dynamics, they set about lobbying for a committee to evaluate legislation and policy to ensure the improvement of the quality of life and status of women. A supportive caucus did not serve this purpose, and once a committee was set up to deal with the broader substantive issues the caucus died. These important transformative innovations created a framework within which to address ongoing gender equity. They also allowed for women's increased participation in policy formulation. But they were less successful in changing the dominant mode of debate. This leaves the public with the impression that women are not participating in Parliament – and women's real contribution to the work of governance remains hidden.

REPRESENTATION AND THE DILEMMAS OF DIFFERENCE IN SOUTH AFRICA'S DEMOCRACY

In South Africa, the civil engagement of women in constructing the new constitutional framework is evident in a variety of interventions. Women were involved in the general struggles of trade unions and civic organisations against apartheid controls, but their participation in struggle also took specific gendered forms. In the 1950s and later, in the 1980s and 1990s, they organised in their own separate and autonomous organisations, forming separate bodies like the ANC Women's League (ANCWL) and the Federation of South African Women (FEDSAW), in order to express a collective will which required of the state a specific response.

Excluded from the political process, oppressed groups made themselves politically relevant by conscious mobilisation and action in the public realm. They forced a response and reaction from those with political power. Women, along with other excluded groups, adopted a range of strategies to influence state outcomes.

In the early1990s, for instance, when the failure of past states to build sufficient houses, coupled with the increased rate of urbanisation, led to a chronic housing shortage, and local authorities evicted residents for non-payment of rates, women in Soweto protested against the allocation of houses to women who were prepared to exchange sexual favours with officials. Their protest action took the form of land invasions. In response to the state's attempts to remove them from the land they stripped off their clothes in a symbolic act which resonated with their version of a sexual contract

(Meintjes 1996). Women's citizenship is structured around their identity as homemakers, mothers, and sexual beings. There are many symbolic identities embedded in the act of stripping. One of them is the shaming of the officials (men) who have stripped women of their right to land and shelter, preventing them from fulfilling their role as adult women. Just as the context of the time determined the shape of state action, so it shaped the nature of women's mobilisation, organisation, and strategies for change. A dominant theme in South African women's politics throughout the twentieth century was the mobilisation of women as mothers. It is important to emphasise that this was a call among nationalists and socialists, it was not an overriding theme of liberal women's politics in South Africa.

The patriarchal nature of some segments of South African society and its family institutions presents particular political challenges. In the context of a strong patriarchy an independent claim as mother is in itself radical. The socialist movement in South Africa shared this radicalism with the nationalists. In turn, South African socialism was heavily influenced by Soviet thinking about women's emancipation and motherhood as markers of women's identity. Appealing to and constructing the identity of motherhood did two things. It mobilised women for a broader political struggle but it also located them in a traditionally acceptable role. During every phase of the political struggle in South Africa men felt uncomfortable and threatened and were sometimes violently opposed to women's involvement. Rallying around motherhood made it easier for women to step into the political space, and harder for men to object.

One way of interpreting the emphasis on motherhood is in term of Elshtein's argument that a politics based on the values and practices of mothering would lead South Africa to a more ethical polity. Given that women and children constitute the poorest and most vulnerable in society, it is tempting to punt the idea of a new moral order based upon the idea of 'family values' if one were not aware of how these ideas have been abused in nationalist and socialist ideology.

This claim to enter political space as mothers posed problems for feminist theory. According to Mary Dietz the problems are twofold. Women cease to act on their own behalf, collapsing their interests into those of the family, and they fail to address the very real questions of gender oppression and 'the articulating of a political vision' which would flow from that understanding (in Phillips 1998, 11). In contrast, Susan Okin suggests that women are different from men, both in biological terms and in relation to politics. Their different relationship within politics and society to that of men and children makes them different. This is not to embrace essentialism, but to acknowledge the fact of gender differences. Jane Mansbridge argues that while there is the danger of essentialism, and in fact there is little difference between the sexes, the social elaboration and interpretation of those differences is considerable (Mansbridge 1999). The feminist debates of the 1980s over the issues of race and class difference shifted the focus from motherhood as an essential unifying factor to an acceptance of differences between women.

The 1970s and 1980s saw the emergence of small groups of white women who, influenced by western feminism, organised around issues of violence against women and engaged in feminist consciousness raising. This activity was not initially seen by anti-apartheid activists as 'political' until the state stepped in to ban the first women's movement magazine in the early 1970s. This action brought a women's agenda into the mainstream of white student anti-apartheid politics. Black women's activism in the same period was mobilised into the Black Consciousness Movement. But it was in the early 1980s that women's organisations were formed by an amalgam of women who came from different ideological homes. That decade brought together young activists and older women who had been involved in the earlier struggles of the 1950s. The context of a broader political struggle and movement gave salience to these groups and to their claims.

The broadening alliances of organisations across racial and class divides in South Africa brought disparate ideological perspectives and understandings of race and gender oppression and sexual orientation into joint action for the achievement of one aim – liberation from apartheid. The outcome was a continuing dialogue about what emancipation meant, about equality, and about difference. Perhaps equally important was the fact that the internal dynamics of the politics of non-racialism within South Africa also generated a dialogue about compromise and negotiation. The experience of working together for a common objective engendered new understanding and respect for difference. In particular, it was in this period that the articulation of a non-sexist future emerged in parallel with the idea of non-racism. For women, the outcome was a new discourse about non-sexism and the promise of liberation from male as well as from apartheid oppression.

Ironically it was apartheid that enabled women's groups to work through their differences in separate spheres, but also brought them together to negotiate a common position. This same process occurred in the trade union movement and the End Conscription Campaign. The sophisticated negotiation skills and conflict management required for leadership were honed in the struggle. In the most repressive times of the mid-1980s, layers of leadership were developed as people were arrested, detained, or fled the country. This resulted in continuity in the generational profile of the organisations in exile.

In the transition to democracy, women organised specifically to put equality on the agenda of constitutional change. The WNC's Charter reflects the demands articulated by grass roots women throughout South Africa during a wide-ranging consultative campaign and research process which drew in thousands of women countrywide. The campaign created awareness of a constituency of women, and forced political parties to take cognisance of the importance of women's issues. It also created a common understanding between women from different political parties about gender equality.

The Charter, drafted by a team of highly skilled academic researchers, including political scientists, social workers, and lawyers, is carefully crafted and structured to provide an agenda for policy makers and legislation to ensure substantive equality. It captures the demands, needs, and aspirations of a broad range of historically excluded people and a strong component meets the developmental needs of the poor. The Charter represents the terms and conditions under which women defined and entered the political terrain, and engaged the state. Although the WNC did not succeed in making the Charter an addendum to the Constitution, a fact that reflected some of the party political disagreements within the WNC itself, it remains the key to understanding how gender got onto the political agenda.

Political strategies to achieve this objective differed amongst the political parties. One possible strategy was the adoption of a quota. The theory and political practice of quotas as a tool for obtaining greater representation of women in representative bodies is examined in different chapters. In South Africa, the idea that the gender issue should translate into a women's quota for representation on party lists was espoused only by the ANC and even there, the demand was highly contested. Even in 1998, in preparation for the second democratic election, the Women's Development Foundation at its conference 'Women in Governance' failed to get an across-party agreement on quotas and the positioning of women on the party lists. Women in the ANC argued for a 50 per cent quota, the alternate positioning of men and women in a 'zebra-stripe' arrangement. This is unlikely to happen in the future unless there is significant mobilisation around the issue.

Political mobilisation, however, is not solely embedded within electoral or representative politics. In the aftermath of the first democratic elections, the anti-violence against women movement organised around the frightening incidence of public and private violence against women and children endemic in South African society. The campaign of marches and lobbying made it hard for either the media or the government to ignore the issue. The outcome was an alliance forged between certain government departments, namely the Departments of Justice, Health, and Social Welfare, and the non-governmental organisations working in the area of gender based violence. It was then taken up as a policy issue and pushed by the parliamentary joint committee on the quality of life and status of women (Meintjes 1999).

An interesting outcome of this alliance was not simply that it created a new understanding among men of how state and civil society could co-operate, but that it also generated new forms of organisation in civil society. Men began to mobilise against violence against women. In Alexandra, a township outside Johannesburg, a new force for change was identified in the work conducted by Agisanang Domestic Violence Training Project (ADAPT), an organisation working with violent men who had voluntarily come for counselling. In different parts of South Africa, a men's movement committed to gender equality is slowly emerging. Accompanying this is a growing body of research that explores the different forms of masculinity in Southern Africa (Morrell 2001). Whether this will lead to a shift in the culture of violence against women remains to be seen. It is also unclear whether organisation and mobilisation against gender based violence will translate into the political will on the part of Parliament to ensure an appropriate legislative framework other than the flawed Domestic Violence Act to deal with sexual offences.

ELECTORAL POLITICS: AN OPPORTUNITY FOR THE POLITICISATION OR DEPOLITICISATION OF WOMEN'S ISSUES?

In the aftermath of apartheid there was, largely as a result of the activism of the WNC, a period of policiticisation of women's human rights issues, as well as a focus on gender equality. However, in the period since the first elections the institutionalisation of parliamentary politics has completely altered the nature of politics in South Africa. The demise of popular political activism was accompanied by what has been called the professionalisation and 'NGO-isation' (Lang 1999) of politics – namely, the emergence of new organisations, issue-based NGOs frequently carved out of existing social movements and dependent upon donor funding for their existence.

Feminists and women's organisations have reacted differently to this process. Some view it as an appropriate development that makes organisations more focused and therefore more efficient. Others point to the erosion of the extensive network of co-operation that existed in the larger, more diffuse women's organisations and offered spaces for ordinary women, empowerment and opportunity. Still others have suggested that the fragmentation of the social movement and the absence of a presence of organised women is not unrelated to a backlash against women's issues and women themselves as well as to a rise in levels of violence in society. This in turn has led to a new awareness of the dangers inherent in a society that does not valorise women. Although the emergence of a men's movement opposing violence is a positive development, there is still a strong sense of men's privilege embedded in all aspects of social life in South Africa. This calls for the continued mobilisation of women, and other marginal groups, including the working class and the poor.

The context in which there has been a reaction against the gains made by women is explained as much by the impact of globalisation as by the strong patriarchal elements embedded in South African society. Women's mobilisation around their own issues during the campaign and life of the WNC brought to the fore the issues of women's rights to substantive equality. The Charter highlighted the nature of women's needs in the broadest terms, and provided an agenda for change. The significance of this campaign to put women's equality with men on the public agenda was to generate a broad consensus and consciousness in society, and especially amongst political leaders, of the importance of women's rights as human rights.

However, the institutionalisation of gender issues and the setting up of the mechanisms to ensure that women are integrated into all levels of government and governance have tended to ghettoise the issues. Parties are inclined to allocate responsibility for gender issues to women gender activists in the party and in government. Gender is translated into the idea that these are women's issues, and not men's. This is so whether one is talking about reproductive rights, which are about women's health and the right of women to control their own bodies, or about responsibility for caring for Aids sufferers. The burden of Aids is acknowledged to rest largely upon the shoulders of women. The fact that these issues are also the concern of men, and of society in general, has yet to filter into the public consciousness.

Thus a sense of the values embedded in gender identities, particularly the issue of what it means to be a woman in this society, remains to be problematised. The righteous anger that surfaces among women and is paralleled by the righteous anger of black people over race privilege, is linked to the promise of substantive equality and its lack of fulfilment. Not only does full equality elude women, worse, they are still seen as inferior and many retain an internal sense of inferiority. It is a truism that participation as an equal requires more than a formal shift to legal equality. In many ways the radical feminists were right, we have to rethink gender relations and gender power at the coalface of personal emancipation.

Institutions still constitute an enormous barrier to gender equality. Although they have proved capable of dealing with men of 'other' races and cultures, and even of different sexual orientation, unless women present themselves as being 'like men' and participate in politics in conventional terms, institutions are resistant to and unable to incorporate them. The incremental changes to parliamentary procedures have made inroads but they have not markedly changed attitudes. Women still need safe spaces in which to organise and empower themselves. The critical mass remains the key in institutions at all levels.

2

MAKING A DIFFERENCE? WOMEN'S STRUGGLES FOR PARTICIPATION AND REPRESENTATION

Cathi Albertyn, Shireen Hassim, Sheila Meintjes

Between 1990 and 1994 South Africans negotiated the establishment of a new democracy founded upon the principles of equality, freedom and human dignity. The 1993 Interim Constitution enshrined that early vision. One of the significant features of the new dispensation was the place it accorded to women, envisaging a society in which there would be equality between men and women and between people of all races. This was more than a formal idea of equality, it affirmed women as full and equal citizens. In the words of the then President, Nelson Mandela, South Africa would not be completely free until 'women have been emancipated from all forms of oppression' (Mandela 1994, 2). This is echoed in the Beijing Platform for Action:

> Women's equal participation in decision-making is not only a demand for simple justice or democracy but can also be seen as a necessary condition for women's interests to be taken into account. (Beijing Platform for Action 1995, para 181)

The constitutional inclusion of women at the heart of the new democracy was the result of long gender struggles both within and outside of the national liberation movements. When the representatives of the first Parliament of the 'rainbow nation' took their seats in May 1994, the fact that 109 of 400 (27%) members were women (placing South Africa seventh in the world) was widely seen as concrete evidence of women's place as full and equal citizens of the new democracy. Conventional wisdom in international gender documents was that the increased representation and participation of women in Parliament was not only 'a good thing', it would also have a positive impact on the gendered nature of the laws and policies of the country.

Why is women's greater representation so important? What are the political and theoretical arguments that underpin and justify the call for the equal representation of women in legislative bodies? Historically, women achieved the vote after men of their class in most countries of the West. This is significant, because it meant that women came into institutions that had already developed procedures and conventions that were literally 'man-made'. In South Africa, the move from a whites-only to a fully democratic political system, also saw a shift from a Westminster model of democratic representation which did not expressly include identity (race, gender, ethnicity) and which emphasised political parties. So how does the issue of women's representation fit into the debate? We bring two discourses together, one theoretical, the other historical, and locate our theoretical justifications for the continued and increased representation of women in South Africa within indigenous historically based concepts and practices of democracy and equality. This discussion gives greater weight to the ANC and the aligned United Democratic Front (UDF) because of their dominance in the struggle against apartheid, and the leading role played by the women's sections of both organisations.

Finally, we ask whether the increased presence of women in the legislature makes a difference to the institution and its work. Should we continue to find ways to maintain and increase the representation of women in our legislatures? We conclude that the representation of women is not only politically and theoretically justifiable, but that the evidence available about the working of Parliament after 1994 suggests that a more representative parliament is a more effective institution. We note some of the challenges that face women in Parliament in the new millennium and conclude that any changes to the electoral system must promote the continued representation of women.

THE POLITICAL CONTEXT

In South Africa, the achievement of women's greater representation is directly linked to the electoral system. Many would argue that South Africa's system of proportional representation based on national lists with a 30 per cent quota for women on the list of the majority party, the ANC, is tailor-made for enhancing the representation of women (Matland 1998). However, the principles and technical rules of this electoral system emerged from a wider set of political conditions in which there was no simple relationship between a political claim for women's equal representation and the principles and rules (in law or in political party constitutions) that guaranteed this. Indeed, gender was not a consideration in the actual choice and design of the electoral system, but was initially inserted at a party political level.

The entry of a significant number of women into Parliament in the post-1994 period was the result of a dual trajectory of political and gender struggles. While the political struggles generated the key principles and rules of the new democracy, gender struggles within the ANC alliance, and more widely, meant that women were able to ensure that the system of proportional representation would work to their benefit. In particular, the broad and inclusive understanding of democracy that emerged from the struggles against apartheid provided an enabling environment for the entrenchment of gender equality in the new democratic order.

South Africa's new democracy is rooted in the struggle against racial exclusion, dispossession and oppression framed (at least from the 1950s) by the principles of inclusion, equality and non-racialism. The 1955 Freedom Charter stated that:

> South Africa belongs to all who live in it, black and white, and ... no government can justly claim authority unless it is based on the will of the people. Every man and woman shall have the right to vote for and stand as a candidate for all bodies which make laws.

During the 1980s, when still in exile, the ANC publicly stated its support for 'genuine negotiations ... aimed at the transformation of our country into a united and non-racial democracy' (ANC 1987). It was only when the ANC was unbanned after 1990 that these principles of negotiation and transformation were developed into policy.

A broad consensus on the principles of liberal democratic representation was apparent in the 1991 Declaration of Intent of the first Convention for a Democratic South Africa (CODESA I) which stated that South Africa would be:

> A united democratic non-racial and non-sexist state in which sovereign authority is exercised over the whole of its territory. A multi-party democracy with the right to form and join political parties and with regular elections on the basis of a universal adult suffrage on a common voters roll; in general the basic electoral system will be that of Proportional Representation.

The Declaration of Intent was signed by all the major players. Only the apartheid bantustan, Bophutatswana, eventually refused to sign. Within the ANC the internal debates crystallised in a policy document, the 1992 'Policy Guidelines for a Democratic South Africa', that committed the ANC to an inclusive, accountable, and participatory multi-party democracy, with periodic elections, and an electoral system based on proportional representation (PR). The Westminster system of constituencies was to be replaced by PR, with representatives chosen by the party, according to national and regional party lists, which were to be compiled with due sensitivity to gender.

In the Working Group of CODESA responsible for crafting the constitutional principles of the new democracy the idea of democratic representation and the nature of the electoral system were not disputed. However, the Working Group deadlocked over the balance between national, regional, and local government, and the participation of political minorities in a future constitution. A PR system had particular benefits for all parties. The fact that proportional representation provided more accurate representative support for smaller national parties (that could be disadvantaged by a constituency system) meant it obtained the support of other key players, including the National Party (NP), the South African government, and the small but vociferous Democratic Party (DP). For the ANC, a system of proportional representation based on a national list system would mitigate against regionally based ethnic mobilisation and would provide fair representation for the purpose of a Constituent Assembly that was to draft the final Constitution. The Inkatha Freedom Party (IFP), with its regional power base, was the only party to oppose PR based on national lists.

However, underlying the agreement on PR were very different political and philosophical assumptions about the nature of democracy. The South African government and the National Party had demonstrated a significant shift from a racially based franchise to one-person-one-vote, but sought this within a democracy that provided strong guarantees for the participation and representation of political minorities, rather than disadvantaged groups. The Democratic Party located its support for PR within a more traditionally liberal understanding of democracy that allowed few limitations on individual political freedom and would not tolerate any form of mechanisms to enhance group participation. In this context the DP would continually reject the notion of a quota. The IFP was concerned with the establishment of democracy based on a federal system with strong regional autonomy. The ANC and its negotiating allies located the electoral system within a broad understanding of a participatory, inclusive, and accountable democracy that drew its inspiration from decades of struggles against oppression and exclusion.

The broad and substantive understanding of democracy created the enabling framework for women to make a range of claims for gender equality. It also gave space to the idea of gender representation and eventually allowed women to assert their claims for inclusion by providing for a 30 per cent quota of women on the party lists.

WOMEN AND POLITICAL PARTICIPATION

Women's struggle for political participation and representation took place, for different groups of women, at different historical moments. Cherryl Walker's germinal study, *Women and Resistance in South Africa*, was the first to chart the contours of the political demands of different groups of South African women for civil rights and equality with men. She examined the racial dynamics of women's claims to political participation in the first half of the twentieth century.

A significant moment for women, as Walker's study shows, was the first congress in 1955 of the Federation of South African Women (FSAW), a broad front of women's organisations formed in 1953 to improve the conditions under which women lived in South Africa. In its 1954 'Women's Charter', the FSAW established the principle of full equality with men and challenged gender stereotypes. The Charter's claims for full equality were spelled out in the following terms:

> As women there rests upon us also the burden of removing from our society all the social differences developed in past times between men and women, which have the effect of keeping our sex in a position of inferiority and subordination.
>
> We shall teach the men that they cannot hope to liberate themselves from the evils of discrimination and prejudice as long as they fail to extend to women complete and unqualified equality in law and in practice. (Quoted in Walker 1982, 280-81)

This double focus on the representation of women and the demands for equality remained a theme within the coalition of organisations which fought against apartheid, both in exile and internally, during the following decades and in very different contexts.

During the struggles against apartheid, women found both integrative and independent strategies to ensure the inclusion of their demands. The specificity of the historical context makes it important to understand how these demands were made, and with what effect. During the 1950s, demonstrations against pass laws and the introduction of Bantu Education spurred nation wide protests and demonstrations. The FSAW played a leading role in these protests, the most famous of which was the march of 20 000 women to the Union Buildings on 9 August 1956. Twenty years before the women's movement emerged in the West, South African women saw clearly the duality of their struggle and politicised their gender claims. The FSAW articulated women's demands in both the 'Women's Charter' and a document entitled 'What Women Demand', compiled in preparation for the Congress of the People in 1955 (Walker 1982, 279 and 285). The demands were framed in terms of women's needs to maintain the integrity of family life. There was a very clear understanding, too, that women were more than housewives and mothers, that they were also workers and political agents. Significantly demands ranged from political representation (the right to vote and 'to be elected to all State, Provincial or Municipal bodies') (quoted in Walker 1982, 287) to the specific needs of women, and to elements which would improve the lives of their children and their communities. They specified the need for maternity leave, clinics, welfare centres, day nurseries, and birth control clinics, claimed their rights as citizens, and argued that the law needed to be changed, in line with social changes in the position of women:

> The law has become an obstacle to progress of the women, and therefore a brake on the whole of society.
>
> This intolerable condition would not be allowed to continue were it not for the refusal of a large section of our menfolk to concede to us women the rights and privileges which they demand for themselves.
>
> We shall teach the men that they cannot hope to liberate themselves from the evils of discrimination and prejudice as long as they fail to extend to women complete and unqualified equality in law and in practice. (Walker 1982, 281)

The rebirth of political activism from the 1970s onwards resuscitated the Freedom Charter. Women's organisations drew links to the Charter to press for demands framed in the context of a world in which feminist consciousness had made a mark. Within the popular struggles of the 1980s, however, a new conception of grass roots participatory politics and the notion of 'organs of people's power' emerged to create a new democratic framework for liberation. In this context, the nature of women's engagement in liberation politics was an important mobilising force, and broadened the scope and understanding of the meaning of democracy. Women's organisations continued to articulate the problems of domestic subordination as a political issue to be addressed within mainstream politics. At political rallies, for instance, they refused to play the role of 'chief cook and bottle-washer'. In exile, debates unfolded in the ANC about the need to end women's subordination. The suggestion that women's concerns were merely social ones, related to their role as carers, was vociferously rejected. Instead, women deftly inserted the issues of subordination into mainstream debates and argued that women's issues were political. This was the battle that took place at the 1985 UN Women's Decade Nairobi Conference (Daniels 1992, 21). These debates were aired also in the ANC Women's Section.

In 1985, Oliver Tambo, President of the ANC, made a joint pledge with Sam Nujoma, the South West African People's Organisation Namibian president that they 'would not consider our objectives achieved, our task completed or our struggle at an end until the women of South Africa and Namibia are fully liberated' (Westcott 1990, 4). This echoed the views of other liberation movements, such as Frelimo, whose leader, Samora Machel, as early as 1973, said 'The liberation of women is a fundamental necessity of the revolution'. Yet the official ANC line when South African women met at the Nairobi Conference in 1985 was that the issue of women's emancipation was viewed as secondary to that of national liberation. This belied the very real contest occurring within the ANC about the need for a strong commitment to women's emancipation and the need for women to organise autonomously. In 1987 the ANC resolved to set up a national commission on women, the task of which was to monitor gender issues, ensure women's representation, and implement affirmative action.

The demands of women were expressed in terms both of national liberation and of everyday life concerns. But there was a tension in this dyad. Women's participation in anti-apartheid struggles, such as the schools boycotts in the 1970s, and in the consumer boycotts in support of trade union demands, were significant (Meintjes 1998, 72). Within the country women organised autonomously in order to pursue their separate interests. At the same time, though, they participated in the broad front formed in 1983 through the UDF. But the 1980s struggles also imbued women with a much stronger sense of their independent identities as women, with specific and different needs from men. The struggle to have women's emancipation seen as a crucial aspect of national liberation was not entirely successful.

In January 1990, the Women's Section of the ANC held the Malibongwe Conference in Amsterdam, meeting with internal women's organisations to address the role of women in national liberation. There was extensive discussion of the place of women and the relationship of gender politics and national liberation politics (Singh 1990, 23). The absence of women's leadership and participation was pinpointed as part of the specificity of women's oppression and as an obstacle to the development of non-sexist policies.

In May 1990 the National Executive Committee of the ANC declared its commitment to the equality of women, and recognised that patriarchy inhibited the acceptance and development of women's leadership. In a statement the NEC said 'Patterns of discrimination and inequality are not self-correcting ... To break this cycle we need to take affirmative action within the ANC ... Women's right to democratic participation in all decision-making must be there in principle and in practice' (ANC NEC 1990). Women were urged to take the lead in driving the process of 'creating a non-sexist South Africa'. In the same year the ANC Women's League (ANCWL) was relaunched in South Africa. The context, however, is important to recall. The country was in the throes of nation-wide violence, and there was a virtual state of war in Natal. In this situation, the ANC-South African Communist Party (SACP)-Congress of South African Trade Unions (COSATU) alliance had difficulty in finding a coherent political strategy to balance the relationship between popular participation in politics and mass struggle against apartheid. This made it very difficult for the ANC to organise itself into a political movement despite the support of the former UDF structures. Thus women's participation and a women's agenda were not seen as priorities by the ANC. The ANCWL received little more that rhetorical support from the movement, and was in fact starved of resources to develop its own organisational capacity (Meintjes1990, 15-16).

After the December 1990 Consultative Conference, in preparation for the July 1991 National Conference of the ANC, the ANCWL proposed a 30 per cent quota for women in the NEC as one mechanism for enhancing women's leadership.

Thereafter, there was a much more careful assessment of the problems of 'patriarchal dominance' as the process of ensuring that a woman's agenda emerged in national politics ensued. The notion of a coalition of diverse interests to influence a gender sensitive constitution making process came to be seen as the only way that a shift could be effected. The combined pressure of women inside the ANC, and women from trade unions, from other political parties, and from diverse women's organisations in civil society became a practical and feasible option. Inside the ANC, the Emancipation Commission's Deputy Chairperson, Frene Ginwala, and the ANC Women's League spearheaded the process of calling a conference to form a Women's National Coalition as part of the strategy to ensure the inclusion of women's interests in the negotiated constitution making process. An initial meeting was held in September1991.

The ANCWL was not alone in pursuing an agenda which would open space for a sexually inclusive citizenship. The Democratic Party had within its ranks a few strong voices pushing for equality, notably Dene Smuts, Carole Charlewood, and Gill Noero. In the National Party, Sheila Camerer had also taken up the cudgels for gender equality. The IFP had within its ranks, also, the Inkatha Women's Brigade, which ensured that women were included within the negotiating teams at the Conference for a Democratic South Africa (CODESA). These voices were significant in pushing for gender equality, and women's representation, in the constitutional negotiations. Voices from civil society, such as the Women's Legal Rights Committee (which later formed part of the Women's Lobby), spearheaded by Babette Kabak and Doris Ravenhill, were indefatigable, too, in their pursuit of ensuring a profile for women in politics.[1]

The ANCWL made separate representations to CODESA on the principles of non-sexism and equality, and commented in detail from a gender perspective on its terms of reference. The ANCWL objected to the fact that so few women were part of the CODESA working groups, and argued that women should 'participate in the political process and [be] part of drawing up a new constitution'. In collaboration, women from the ANC, DP, and NP called for the establishment of a gender advisory committee which would review all documentation produced by the different working groups (*WIP* 1992, 81:16). This was indeed set up, but very shortly thereafter the talks broke down.

The Women's National Coalition articulated its mandate in two ways. The first was to draw up a Women's Charter which formulated and reflected the socio-economic and political needs of the diversity of women in South

Africa in the 1990s. The second and equally significant mandate was expressed by Frene Ginwala at the first meeting of the WNC, 'Women must start thinking about getting women into the constituent assembly or whatever final constitution-making body is agreed. If we elect a body dominated by patriarchal men then all our efforts will be in vain' (Meintjes 1992, 17). The representation of women by women in political life was seen as a significant element in ensuring that women's interests would be taken seriously. The WNC was an important vehicle for engaging the debate about gender equality and the needs of women in a new democratic dispensation through its campaign for a Women's Charter.

But discussion and debate about how women should engage in politics and in elections came from many sources, not simply the WNC. Towards the end of 1992, in its journal *Democracy in Action*, the Institute for a Democratic Alternative for South Africa (IDASA) focused on the significance of elections for the democratic process. In order to engender debate on questions of women's representation in governance, IDASA, with a steering committee of Durban-based gender activists, hosted a workshop in Natal in December 1992. This workshop was the first to raise debate about the need for a multi-pronged approach to the issue of women's political participation and representation in government and Parliament. Comparative experience was also drawn into the debate, when women from the Philippines, and from Uganda, Sierra Leone, Bangladesh, and Zimbabwe participated in the discussions. Their experiences showed that women were often sidelined in the electoral process. They believed one of the reasons for this was that women's issues tended to be seen in terms of 'development'. Paradoxically, although development was at the core of any country's economic health, political parties tended to de-politicise the issue during elections effectively removing from the electoral gender many issues at the heart of women's concerns.

During the second round of talks, which produced an Interim Constitution, an electoral system was agreed upon and by mid-1993, the issue of elections was firmly on the agenda and voter education and training programmes for elections were being set up. By this time the WNC had created a significant space for women's concerns to be debated nationally. In May 1993, the WNC held an international conference in Johannesburg to debate issues raised earlier in Durban. In particular, at issue was the kind of government machinery which could most effectively allow for an improvement in the gender sensitivity of government. At this conference the notion of a 'package' of institutional mechanisms first mooted at the IDASA workshop was finally accepted as a strategy to improve the status of women in the new democracy.

The WNC, in collaboration with the Voter Education and Elections Training Unit (VEETU) set up by the Kagiso Trust, argued that the participation of women in voting was important, since they constituted 53 per cent of the electorate in South Africa (Cullinan 1993, 23). The pressure exerted by women inside and outside the Negotiating Council ensured that a special clause dealing with the role of women was added to the Electoral Code of Conduct. This clause attempted to protect the independent participation of women in the political process. Equality was to be the hallmark of this participation. Women were to be given free access to all public political meetings, facilities, and venues. Women's right to communicate with political parties and organisations was to be respected. Finally, parties were required to refrain 'from forcing women to adopt a particular political position or to engage in, or refrain from engaging in, political activity' (*Negotiation News* 13 1993, 16).

Inside the largest political party in South Africa, the ANC, the quota quietly found its way into the drawing up of the party lists for the 1994 elections, testimony to the extent to which the issue of equality and the quota debates at a national level had influenced at least the leadership of the party.

REPRESENTATION

One of the dilemmas for democrats is that representative democracy may be procedurally fair, but need not translate into participatory, substantive democracy for all citizens. Women, for instance, who form the majority of voters, are under represented in most legislatures. So although representative democracy in theory offers the opportunity for citizens to select and remove from office their chosen representatives, in practice it neither provides all citizens with representatives with whom they can identify, nor with proper accountability (Hirst 1990, 2). Free and fair elections do not necessarily reflect the diversity of interests and identities in society.

In South Africa, two broad approaches to the problem of women's representation are discernible. The first focuses on social and economic inequalities as an explanation for women's exclusion from the public political sphere, and rejects tampering with conventional electoral procedures as a solution to the absence of women. The second radically questions the institutional underpinnings of representative democracy, and argues for special mechanisms to ensure representation of women. The first reflects the liberal position adopted by the Inkatha Freedom Party and the Democratic Alliance, and, paradoxically, by the more radically Africanist Pan Africanist Congress. The second, adopted by the ANC, views democracy from a substantive position and supports the creation of special mechanisms within the party to increase the numbers of women representatives, despite divisions within its constituency.

The liberal perspective sees the issue of under-representation in procedural and individualistic terms, as reflecting social and economic inequalities (Williams 1998, 4). In this view, neither the political institutions nor the electoral system is at fault. For liberals, the solution to these socio-economic problems lies in developmental opportunities for excluded groups. Liberals oppose special electoral mechanisms to enhance the political representation of disadvantaged groups. Such mechanisms might impinge on the individual choice and freedom that are the hallmarks of liberalism.

Radical opposition to institutional reform for excluded groups bases its argument on the dangers inherent in promoting group representation as against popular democracy. Representation on the basis of identity, that is the representivity of groups, could lead to elite manipulation and undermine the accountability of party leaders to party members. The radical critique often goes further, to suggest that representative democracy is, in itself, flawed. Paul Hirst argues that 'Modern representative democracy has predominantly functioned as a means of legitimating governmental power, rather than of making government effectively accountable and open to public influence... While mass democracy gives the electorate a real power to choose some of the major ruling personnel, it also routinizes and minimizes political participation' (Hirst 1990, 3-4). This would suggest that the nature of representation – in particular the relationship between electoral constituencies and representatives – needs to be examined at least as closely as the right to representation per se. In South Africa, at a workshop on women in democratic government held in 1992, delegates grappled with 'exactly whose interests they would represent if they were elected to parliament' (Schefer 1992). The dilemma of 'dual representation' is explored in greater detail in Chapter 5.

Social democrats argue that special electoral mechanisms are useful in levelling the inequalities and historical exclusion of certain groups (Williams 1998, 3). This was the position adopted by the ANC in relation to a women's quota. A third influence is the gendered analysis of institutions which, in similar vein to Williams, argues that institutions are not separate from their outcomes. As Goetz contends:

> Understanding institutions as historically constructed frameworks for behavioural rules and as generators of experience contributes to understanding why it is that when new agents (such as women) and orientations (such as gender equity) are introduced to institutions outcomes can be so little changed. Institutional rules, structures, practices and the identities of the agents which animate them may continue primarily to serve the political and social interests which interests were designed to promote in the first place. (Goetz 1998, 6)

All these perspectives raise three broad questions. First, should there be affirmative action to break through historical inequalities? Secondly, what are appropriate mechanisms of accountability in identity politics, as in the case of women, where a range of intersecting interests, such as race, class, ethnicity and age, for instance, come into play? Finally, if as Goetz suggests, the under-representation of women is not merely an unintended consequence of institutional practices, then is the demand for parliamentary representation not merely reproducing a limited equality and democracy?

FEMINIST ARGUMENTS FOR AND AGAINST GROUP REPRESENTATION

Several arguments raised in feminist debates highlight the value of better and more representation of women. However, there are considerable differences in the extent to which feminists are prepared to support formal institutional mechanisms to 'unblock' women's access to representation. The five arguments outlined below, although not necessarily categorically distinct, enable us to clarify the different implications of foundational claims. It is also worth noting that we deal here with arguments *within* democratic theory and politics; arguments do exist for special representation of women in undemocratic political systems (e.g. under military regimes in Nigeria, women's special representation was promoted as a political strategy). All five arguments posit mechanisms to increase women's representation as a group in democratic politics. Fundamental to all is that the presence of women in legislatures in proportionate numbers is a necessary, if not sufficient condition for the raising of gender awareness.

The first argument is based on the legitimacy of democracies. Jane Mansbridge argues that descriptive, or 'mirror', representation (women representing women) is desirable in representative democracies because 'democratic deliberation and aggregation are most legitimate when political interests are represented in the decision-making assembly in proportion to their representation among the population' (Mansbridge 1999, 2). Mansbridge's argument is similar to Dahlerup's critical mass argument in the Scandinavian context, where a thirty per cent presence in national legislatures is seen as the key to the effective representation of women because the greater the number of women in politics, the greater the likelihood that issues of gender inequalities will be raised and dealt with in policy terms. Mansbridge, however, is concerned about the legitimacy of representative democracy, rather than merely the effectiveness of particular group interests, or of fairness (Williams). Mansbridge argues that the deliberative functions of a democracy – 'understanding which policies are good for the polity as a whole, which policies are good for a representative's constituents, and when the interests of various groups within the polity and constituency conflict' demand a fully representative legislative body (Mansbridge 1999, 4).

The second argument is based on justice, on the notion that the exclusion (or absence) of women from political activities is unfair and discriminatory. Williams, for example, emphasises that the distinctive quality of democracies is the extent to which there is fair representation of citizen's interests and identities. This argument does not necessarily imply that the content of politics will change substantially as a result of women's greater participation. Anne Phillips argues that justice-based claims can be made independent of outcome claims in radical liberal versions of democracy (Phillips 1989). However, this conclusion is certainly supported by some justice-based theorists such as Williams.

The third argument, stemming from the 'ethics of care school', suggests that women bring a different set of values, experiences and expertise to politics. These values are the result of biology (women are inherently nurturing) or in a social-relational context (women's roles in society, mainly their caring and reproductive tasks, result in a different set of concerns and style of politics from that of men). In either case, it is argued that women's greater involvement will change the content of politics (Meehan and Sevenhuijsen 1991).

The fourth argument originates from a notion that the interests of men and women are different, and often in conflict and therefore men cannot represent the interests of women. Although Iris Marion Young bases her argument within a frame of justice, her call for a policy veto for particular groups places her within this category (Young 1990). In this case, it is argued that women's greater involvement will change the content of politics.

A fifth, more pragmatic, approach agrees that the mere presence of women does not necessarily translate into the representation of women's interests, but nevertheless argues that it increases the probability that gender equality concerns will be addressed. Some of the women elected will have the ability (or even inclination) to address gender, but the cumulative effect of their presence will affect Parliament.

This argument is the most likely to be effective in South Africa as it makes no normative judgements about fairness, or essentialist arguments about women's difference. Rather, it is an argument posed at the most general and pragmatic level and is relatively detached from assumptions about what kinds of policies are best for women, or what kinds of substantive changes are needed to empower women. For this reason, it is an argument that can be made within any political party or NGO, regardless of its particular ideological direction. The substantive content of the roles of women representatives in Parliament then becomes a matter of political (and electoral) contest, not just between political parties but between women.

SPECIAL MECHANISMS FOR INCREASING WOMEN'S REPRESENTATION

The most significant differences between feminists relate to the manner in which women's representation should be advanced. For Mansbridge, fixed formal mechanisms such as affirmative action quotas carry their own particular dangers. 'They assume, for example, that any "woman" can stand for all "women", and "Black" for all "Blacks". They do not respond well to constituents' many sided and cross-cutting interests' (Mansbridge 1999, 21). Her solution is that there should be more fluid mechanisms, although it is not clear how effective these would be. Mansbridge offers a continuum of least fluid to most fluid forms of institutionalising what she calls 'descriptive representation'. These are quotas in constitutions, in law, in party constitutions and in majority-minority districts; quotas in party decisions, proportional representation and cumulative voting. Most fluid are a number of enabling devices, such as schools and funding for potential candidates, limits to, or public funding of nomination campaign expenses, formal search committees within parties to identify potential candidates from excluded or disadvantaged groups, scholarships for such groups, and daycare facilities for elected representatives (Mansbridge 1999, 21). None of these strategies is mutually exclusive, and in South Africa several of them already co-exist.

Iris Marion Young goes much further in her proposal for increasing the extent and effectiveness of women's representation, arguing that marginalised groups should have special representation, including veto power over decisions that affect them. Young is not concerned with representation in itself, but with the extent to which representation can facilitate interest articulation of oppressed groups, that is, qualitative representation. She argues that while privileged groups can rely on access to decision-making processes, oppressed groups are disadvantaged. Thus institutional mechanisms and public resources should support their collective organisation and self reflection, provide obligatory mechanisms for their participation in drawing up public policies, and institute veto powers on issues that affect them directly, such as reproductive rights for women (Young 1989, 261-2).

While Young's proposals about mechanisms for aggregating group interests have been well received, her proposal for a group veto is seen to be antithetical to liberal representative democracy. In South Africa, some corporatist mechanisms do exist for decision-making. The most notable is the National Economic Development and Labour Council (NEDLAC). This council has four chambers – government, business, labour and development – that can initiate public policy, and discusses legislative and policy initiatives emanating from the state. While NEDLAC does not give the non-state actors (primarily labour and capital) the power of veto, it does impose consultative processes and consensual politics in key areas of decision-making. There have been two problems with this route, however: firstly, there are myriad ways in which the power of NEDLAC can be eroded within the present system; and secondly, although women are represented within it as a distinct group, their presence is marginalised within the 'development chamber'.

The most common argument against special group representation is that it could lead to the proliferation of endless 'interest groups' demanding special representation. Counter to this is that the political process establishes which interests are salient at any given period in a country's political history. In Mansbridge's argument, where interests are crystallised such group representation is the outcome of democratic politics. In South Africa, political processes have determined that race and gender differences are primary and need to be proactively addressed. The result has been the introduction of institutions such as the Office of the Status of Women (OSW) within government. In this context the issue is how to extend this general commitment to the representative sphere.

ACCOUNTABILITY

Does representation, however imperfect, ensure accountability – that other value of a democratic system? Descriptive representation *à la* Mansbridge does not ensure that women representatives will in fact have a strong relationship to their constituents, or that male representatives with a commitment to gender equality may not advance women's agendas more positively than women who are not gender-aware. Indeed, South Africa provides a counterfactual case to descriptive representation: attention to gender equality has been facilitated by broad party support, and by civil society activism rather than primarily by women representatives.

Young's proposal of a veto right for particular groups also fails to resolve the problem of ensuring accountability. Group representation is unable to account for different ideological and socio-economic interests among members of the same group. Her veto right is admittedly buttressed by structures which promote the self-organisation of groups, within which, presumably, mechanisms of accountability could be carefully constructed. However, the women's movement, for example, is not represented by a single organisation of women, nor is it entirely desirable that it should be. Differences between women will impact on the kinds of policies particular constituencies may advocate; it is quite conceivable that different economic or even ideological interests will lead to contestation among women over policy priorities. For these reasons, it is preferable to have mechanisms that increase the representation of women within all parties rather than those which seek to treat women as a coherent and distinct group.

Different electoral systems give rise to quite different constituency relationships. In the PR system, issues of direct accountability to smaller constituencies can be accommodated where MPs are allocated to particular areas. But it is not simply geographical accountability that is important. Other interests also need to be accounted for in the political system: political parties, the constituencies parties claim to represent, and the values and issues they claim to carry into the representative sphere. The issue of accountability is further developed in Hassim's chapter.

The struggle of South African women, as we have seen, culminated in the acceptance of their right to represent and be represented. It secured gender rights in the Constitution, and for ANC women it secured positions on the party's electoral lists through the quota. It also secured a plethora of institutional mechanisms in the state for the promotion of gender equality and placed the question of women representatives on the agendas of all political parties, even though no other party has adopted a fixed quota.

MAKING A DIFFERENCE: WOMEN IN GOVERNMENT, WOMEN IN INSTITUTIONS

Have women really made a difference in the South African Parliament? Has the presence of women meant that women have acted broadly in the interests of women? In particular:

- Have women parliamentarians influenced or supported laws that benefit women?
- Have women introduced different perspectives into all the laws in Parliament?
- Have women impacted on the issues that are debated in Parliament?
- Have women affected the rules and norms of the institution itself?

Most international and local research has tended to concentrate on the mechanisms for getting women into Parliament and on the barriers to full and equal participation faced by women within the institution. Less work has been done on the actual impact of women on the nature and the work of legislative bodies. Not surprisingly, most of the research has, been carried out in those countries with high numbers of women in Parliament. Generally it is suggested that greater numbers of women in legislative bodies have resulted in increased attention to laws and policies dealing with families, women, and children (Reynolds 1999; Lovenduski and Karam 1998; Edwards 1991). There is also some support for the idea that women can impact on the nature of the institution itself once they achieve a critical mass. Lovenduski and Karam (1998) note that women in Scandinavian legislatures at national and local level have influenced the nature of politics in a number of ways, including a greater prioritisation of family obligations and more accessible debates.

In South Africa, the years between 1995 and 2000 saw the enactment of an impressive list of laws relating to women. These include:

- Legislation on reproductive rights (the 1996 Choice on Termination of Pregnancy Act);
- The 1996 Commission on Gender Equality Act;
- Improved legal protection against domestic abuse (the 1998 Domestic Violence Act);
- The removal of discrimination in customary marriages and of women's minority status in such marriages (the 1998 Recognition of Customary Marriages Act);
- Protection against discrimination in the workplace and other

forms of private and state discrimination (the 1997 Employment Equity Act and the 2000 Promotion of Equality and Prevention of Unfair Discrimination Act);
- Improvements to the system of private maintenance (the 1998 Maintenance Act).

Within Parliament special debates and resolutions on gender issues have raised a symbolic awareness of the place of women in the new South Africa and have sought to hold government broadly accountable for its commitment to gender equality. In addition, there have been some significant sectoral initiatives relating to gender. The Women's Budget a project that emerged jointly from the Joint Standing Committee on Finance and civil society organisations is a particularly celebrated example.

However, these achievements are not in themselves evidence of the impact of women in Parliament. They must be assessed in relation to the experiences of women parliamentarians within the institution and their actual role and participation in law making processes. They must also be placed within the broader context of the political values of the state, the rules and ideologies of political parties, the particular nature of Parliament and its place within the overall policy development and law making processes of the state.

Most research has tended to focus on the experiences of women in Parliament and the obstacles they encounter in their work, rather than to analyse the actual role of women in influencing particular laws and issues for women or introducing a gender perspective into the way in which all laws are discussed and understood. This research emphasis is largely driven by the needs of women parliamentarians themselves, many of whom have felt excluded and marginalised within the institution.

Lovenduski and Karam (1998, 131) suggest that before women can make a substantial impact on Parliament or can seek to change the rules of the institution, they have to be able to learn them and to use them. Several studies document the fact that many women lack the knowledge, information, and skills to participate effectively in the South African Parliament (Serote et al 1995; WEU 1998; Budlender et al 1999). This has resulted in a reduced level of participation by many women. However, there is also evidence in this research that women have made a difference.

ENGENDERING THE INSTITUTION

The question whether the presence of women has contributed to making Parliament a more gender sensitive institution raises difficult issues. We have already identified the way in which 'gendered preference systems' are 'embedded in the norms, structures and practices of institutions' and thus 'serve the political and social interests which they were designed to promote in the first place' (Goetz 1998, 6). Parliamentarians themselves have commented that Parliament has long established (masculine) priorities, hierarchies, culture and power. Women may often find it easier to accept these constraints and work within the institution rather than change it (Pregs Govender, Second Women's Budget 1997).

Nevertheless, research carried out in 1999 for the European Union Parliamentary Support Programme found 'virtual unanimity' among the parliamentarians interviewed 'that having women in Parliament had made a difference' (Budlender et al, 74). This difference not only related to a greater attention to women's issues and to increased priority given to social issues, but also to the role of women in influencing the environment of Parliament. The elements of the 'boys' club' in the rules, facilities, debating style, committee system, legalism, and general culture of Parliament are well documented (Serote et al 1995; WEU, 1998; Budlender et al 1999). Budlender et al's research suggests that women have had some influence over the rules, norms and culture of the institution. Several of their interviewees who were members of Parliament believed that women have changed 'the atmosphere in Parliament to a "softer" or more "homely" environment, with less conflict' (Budlender et al, 74). Their presence had also challenged sexist prejudices and 'disproved a previous misconception that women were incompetent' (Budlender et al, 75). The increase in representivity in appointments to positions in government and institutions was also attributed to the presence of women in Parliament.

At the same time, other interviewees felt that women had had to adapt to an institution with 'insufficient toilets, lack of attention to sexual harassment, fewer opportunities, sexist remarks, undermining of women in committees, disrespectful treatment of the women's caucus and double standards in respect of personal conduct' (Budlender et al, 76-7). In a survey for the parliamentary Women's Empowerment Unit, it was argued that while women were making an impact; political parties and Parliament were often not affirming of them. 'Many MPs and MPLs [Members of the Provincial Legislature] feel disempowered by the structure and procedures of the legislatures, and this is intensified for women who face a male-dominated ethos extending to the fact that most committee chairpersons are men' (*WHIP* 18 Sept 1998).

The South African experience suggests that Lovenduski and Karam may be correct in arguing that women's mere presence in legislatures will

> inevitably change existing arrangements and procedures, parliamentary timetables, places of meeting, childcare provisions, working hours and travel arrangements may be changed to make these more suitable for women. (1998, 146)

The long-term impact of even these minimal changes should make Parliament more accessible to women (thus increasing the possibility of women entering it).

The available research suggests that women have made some inroads into the institutional culture and mainstream discourse of Parliament. Serote et al's (1995) analysis of parliamentary and committee debates found that women raised gender issues substantially more than men and introduced gender analysis into some of the debates. However, gender was not part of the mainstream discourse of Parliament (1995, 67). The WEU research found that women made an 'important contribution' to parliamentary debates, but did not analyse the substance of this contribution. There is, however, evidence of a direct link between women in Parliament and a greater attention to gender issues in the National Assembly itself. In particular, women have used Parliament to raise symbolic and public awareness on gender issues and to exercise a broad oversight function on the government's progress towards gender equality.

The symbolic function was initiated in August 1994, with the call for 9 August to be celebrated as National Women's Day in South Africa (*Hansard* 9 August 1994, col 1002). This has been followed in subsequent years by several debates and parliamentary resolutions on women's position in society and progress towards gender equality. The Women's Charter for Effective Equality was presented to the President after its adoption by the

Women's National Coalition in 1994 (*Hansard* 9 August 1994, col 1002). In 1995, the year of the Fourth World Conference on Women in Beijing, Parliament's attention was drawn to the Convention on the Elimination of All Forms of Discrimination Against Women (CEDAW) and the Beijing Platform for Action (*Hansard* 9 August 1995, col 3513). From 1996, debates on women and gender in Parliament were dominated by the issue of violence against women and children.[2]

Women in Parliament have also used parliamentary resolutions to hold government accountable for improving the status of women. Early resolutions called for the integration of gender in the government's Reconstruction and Development Programme (*Hansard* 9 August 1994, col 1002), the ratification of CEDAW (*Hansard* 8 August 1995, col 3513), and for reports of progress in terms of CEDAW and the Beijing Platform for Action (*Hansard* 7 March 1996, col 420). From 1996, the emphasis again shifts to the prevention and eradication of violence against women,[3] together with the allocation of greater resources for gender structures and policies.[4] At the end of its first term Parliament passed a resolution setting out the objectives for the next five years, noting that the legislative framework established during the first term should be fully implemented by government with sufficient resources. This monitoring role has also been driven by Parliament's joint monitoring committee on the Quality of Life and Status of Women (CQLSW), formed in 1996, which directly oversees government departments by requesting reports on progress towards gender equality and publishing their findings. In this way, Parliament has been used as an important mechanism of accountability between different sections of the state.

THE TASK OF LAW MAKING

The nature of the relationship between the development and enactment of laws relating to women and the fact that women are present in Parliament must be understood within broader political processes, of which Parliament is but one element. These include a Constitution which has equality as one of its founding principles, a political commitment to gender equality within the ruling party, and an historic moment that saw a flurry of 'law making' as the new ANC government sought to reshape the legal and social boundaries of society. At the same time, the parallel and interactive activities of women's organisations in civil society, and key individuals in positions of decision-making in a variety of state institutions and the international arena shaped a positive policy and legislative agenda on reproductive rights, violence against women, customary law, anti-discrimination, and other laws (Albertyn et al 1999).

Within this context Parliament played a role that facilitated civil society involvement in law making processes and allowed parliamentarians to impact on many of the draft laws. Indeed, the new 'People's Parliament' had rejected the rubber-stamping of executive decisions that had characterised its apartheid predecessor. Instead, the portfolio committees saw themselves both as watchdogs over the executive, using their oversight power to call ministers to account, and as law makers, sometimes making substantive changes to some of the laws that came before them. In addition, the formation of the CQLSW provided a focal point for gender activity.

Research on women's role in law making processes confirms that it created greater opportunities for women both in Parliament and, in some instances, in civil society. In the process of shaping and approving the Choice on Termination of Pregnancy Act, Parliament investigated the problems caused by the previous restrictive law. This process demonstrated the significance of a diverse and representative Parliament as the presence of women and men, but especially black women, gave a voice to those who had, in the past, been absent. It allowed the discourse on abortion to shift from questions of criminality and morality to women's rights, especially women's choices within a broader context of women's health and poverty (Albertyn et al 1999). Here the presence of women, as well as the broader climate of human rights and gender equality, was critical to the emergence of a new discourse and a women friendly law.

Women in Parliament also played an important role in determining the content of the Commission on Gender Equality Act. A special ad hoc committee was formed to consult women and report to the Minister. Again, women were central to determining the content of the law.

The trio of women's Bills relating to domestic violence, customary marriage, and maintenance that came before Parliament in 1998 tell a slightly different story about the impact of women. The Bills were drafted by the South African Law Commission, with significant input from organisations in civil society. However the CQLSW played a key role in lobbying within government and in Parliament to ensure that the bills came before Parliament before the 1999 general elections (Albertyn et al 1999). The CQLSW also held workshops to educate women parliamentarians about the content and impact of the Bills and to enable them to participate in parliamentary debates. It worked jointly with the Portfolio Committee on Justice to refine the content of the law and ensure a gender perspective. In these instances, women played an important political role in advocating the speedy passage of the laws, and a technical role in working with the Justice Committee to fine tune the content.

The participation of civil society organisations in parliamentary portfolio hearings is crucial if the gendering of the policy process is to be ensured. The expertise brought to Parliament by the engagement of civil society organisations is invaluable in bringing specialised knowledge into the legislative process. Perhaps even more significant is the relationship between the CQLSW and women's organisations in civil society in facilitating this engagement with other parliamentary portfolio committees, which brings a gendered perspective to all the committees. Therefore the presence of women parliamentarians and a portfolio committee dedicated to furthering women's equality are crucial elements in the political process to advance gender equality in society as a whole.

There are few examples of the engendering of more 'mainstream' laws and issues. Perhaps the most salutary one is the work of women in the Joint Standing Committee on Finance (JSCOF) and the development of the Women's Budget Initiative (WBI). Originating amongst ANC women and endorsed by the Transitional Executive Council's Report on Women and Finance, the WBI was steered by the working group on gender and economic policy of the JSCOF and civil society organisations (Govender 1996, 3-4). This research project sought to analyse the gender impact of the South African budget on all government departments. Linked to it have been several key advocacy issues relating to the 'engendering' of the budget. In this respect, women parliamentarians, in partnership with civil society, have influenced the transformation of the budget and the budget process into one that takes more account of women.[5]

Thus the role of Parliament and women parliamentarians in influencing the substance of laws has differed according to the issue and the portfolio committee. From the evidence that exists it seems as if women have had the greatest impact on issues that traditionally concern women – reproductive rights, violence, customary law, and maintenance rather than on all laws and issues. If finance has been a crucial exception to this pattern, it is because of conscious and strategic interventions by women parliamentarians and civil society. The establishment of the CQLSW has been critical in enhancing women's ability to shape the passage of laws. Secondly, it seems that women's presence in committees may play a crucial watchdog function, serving to maintain a consciousness of gender issues even if no real gender analysis emanates from the committee. Finally, there are significant examples of key areas, such as finance, where women have begun to make a real impact in mainstreaming gender.

THE DIFFERENCE WOMEN MAKE

The first five years of a democratic Parliament in South Africa clearly demonstrated that if women are actively present in Parliament, in numbers that make them effective, they can begin to act in the interests of women (as they define them) (Phillips 1991, 72). This 'presence' ranges from active political and technical intervention in law making and policy issues to the 'moral force' in favour of gender created by the mere presence of sufficient numbers of women. In South Africa, women have also used Parliament to raise awareness of the status of women and to hold government broadly accountable for improving that status.

The research also suggests that with greater skills and training this capacity to act will be enhanced as more women are able to participate effectively (Budlender et al 1999). In South Africa the question is no longer whether women can make a difference to Parliament, but rather how much difference they can make.

CONCLUSION

In South Africa, as the new century and young democracy unfold and develop, the challenges for women in Parliament will change. These include equipping themselves with increased skills to participate in politics in a context of different political needs. The first Parliament was characterised by what might be called 'grand legislative schemes', in the second Parliament the implementation and delivery of policies required much greater attention to more detailed and concrete laws – in which more advanced technical skills were needed. Greater importance was attached to the capacity of the state, both its representative and its administrative institutions, to oversee the implementation of laws, the allocation of resources, and its accountability to the electorate.

The presence of women in Parliament made a difference in the promotion of a greater consciousness of the need to meet women's needs. It also led to new forms of institution building that sometimes crossed conventional party lines. The internal cooperation was matched by attempts to link up with women's organisations in civil society in determining a policy agenda in Parliament that would answer the needs of women. Whilst debate about changes to the electoral system were engaged in 2001, the importance of promoting the participation and the continued and increased representation of women has been underscored.

NOTES

1. This paragraph draws on the experience of the authors.
2. Resolution on Violence against Women and Children, *Hansard*, 7 November 1996, col 5386; Special debate on violence against women and children *Hansard*, 11 March 1999, col. 481; Resolution on the Prevention of Violence Against Women, *Hansard*, 25 November, 1997 col 6266; Women's Day Resolution, *Hansard*, 19 August 1997, col 4144.
3. In November 1996, a resolution was passed asking government to report on what it had done to eradicate violence against women (*Hansard* 7 November 1996, col 5386); In November 1997, a parliamentary resolution called on government to pass laws and report on progress in eradicating violence against women (*Hansard* 25 November 1997, col 6266).
4. In 1997, a resolution called for greater resources to be given to the CGE, the OSW, and the Parliamentary Joint Monitoring Committee (*Hansard* 19 August 1997) and in 1999, a resolution on International

Women's Day called for the fairer allocation of resources to women (Hansard 5 March 1999, col 1365).

5. For more details on the Women's Budget initiative see the IDASA publications edited by D Budlender on the three Women's Budget research projects in 1996, 1997 and 2000.

3

CITIZENSHIP AND GENDER EQUALITY: THE IMPLICATIONS FOR FREE AND FAIR ELECTIONS[1]

Glenda Fick

Every citizen has the right to free, fair and regular elections for any legislative body established in terms of the Constitution. (Constitution of the Republic of South Africa Act 108 of 1996, subsection19 (2))

> The Constitution of the Republic of South Africa provides for a common South African citizenship. It states that all citizens are equally entitled to the rights, privileges, and benefits of citizenship and that they are equally subject to the duties and responsibilities of citizenship (Constitution, sections 3(1) and 3(2)). It also guarantees equality, universal adult suffrage, and certain political rights.

CITIZENSHIP AND EQUALITY

To conceive of citizenship as gender blind is problematic if the objective is to ensure the participation of women in the political realm. A concept of citizenship that is male orientated is equally detrimental to gender equality. However, such a view of citizenship is pervasive. Both citizenship and nationhood, to which it is closely related, may be seen as masculine concepts reflecting masculine values (Enslin 1995, 342).[2]

Walby (1994, 379) notes that the problem with the recent social science conception of citizenship is that it has been concerned with the relationship of class to social integration and that it omits gender. She refers to the work of Marshall (1950, extract reprinted in Clarke 1994) who regards citizenship as a contested issue, a complex interplay of political, social and civil rights. However, he does not even think about the attainment of gender equality as a component of the complexity of citizenship.[3] McLaughlin's (1992, 236) formulation of citizenship, in which he presents a maximal and minimal view of citizenship, is more flexible and leaves room for considerations of gender. In the maximal view, the identity conferred by citizenship would mean more than the possession by a person of a passport or the right to vote and an unreflective 'nationality' – all features of a minimal view of citizenship. A fuller or richer identity is conceived in social, cultural, and psychological terms. A minimal view would concentrate on a formal legal identity conferred on an individual by citizenship. Hassim and Gouws suggest that formal citizenship 'establishes an equality within the political community, regardless of the racial, class, ethnic or gender identities of individuals' (Hassim and Gouws 1998, 55). Cock and Bernstein remind us that Mary Wollstonecraft, in 1792, 'called for equal civil and political rights for women, but [was of the view that] their service to the state and identity as citizens was expressed through their motherhood rather than through the military service then demanded from male citizens' (Cock and Bernstein 1998, 24). This distinction between men as soldiers or workers and women as mothers has determined different perceptions of citizenship and the extent to which citizenship has accommodated men and women.

In contrast to the gender blind notions of citizenship proffered by Marshall and, perhaps, McLaughlin, other writers have explored feminist perspectives in relation to citizenship. Pateman argues that 'civil society is a social contract formulated as a contract among men because women cannot participate fully as equals with men due to their subordinate position within the private sphere' (Hassim and Gouws 1998, 55; Pateman, 317), Dietz (1985,19) recognises citizenship as an activity as well as a concept.

> [Democratic] politics [is] the collective and participatory engagement of citizens [women and men] in the determination of the affairs of their community. The community may be the

> neighbourhood, the city, the state, the region or the nation itself. (Dietz 1992, 75)

Dietz urges a focus on the 'activity of citizenship' which will place women in a position 'to claim a truly liberatory politics as their own' (Dietz 1992, 76). What is this activity of citizenship? It is a continuous activity, and a good in itself. It would entail public debate and discussion inspired by the principle of freedom and the goal of self-government. It would also entail 'organised movement with expressly political goals and democratic activities in which feminist citizens challenge the "givens" and seek to revitalise democratic values' (Dietz 1985, 35). Participation in elections and the electoral process could certainly form a part of what Dietz would view as the activity of citizenship.

Dietz believes that these democratic values and practices must be transformed into a feminist theory of citizenship. This will require feminists to become political thinkers. However, she warns that feminist democracy must not be 'womanist', in other words, it should not presuppose the superiority of women. If an attitude of superiority is allowed to develop, the democratic ideal that feminist democrats are seeking to promote will be lost. Furthermore, feminist democratic thinking and its commitment to citizenship must allow for the participation of men.

In her view of active citizenship, individuals are the creators of their social and political identities, and with sufficient determination as 'prime movers', are thus capable of changing them. On the one hand, the ongoing activity on the part of women (and men), which Dietz urges, is necessary for women's self-government and for addressing gender equality. On the other, she might be too optimistic in assuming that women have the time (given their multiple roles in society) and the public space and recognition to take their political lives into their own hands as 'prime movers', and to achieve the revitalised citizenship she envisages. It seems more realistic to suggest that women will have to be regarded as a political force by men (and other women) before their debates and other active involvement in the public realm will be accorded due recognition. This goal may be achieved by addressing the inequality experienced by women as a result of their productive, reproductive, and community management roles and responsibilities.

Dietz's view of citizenship suggests an activism in the public sphere. It seems to rely on a perception of a public sphere characterised by equality (including gender equality).

Also addressing the issue of citizenship in relationship to gender, Sylvia Walby (1994, 390) believes unequivocally that 'politically, citizenship has been central in the forms of gender relations over the last century'. Walby argues that women did not enjoy social and civil rights as benefits of citizenship until after they had received the political rights also recognised as crucial to citizenship. She points out that the ordering of civil rights *before* political rights can legitimately be questioned (as it was by early feminists) if one is not white and male and contends that in giving effect to citizenship, women's rights, including the right to vote and to stand for office, should be given high priority. One way to achieve this is to claim greater social benefits in order to make the achievement of political rights a possibility. She thus advocates a form of social citizenship.

Social citizenship would comport with a notion of citizenship that encourages women's political activism and regards the right to vote and to stand for office as important for the achievement of full and equal citizenship. However, advocates of social citizenship do not regard active citizenship for all as being sufficient to address gender inequality. Rather, social citizenship recognises the idea of citizenship at the political, social, and economic levels and seeks to give rise to a form of citizenship that addresses inequality at all these levels. Social citizenship would propose that 'citizenship is about gender and the transformation of the form of patriarchy as much as it is about class, nation/ethnicity, and capitalism' (Walby 1994, 391).

Walby suggests that one way of accomplishing such a transformation would be for women to form alliances with political movements. For example, if the labour movement were to demand and ensure the benefits of social citizenship and these social benefits became available to women, the latter might become less dependent, in the private realm, on the 'arbitrary will' of their male spouses and partners. The central issue in her argument is, then, that in relation to gender political citizenship is more important than has been believed.

Walby sees the introduction of a welfare state as one way of addressing the institution of patriarchy (the basis of gender inequality) and of changing it. In her view, through the welfare state, certain forms of domestic life will become socialised through state provision of services such as schools, nurseries, hospitals, and other resources generally associated with the private realm. Thus a welfare state could improve the lives of women in the private domain even though it might not completely address the situation of economic hardship common to many women. Liebenberg, writing in the South African context, suggests that 'the idea of "social citizenship" thus captures the full dimensions of an individual's sense of belonging within society. Social inclusion and participation in democratic institutions not only depends on the guarantee of formal civil and political rights, but also on socio-economic rights' (Liebenberg 1999, 59).

The activism associated with Dietz and Walby's view is to be welcomed in the South African context. It poses a challenge to women (and men)[4] to do what is necessary to overcome gender inequality. Arguably, social citizenship addresses gender inequality in a more direct and substantive way than Dietz's 'prime movers' in achieving full citizenship. This is because social citizenship could address what lies at the core of gender inequality, namely, the institutionalised patriarchy, which is epitomised by the vast disparities between men and women in socio-economic and political power, and the disparities based on race and class so prevalent in South African society. This is particularly the case in communities in which the traditional gender roles of women are firmly entrenched and in which women do not have the resources to become prime political movers. Dietz's 'prime mover' notion suggests that women can simply step out of their position of inequality and, through political activity, claim the citizenship that is rightfully theirs. This idea of citizenship disregards the deeply rooted institutionalised societal relations promoted by the family and the state that result in gender inequality.

The fact that citizenship is the starting point for the exercise of constitutionally protected political rights that guarantee participation in an election is recognised, in the first place, by South Africa's Constitution which expressly accords political rights only to citizens (Constitution, section 19).[5] It is also recognised in the Electoral Act 73 of 1998 which provides that only South African citizens may register to vote in an election (section 6). Gendered notions of citizenship, extended to free and fair elections, share the common goal of affording women the opportunity of participating in framing policy, and determining who will exercise political power. These notions of citizenship ensure that women are not discriminated against and that (like men) they enjoy the full benefits of universal adult suffrage.

Equality[6] is pertinent both to the concept of citizenship and to its relation to gender. According to the constitutional directive, equality must apply to citizenship. All citizens are equally entitled to the rights, privileges, and benefits of citizenship. Furthermore, no citizen may be deprived of citizenship. Citizenship must be maximally construed to include full political involvement on the part of citizens. To guarantee women equal access to all constitutionally protected rights, including political rights, an interpretation that gives effect to social citizenship and a substantive interpretation of equality are essential. Giving effect to substantive equality would require an assessment of the social and political position of women (and men) in a particular society. Such an assessment would reveal an imbalance of power between men and women, brought about by disparities between them in the political and socio-economic arenas (Gasa 1998, 321).[7] Liebenberg pertinently points out that women face multiple institutionalised barriers in society. These include the unequal burden of reproductive and caring work, labour market discrimination, discriminatory religious and cultural laws and practices, lack of representation in political and economic institutions, and widespread violence against women. Even when women do gain access to social and economic rights they are frequently discriminated against in the exercise of these rights (Liebenberg 1999, 60).

Longstanding and deep-rooted practices of gender discrimination are difficult to address through formal equality (constitutionally and legislatively provided for). What is needed is substantive equality or 'equality of result'. Dahlerup (1998, 95) explains that the argument for equality of result 'is based on the experience that equality as a goal cannot be reached by formal equal treatment as a means'. If social and economic barriers exist in society, 'compensatory measures must be introduced as a means to reach equality of result'.

In the area of political life (as in other areas), women in South Africa qualify as a category of persons disadvantaged by unfair discrimination on the bases, *inter alia*, of sex and gender. The lasting negative effects of unfair discrimination on societal groups have been recognised in South Africa. In order to address such discrimination, a concept of 'restitutionary equality' akin to Dahlerup's 'compensatory measures to introduce equality of result' has been advocated (Albertyn and Goldblatt 1998). In *National Coalition for Gay and Lesbian Equality v Minister of Justice* (1999 (1) SA 6 (CC)) the Constitutional Court stated 'Particularly in a country such as South Africa, persons belonging to certain categories have suffered considerable discrimination in the past. It is insufficient for the Constitution merely to ensure, through its Bill of Rights, that statutory provisions that have caused such unfair discrimination in the past are eliminated. Past unfair discrimination frequently has ongoing negative consequences, the continuation of which is not halted immediately when the initial causes thereof are eliminated, and unless remedied, may continue for a substantial time and even indefinitely. ... One could refer to such equality as remedial or restitutionary equality' (paras 60-61).

A commitment to social citizenship will go a long way towards ensuring that an appropriate strategy and 'compensatory measures' (legislative and otherwise)[8] to achieve 'equality of result' are put in place. In this regard, Gasa writes 'in order to address gender-differentiated responsibilities and differentiated access to resources and decision-making, a comprehensive and systematic strategy is needed' (Gasa 1998, 321). In order to address unfair discrimination experienced by women in the political sphere such 'restitutionary' or 'compensatory' measures should also extend to the context of elections.

In most societies universal adult suffrage, guaranteed to all citizens, has different implications for men and women. The founding provisions of South Africa's Constitution (section 1) include universal adult suffrage, a national common voters' roll, regular elections, and a multi-party system of government to ensure accountability, responsiveness and openness.[9] These values are of direct relevance to gender equality in the context of elections seeking, as they do, to create a public sphere of equality between women and men. However, in other respects, the public sphere defines a place for men but not for women.

Hassim and Gouws (1998, 56) observe that 'viewing the public sphere as the sphere of free equals does not capture the reality that women's unequal position within the family establishes the boundaries of their public participation'. Gender equality must influence the substance of constitutionally protected rights that ensure public participation. For this reason, the values of equality, dignity, and non-sexism need to be extended from the public sphere in which elections occur to the private sphere. Notwithstanding the constitutional values and guaranteed political rights, the political involvement of women is often clearly demarcated along lines of gender discrimination.

Social citizenship is the starting place for addressing the bases of gender discrimination. According to Liebenberg (1999, 59) it is a prerequisite for full and effective participation in democratic processes that citizens have access to the basic necessities of life, including water, shelter, basic education, and health care. She writes that unless citizens are capable of satisfying these basic human needs they become caught up in a struggle for survival. Even though they may cast their votes in elections every five years, they are marginalised from real political, economic and social power. As illustrated elsewhere in this chapter, the scenario described by Liebenberg is particularly applicable to women in South Africa. Hence, it is essential to adopt all measures which will address and remedy unfair discrimination, based on sex and gender, while guaranteeing full political rights.

CONDITIONS NECESSARY TO ENSURE GENDER EQUALITY IN A FREE AND FAIR ELECTION

The Convention on the Elimination of All Forms of Discrimination Against Women (CEDAW), described as the 'definitive international legal instrument requiring respect for, and observance of human rights of women' (Kathree 1995, 421), was ratified by South Africa in 1995. Article 7 of CEDAW reads:

State Parties shall take appropriate measures to eliminate discrimination against women in the political and public life of the country and, in particular, shall ensure to women, on equal terms with men, the right:

(a) To vote in all elections and public referenda and to be eligible for election to all publicly elected bodies;

(b) To participate in the formulation of government policy and the implementation thereof and to hold public office and perform all public functions at all levels of government;

(c) To participate in non-governmental organisations and associations concerned with the public and political life of the country.

The Convention establishes the international human rights standards necessary for the participation of women in public life. South Africa's Constitution contains provisions relating to the political rights of all citizens as well as certain provisions aimed at achieving a free and fair election, which, in itself, is considered to be a constitutional imperative. The Constitution emphasises equality as one of its central democratic values, and must be interpreted by law and policy makers to ensure that gender equality is central to electoral law[10] and policy. Such an interpretation will enhance the free and fair nature of an election.

In South Africa the Electoral Commission is the independent, impartial state organ responsible, *inter alia*, for ensuring free and fair elections. It also has the responsibility of managing such elections. In accordance with CEDAW and the constitutional value of equality, there is a clear obligation on the Electoral Commission to give effect to gender equality at every level when it manages an election (Electoral Commission Act 51 of 1996, section 5(1) a) and b). Gender equality must be an integral part of all the Electoral Commission's formulation of policy regarding matters such as recruitment of Commission staff at all levels, electoral processes, voter registration, demarcation of boundaries, and voter education (Electoral Commission Act 1996).

The Right to Vote

Universal adult suffrage means that all citizens who have reached the minimum voting age of 18 years, and whose names appear on the voters' roll (Electoral Act 73 of 1998, section 8), are entitled to an equal vote. Any factors affecting the impartiality of the vote (and resulting in discrimination) must be addressed and eliminated. Implicit in the equality of the vote are a number of issues. First, it is imperative that a citizen's right to vote, on a non-discriminatory basis, in the election of legislative bodies is guaranteed. Second, the right to vote must be exercised equally with other voters and must carry equal weight. So the report that at a voting station in the North-West province married women were required to produce a marriage certificate before they voted notwithstanding the fact that they had registered as voters (Mathye and Motara 1999, 71) was effectively a violation of the rights of those women.

The establishment of voting districts, voter registration, delimitation of constituencies (when appropriate)[11], and voting procedures[12] must take gender equality into account. An interpretation of equality that results in substantive equality must be adopted in order to ensure that unfair discrimination is avoided. In relation to the various issues associated with voting policy-makers and legislators must bear in mind that the domestic responsibilities of household management, rearing and caring for children and the elderly, together with being economically active, could make it difficult for women to get to registration and voting stations. If these stations are not located close to where women live and work, absence of transport combined with lack of financial resources are barriers to participation. This particularly applies to rural women (Baden, Hassim, Meintjes 1998, 9). [13] These problems are exacerbated by women's onerous agricultural and domestic obligations and by the restrictions placed on their mobility by patriarchal controls.

Motara (1999, 17) writes that 1 589 690 more women than men registered to vote in South Africa's 1999 election. More women than men registered in all provinces except Gauteng (*The Star*, 24 April 1999).

In a study of rural women's participation in the voter registration process on 6 and 7 March 1999 conducted by the Commission on Gender Equality (CGE) in the Northern Province, Eastern Cape, KwaZulu-Natal and the Western Cape interviews were conducted with 173 women after they had registered. They were asked twenty-nine questions addressing socio-economic considerations, literacy levels, culture, administrative infrastructure, and the political environment. The first three provinces were chosen because they were identified as having a large rural population and because in these provinces the number of rural women exceeded the number of rural men and of urban women and men. The Western Cape was chosen because its political leadership differs from that in the other provinces and because large numbers of women work on farms in the province. Results revealed that rural women were motivated to vote for two main reasons. First, they believed they must vote if they wanted to change their circumstances, and secondly 'women are conscious that they must vote to put their leaders in power' because these leaders would, in turn, implement measures to improve women's lives.

The CGE found that, 'many women felt that the registration process was satisfactory' (Motara, 1999, 29). However, certain problems were identified. These included long queues that created difficulties for women, who bore household responsibilities which included walking long distances to fetch water, or caring for young children, the sick, and the elderly. Additional problems included the fact that some potential women voters did not have the required identity document for purposes of registration, while others lacked the money to obtain the appropriate documents. Interestingly, the CGE study revealed that '[o]verall, women were satisfied that [registration] venues were accessible' (Motara 1999, 30). However, certain women reported problems with gaining access to the voter registration stations.

The Electoral System

Closed list proportional representation was a central feature of South Africa's democratic elections in 1994 and 1999. There is a body of literature which reveals that the best predictor of women's electoral success is the party list proportional representation system, and that the non-list proportional representation system, including single member districts, is least likely to increase the representation of women (Ballington 1999 and in this volume). As detailed in other chapters in this volume election results have certainly painted a positive picture for women in South Africa. The numbers – 27.7 per cent of women elected to the National Assembly in 1994 and 29.75 per cent in 1999 – compare favourably with international figures with the world average for women in the lower houses of parliament currently standing at 11.7 per cent[14]. However, it is worth noting that in the Nordic countries the average is 36.4 per cent (Lovenduski and Karam 1998, 126-127).

It is conceded that 'the fact of having women candidates [on lists] and, eventually, women in the legislative assembly, does not of itself bring any guarantee of commitment to gender equity' (Jacobson 1994). However, as citizens, women must be guaranteed the opportunity of being elected to hold office. Once in office, like male representatives, women have the chance to exercise political power and participate in decision-making. The presence of women in political life dilutes the male dominance of the political realm. Lovenduski and Karam (1998, 127) suggest that notwithstanding the 'institutional masculinity' of parliaments the world over, women today are 'organizing, mobilizing, motivating and advancing' other women from inside the world's legislatures. They are 'devising strategies and taking action to promote issues relevant to women and facilitate changes in legislation' (1998, 127). A commitment to gender representation by political parties in the compilation of their lists is, therefore, essential to ensure that women and men will have equal opportunities to enjoy the benefits and privileges of citizenship, one of which is the chance to hold office. When placing candidates on lists, political parties must also be particularly judicious in ensuring that representation for both rural and urban women.

VOTER EDUCATION

There are at least two aspects to voter education in respect of gender equality. First, women must be acquainted and familiarised with the process of voting. If this is achieved the process is demystified and, more importantly, women can go to the polls feeling confident about how to vote. Voter education programmes should explain complex electoral processes in a manner that will be understood by illiterate voters (the majority of whom are women) (Mbere 1999, 41).[15] As a group, men are more literate and are likely to have access to information on the electoral process through the written media and voter education programmes.[16] Appropriate and ongoing voter education programmes will thus empower women to exercise a fundamental right attached to citizenship.[17]

Secondly, voter education programmes need to ensure that an understanding of and a commitment to gender equality[18] permeate the entire electoral context. Voter education should be designed to shift and deconstruct deeply rooted stereotypes that cast men in roles of leadership and dominance and women in roles that are more subservient and passive (Mbere 1999, 40).[19] According to Mbere, '[r]ural women participating in voter education in the Free State raised specific concerns around continuing inequalities associated with culture and the exclusion of women, the elderly and those with disabilities from decision-making and participation in community affairs'(Mbere 1999, 40). Certain voter education material depicted women in stereotypical roles such as 'tea ladies' and teachers, while men were depicted as judges or builders.

Indeed, in the context of voter education, women educators may well find themselves at the receiving end of such stereotyping. This was the experience of women who conducted voter education in preparation for the 1994 South African elections (Ballington 1999, 5).

Participation in election-related activities

– Freedom of opinion and freedom of expression –

Because women are often more culturally, socio-economically, and politically disempowered than men, they are less likely to express provocative or controversial opinions to those individuals who are perceived by them to be in powerful positions. The latter would include their fathers, male partners, and employers. Women may, therefore, be more susceptible to intimidation than men. This danger appears to be recognised by the drafters of the Electoral Act 73 of 1998, in the section entitled 'The Role of Women', whose aim is to ensure that women are free to engage in any political activities.[20]

Politics and the activities associated with it provide fertile ground for the intimidation of women in the exercise of their political rights. Ballington offers some examples. '[M]any women have reportedly complained that they could not vote for the party of their choice because husbands, fathers and in-laws, or chiefs told them whom to vote for' (Ballington 1999, 4). It seems likely that the expression of an opinion contrary to that of a woman's husband or father might result in a form of abuse or violence against her.

In 1994 domestic workers reported problems with employers who told them who to vote for (Ballington 1999, 4). One domestic worker said, 'I'm really confused, my madam is telling me to vote for a particular party, at home my husband is telling me to vote for a different party, I'm really torn apart, I don't know who to trust' (Zondo 1994, 58). Whatever her personal opinion may have been, it seems she had little opportunity to express it.

The Electoral Act is alive to the hazards of one person unduly influencing or compelling another 'to vote or not to vote for any registered party or candidate' (s 87) and contains a provision prohibiting an individual from such conduct. Although this provision is not specifically intended to apply to women voters it would be applicable to situations in which undue pressure is exercised by husbands, partners, male relatives and employers over women. Notably, the Electoral Code of Conduct states that no person may abuse a position of political power, privilege or influence, including parental, patriarchal, traditional, or employment authority to influence the conduct or outcome of an election. The Code of Conduct stipulates that no registered party or candidate may use language or act in a way that might provoke the intimidation of candidates, members of parties, representatives, or supporters of parties or candidates. This protection against intimidation may be interpreted to extend to women voters and candidates. It states that no registered party or candidate may discriminate on the grounds of race, ethnicity, gender, class, or religion in connection with an election or political activity. These statutory measures to combat intimidation in the electoral context are important. However, it seems unlikely that many women would lay the criminal charges provided for in the legislation. Women are both economically disempowered and financially dependent on their husbands, partners, male relatives, and employers as well as bound by these relationships.

Another important aspect of free and fair elections is access to the information[21] necessary for the formation and expression of opinions. It is internationally accepted that

> the dissemination of all information must be permitted to the maximum extent possible in order to ensure that the electorate is fully informed. Without a well-informed electorate, it is impossible to guarantee that elections genuinely reflect the will of the people. (Centre for Human Rights, 7)

It is particularly important that information pertaining to elections and the electoral process be available to women. There are fewer women than men in the political arena, and more women than men whose activities are confined to the private realm. Rai (1996, 221) writes '...as political institutions have evolved over the years with men as the major (if not sole) participants, they reflect in their functioning and procedures a male bias that does not allow women to gain easy access to them'. This position is entrenched by the traditional gender roles of men and women. The state and political parties must take all reasonable steps to ensure that any discrimination that flows from this situation is addressed[22]. Reasonable steps would entail ensuring that women have access to all relevant electoral information.

– Freedom of assembly, association and movement –

The right of assembly[23] is recognised as important in the electoral context. Assemblies of people at public demonstrations and political rallies are not only integral to elections, they also effectively allow for the dissemination of information associated with political activity. Intertwined with the right to freedom of assembly is the right to freedom of association, also constitutionally provided for (Constitution, s 18).

Implicit in the rights of assembly and association is the right to freedom of movement.[24] Together these rights guarantee that all citizens, women and men, have the opportunity to attend or participate in peaceful political demonstrations and rallies. The Electoral Code of Conduct states that registered parties and candidates must take 'all reasonable steps to ensure the free access of women to all public political meetings, marches, demonstrations, rallies and other political events' (item 6(d)).

Because of their traditional roles as child minders, caregivers and housekeepers, women are more likely than men to experience difficulty attending meetings and other political gatherings at certain times of the day. In order to enhance the free and fair nature of an election, organisers of such meetings should ensure that the gatherings are arranged at times identified by the women as most suitable for them, and venues for political gatherings should be chosen with a view to ensuring that women are free from any threat of physical violence or intimidation. Access to and attendance at political gatherings must be facilitated. Unless these factors are recognised and addressed 'the full and equal participation of women in political activities' referred to in the Electoral Code of Conduct will have little meaning in practice. If they are not, women will remain marginalised.

– Election campaigns –

Political parties must ensure that issues pertaining to gender equality form an essential part of their election campaigns. Their commitment to gender equality must constitute more than paying lip-service to 'women's issues' and should not be motivated simply by a desire to secure votes.

Freedom of opinion, expression, and movement must be guaranteed to women candidates. The Electoral Code of Conduct recognises these rights by stipulating that every registered party and candidate 'must respect the right of women [voters] to communicate freely with parties and candidates' (item 6(a)). However, women candidates, too, must be guaranteed a full and equal opportunity to campaign and communicate with all sectors of the electorate without fear of intimidation or harassment of any kind.[25] The onus is on political parties and on the electorate to ensure that this opportunity is given.

Political parties must be alert to gender equality and must ensure that they advance the electoral opportunities of women candidates. Women candidates must be allocated equal campaign funding (in an electoral system to which candidate funding would be applicable)(Lowe-Morna 1996, 22)[26] and they must be guaranteed equal media exposure. Colleen Lowe-Morna (1996, 22) points out that the Canadian Progressive, Conservative, and Liberal Parties established funds to provide training programmes and financial support directly to women to assist them with covering expenses such as childcare and housekeeping. She also writes that in the United Kingdom, Emily's (Early Money is Like Yeast) List assists Labour Party women into parliament by making grants available to women seeking parliamentary seats to defray childcare and travel expenses. Lowe-Morna also refers to the suggestion of the Commonwealth Parliamentary Group Task Force that governments consider tax breaks for women candidates, such as ensuring that the cost of childcare during the election period is tax deductible.

The CGE's report on the 1999 elections points out that in media interviews during the campaign period, political parties were not often asked to account for their policies on gender and representivity. One conclusion reached in the report is that '...the failure to access female news sources, the marginalisation of women-related issues in the media, and the often stereotypical treatment of women politicians contributed to an implicit message that gender equality is of secondary importance in our society' (CGE 1999, 46)[27]. The CGE's report correctly states that the political parties and the media share the responsibility of ensuring that this gender imbalance is addressed and is not perpetuated.

– *Secrecy of the ballot* –

The Constitution guarantees the secrecy of the ballot (s 19(3)). Such secrecy is an important contributing factor in giving effect to the true will of the people and serves as the legitimate basis for representative government. In order to give effect to this right, the Electoral Act provides that '[a] voting compartment must screen a voter from observation by other persons while marking a ballot paper (s 70(2))'. Furthermore, the Act provides that '[n]o person may interfere with a voter's right to secrecy while casting a vote' (s 90(1)) . However, it must be recognised that secrecy of the ballot extends beyond the voting compartment. During voter education workshops held prior to the 1994 election, women often sought the assurance that their husbands and employers would not know how they voted.

CONCLUSION

Citizenship, like elections, is crucial to democracy. Under South Africa's Constitution citizenship serves as the starting point for the exercise of political rights while elections provide the avenue for citizens, through their right to vote (and other political rights), to choose their representatives in government. Representative government, in turn, is essential to democracy as it amounts to a form of government by the people.[28]

This chapter has shown that, as citizens, it is generally easier for men than it is for women to be active in political life and to exercise their political will. This fact has important implications for democracy. For this reason one cannot take issue with Mendus's view of the under-representation of women in political life:

> In brief the charge made against democracy is that, for women, it was never more than an article of faith, and when two hundred years of democratization have failed (and are still failing) to deliver equality for women, even faith is giving out. (Mendus 1996, 409)

In this chapter I have proposed that before all is lost and faith does indeed give out completely, social citizenship giving effect to substantive gender equality needs to make its way into the soul of the democratic undertaking in South Africa. The starting point of the entire electoral process must be substantive equality, the recognition of dignity, and political independence. These must become central features of citizenship. After the arrival of democracy in South Africa in 1994, elections remain a central part of this country's democratic endeavours. There is still time for the incorporation of gender equality into the notions of citizenship, political rights, free and fair elections, and representative government – all constitutional imperatives and important ingredients of South African democracy.

NOTES

1. See Glenda Fick, 1999 and Appendix in this volume. 'A Gender checklist for Free and Fair Elections'. Johannesurg: Electoral Institute of Southern Africa (EISA).
2. Enslin suggests that nationhood expresses an ontology that excludes women. She also makes the point that nationhood reflects masculine, even militaristic values. Since citizenship is an essential component of nationhood, it too could reflect such values.
3. Phillips writes that 'Carole Pateman notes that Marshall wrote in a right to employment as part of his conception of citizen rights – but did this just at a point when architects of the welfare state were constructing man as breadwinner-worker and woman as dependent-wife.' See Anne Phillips, *Democracy and Difference*, 78.
4. It is recognised that 'the international debate on gender equality and women's emancipation has moved away from viewing equality as an issue that concerns only women to an understanding of the implications of the unequal power for society as a whole'. See Nomboniso Gasa. 'National Machinery for Gender Equality', 321.
5. This section gives rights to 'every citizen' rather than to 'everyone', the latter being the formula used in, *inter alia*, ss 9, 10, 15, 16, 17, 18 and 21 – all sections that protect rights pertaining to free and fair elections.
6. Equality is guaranteed in s 9 of the Constitution. The right to equality is listed as the first right in the Bill of Rights. Subs 9(1) states that

everyone is equal before the law and has the right to equal protection and benefit of the law. According to subs 9(2), equality includes the full and equal enjoyment of all rights and freedoms. Subs 9(3) provides that the state may not unfairly discriminate directly or indirectly against anyone on one or more grounds, including race, gender, sex, pregnancy, marital status, sexual orientation, and others. Subs 9(4) of the Constitution provides that no individual may unfairly discriminate against another, while subs 9(5) assumes state or private discrimination on the grounds listed in subs 9(3) to be unfair.

7. Gasa writes: 'gender equality examines the unequal division of labour and access to and over resources, and the ways in which women and men are affected by programmes and policies that are supposed to benefit society at large. This analysis encourages an understanding that broad socio-cultural processes and socialization [both] influence the roles which women and men play.'
8. See s 9(2) of the Constitution.
9. Other values on which the South African state is founded, include human dignity, the achievement of equality and the advancement of human rights and freedoms, non-racialism and non-sexism and supremacy of the Constitution and the rule of law.
10. Measures relevant to the 1999 elections in South Africa are the Electoral Act 73 of 1998, the Electoral Commission Act 51 of 1996, and the Political Parties Funding Act 103 of 1997.
11. Delimitation of constituencies was not applicable in the 1999 national and provincial elections in South Africa, but was relevant to the local government elections in 2000.
12. With regard to voting procedures, it is worth noting that the Electoral Act stipulates that the Electoral Commission must allow a person to apply for a special vote if, owing to pregnancy (or infirmity or disability), that person cannot vote at a voting station in the voting district in which she is registered as a voter. However, what may be perceived to be a hint of sensitivity to gender equality in this section is not sustained throughout the Act.
13. According to these authors 'women, especially rural African women, suffer more from poverty than men: overall, 48% of women live in poverty compared to 44% of men, rising to 70% for African rural

women (over 15) compared to 65% for men in the same category.' . See also Janet Small and Lydia Kompe, 1992. 'Organising Rural Women: The Experience of TRAC'. Agenda 12 cites Ginwala et al who write that 71% of African women live in the rural areas. See further Debbie Budlender. 1992. 'Rural Women: The 'also-rans' in the development stakes.' In *Agenda* 12, 27 at 29 Budlender writes that 'rural' is never defined when 'rural women' are referred to. She cites Naila Kabeer, who points out that 'rural' lays open what Kabeer refers to as the 'fallacy of aggregation', or the use of 'non-specific, generic, abstract categories'. The danger of this approach is that the group is then 'portrayed as having all the same needs' and that they will benefit from that same project and that there therefore is no conflict of interests. Budlender confines the category of 'rural women' to women who live in the areas which made up the former homelands, and on farms. A similar understanding of 'rural women' will be relied upon in this chapter.

14. It appears that the relatively high representation of women in the National Assembly can be attributed to the introduction by the African National Congress of the quota system.
15. Mbere's analysis of voter education material revealed that the materials reviewed used simple language, and were clearly illustrated and colourful. Furthermore, responses from users of the material suggested that they were effective in creating awareness of the voting process, democracy, and the right to vote.
16. Baden, Hassim and Meintjes state that more women in the 25 years and above group have no education (18% overall, compared to 23% among African women) than men (12% overall, 16.5% among African men). Twenty-two per cent of women (28% of African women) and 16% of men (21% of African men) had not achieved Standard 3, a minimum for basic literacy.
17. Figures suggest that more than 7 000 women were reached through voter education sessions before the 1999 elections. See Nomtuse Mbere. 1999.'Gender analysis of voter education material'. In *Review of the 1999 General Elections: A Gender Perspective*. CGE, 35 at 40. In a review of voter education materials used to prepare voters for the 1999 general election, Mbere points out that it was not clearly

demonstrated that women would use their votes to elect the party that best promoted the reversal of gender inequality.

18. Ibid. Mbere writes that the '[v]oter education process provided opportunities to link voting to certain gender issues, and encouragingly, the responses showed that these links were often made.

19. Mbere reports that the materials reviewed were largely gender blind. She recommends that '[e]ducation material producers need to move from stereotyping males and females to a balanced portrayal of the roles of both in civil society.' Ibid.

20. See ss 15 and 16 of the Constitution, respectively. Subs 16(2)(c) provides that the right to freedom of expression does not extend to advocacy of hatred that is based, *inter alia*, on gender and that constitutes incitement to cause harm. The type of expression and the causal link between it and the harm envisaged by the section fall beyond the scope of this chapter. However, once it is established that a form of expression is of the type contemplated by subs 16(2)(c), it will constitute expression that is not conducive to a free and fair election. In other words, the section permits a restraint on the right to freedom of expression that is crucial during an election in order to guarantee a political environment for women which is free of intimidation and harm, and one in which their fundamental rights are respected.

21. The right to access to information intended here is different from the right to access to information expressed in s 32 of the Constitution. The latter is aimed at obtaining information, held by the state or any individual, which is necessary for the protection of any rights. The right to access to information in an electoral context guarantees that members of the electorate receive all information about the political parties and/or candidates in order make the relevant decisions prior to exercising their right to vote.

22. See item 9(d) of the Electoral Act which prohibits discrimination on the ground of gender (and other grounds).

23. The right is guaranteed in s17 of the Constitution, which provides that '[e]veryone has the right, peacefully and unarmed, to assemble, to demonstrate, to picket and to present petitions'.

24. S 21(1) stipulates that '[e]veryone has the right to freedom of movement'.
25. Item 4 of the Electoral Code of Conduct lists a number of activities associated with an electoral campaign. Political parties must ensure that women candidates are afforded the opportunity to participate in all such activities free from unfair discrimination, violence and harassment.
26. The author states that the responsibility for assisting candidates in raising funds rests first with political parties.
27. Men comprised 87% of election news sources, women comprised 8%, and 5% of the election stories monitored did not specify the sex of their sources. See The Media Monitoring Project 1999, 'Media coverage of women during the 1999 elections'. In *Review of the 1999 General Elections: A Gender Perspective*, 48.
28. See Constitution, s 42 (3).

4

POLITICAL PARTIES, GENDER EQUALITY, AND ELECTIONS IN SOUTH AFRICA

Julie Ballington

INTRODUCTION

Voting as a process of selection was first encountered in ancient Greece, where it was generally used for decisions put before the democratic assembly. Although various forms of voting have existed throughout the ages, it emerged as a central theme in the eighteenth century with the birth of 'modern democracy'. Political philosophy in this period, together with the English, American and French Revolutions, integrated the idea of the general interest of the people being expressed through elected representatives (Council of Europe 1997, 5). Today the right to vote for elected representatives is constitutionally guaranteed in most democracies.

However, for the most part, women were excluded from the polis at the beginning of the democratic tradition and adult suffrage, as it was progressively introduced, was reserved exclusively for men. The fact that only male citizens could vote and be elected was not seriously questioned until the advent of the suffragists in the late nineteenth century which found expression notably in the writings of John Stuart Mill. The slow enfranchisement of women began in 1897 in New Zealand and was followed by restricted voting rights in Australia in 1902, Finland in 1906, and Denmark and Iceland in 1915 (IPU 1997, 2). Most countries gradually enfranchised women, setting the stage for modern representative democracy.

However, the enfranchisement of women in South Africa was particularly slow.

The passage of time between the demand for and the granting of the franchise to women was considerable but not as great as the decades it took for a significant number of women to be elected to Parliament. National parliamentary politics was for a long time an exclusively male domain and sixty-five years elapsed between the enfranchisement of white women and the presence in Parliament of more than three women parliamentary representatives at any given time. The advent of democracy in 1994 ended white political rule, and gave women a voice in the new democratic dispensation.

In July 1991, at the first ANC conference held in South Africa since the organisation had returned from exile, a quota for women was debated. The debate was something of a debacle. Only 17 per cent of the delegates were women, and a gender policy had not been discussed at any level in the organisation. The party's National Executive Committee was reticent during the debate, and it was clear that the organisation was generally conservative about gender. Although many at the conference, including women, rejected the quota, the debate opened up the whole issue of affirmative action in the ANC. It opened a space, too, for exposing gender oppression (Horn 1994, 37). Most significant of all, however, was that it led to a more strategic approach by the ANC Women's League (ANCWL) in its attempts to establish a national women's agenda.

As a result of the pressure brought to bear on the Executive by the ANCWL the party adopted an internal quota of 30 per cent on its 1994 lists.

The political commitment to gender equality led to the election of a significant number of women parliamentary representatives and brought an end to the idea and practice of the public political domain as the exclusive preserve of men. The number of women legislators increased ten-fold, from a mere 2.4 per cent in 1987 to 27 per cent in 1994 and 29.8 per cent in 1999. The acceptance of the quota is one of three primary factors that explain this achievement. The other two are the politicisation of women's rights during the 1980s in the internal United Democratic Front and in the exiled ANC Movement and the proportional representation (PR) electoral system adopted in 1994.

This chapter examines the participation of women as elected representatives in South Africa and argues that political parties and electoral systems are the major determinants of the notable presence or absence of women in national legislatures. It also suggests that there is not necessarily a correlation between the presence of women parliamentarians and gender sensitive policy. However, it is argued elsewhere in this volume that a critical mass of women representatives does make a significant difference to women-oriented legislation.

COMPARATIVE REPRESENTATION OF WOMEN

Despite the fact that universal suffrage is the norm in most countries, the number of women in national legislatures has remained comparatively low over the decades. The Inter-Parliamentary Union (IPU) estimated that in October 2001 14 per cent of seats in national legislatures worldwide were held by women (IPU Website). The regional average for sub-Saharan Africa in 2001 was 11.8 per cent, slightly lower than the worldwide average. The regional average for the Southern African Development Community (SADC) in July 1999 was 18.4 per cent. Compared with these figures, South Africa's 29.8 per cent ranks favourably.

A number of factors accounts for the regional variations, one of the most important being deeply entrenched patriarchal attitudes and stereotypes of the role of women in both Western and African society (C. Lowe-Morna 2000). In many Southern African countries, like Mauritius and Swaziland, traditional and patriarchal cultures make it difficult for women to enter or advance in decision-making structures (Lowe-Morna 2000). Rule has argued that women face pervasive obstacles in representation caused by social bias, narrow gender roles, restrictive religious doctrines, unequal laws and education, discriminatory socio-economic conditions, male biased party leaders, and the nature of the electoral system (Rule 1994, 15), all of which compound to relegate women to the private realm.

The political party straddles the divide between the patriarchal society and the practice of citizenship, equality and democratic representation (Phillips 1991). It is the party which is the final determinant of women's presence or absence in political institutions and consequently in the public domain. The Nordic countries clearly demonstrate this. One reason why women enjoy a high representation in legislatures in Nordic countries is because many political parties use a quota system to ensure that they are fairly represented on party candidate lists under the list proportional representation (PR) system.

The average of 38.7 per cent of women representatives in parliaments in the Nordic countries contrasts with countries in central and South America, which primarily use list PR systems but where the average representation of women is little over 12 per cent. The PR electoral system affords the opportunity, but does not guarantee the numbers. The critical difference is the stage at which the parties nominate candidates.

While in South Africa the use of the list PR system has been advantageous to women, those who have entered Parliament have done it largely on the ANC ticket, the majority party having committed itself to gender equality. Prior to 1994, the National Party dominated a Parliament elected on a constituency basis, where at any given time between 1910 and 1994, no more than 3.6 per cent of elected MPs were women.

THE ROOTS OF WOMEN'S PARLIAMENTARY REPRESENTATION IN SOUTH AFRICA: 1910-1990

In 1910 the Union of South Africa was formed from four British colonies: the Cape, Natal, the Orange River Colony, and the Transvaal, and was constituted as a self governing dominion. Each of the four territories had a history of electoral politics before Union, but the franchise was limited to white males, and, in the Cape and Natal, was subject to property and education requirements (Lodge 1999). In 1930, the government extended the franchise to 'European' (white) women, partly in response to demands made by some women, but mainly as a means of reducing the significance of the coloured and African voters who were able to vote in the provinces of the Cape and Natal. Restricted and indirect forms of electing and representing 'non-whites' were implemented over the years (Lodge 1999)[1], but it was not until 1994 that universal adult suffrage was adopted in South Africa.

From unification until 1980, the South African Parliament consisted of the House of Assembly (Lower House) and the Senate (the Upper House). In 1980 the Senate was abolished. In 1983, the Tricameral Parliament was established, consisting of the House of Assembly, representing the white electorate; the House of Representatives, representing the coloured electorate; and the House of Delegates, representing the Indian electorate. This arrangement re-enfranchised coloured voters who had been subject to restricted voting rights for many years. As specified in the Interim Constitution of 1993, the Tricameral Parliament ceased to exist on 27 April 1994, being replaced by a Parliament consisting of a National Assembly and a Senate (now the National Council of Provinces). All elections prior to 1994 were contested on a constituency basis under the first-past-the-post (FPTP) electoral system.

White women in South Africa were first enfranchised in 1930 after a suffrage campaign spanning three decades (Vincent 1997, 102). With the support of the National Council of Women, Bertha Solomon, a pioneering feminist and politician, led the campaign for women's suffrage which was eventually extended in Act 18 of 1930 (Herrman 1974, 51) (black women and men were only able to vote in 1994). Although the fight for the vote has always been closely associated with urban and English-speaking women, Vincent argues that some Afrikaner women played a substantial role in the suffrage campaign by contesting the prevailing gender relations (Vincent 1997, 104) and maintains that the issue of women's enfranchisement was, at the time, one of the most controversial issues ever to have been dealt with in the South African Legislative Assembly. Helen Suzman reiterates this point, recounting that some members of the House of Assembly protested the enfranchisement of women. One man proclaimed that 'empty cradles would result', while another stated that 'suffrage would mean dragging women down from the pedestal where she stands remote and revered as a symbol of good influence, into the muddy arena of party politics' (Suzman 1993, 26). These responses emphasise the patriarchal nature of Parliament, where the majority of men held traditional beliefs about a woman's place.

The first woman elected to the House of Assembly (in 1933) was Mrs Leila Reitz of the United Party, who remained there for ten years. The second was Mrs Mabel Malherbe (1933-1938) of the National Party, elected in a by-election, who was also the first woman mayor of Pretoria (Sinclair 1975, 485). They were followed by Margaret Ballinger (1937-1960), the first woman to represent Africans in politics and a leading member of the Liberal Party; Carolina Badenhorst (1938-1943); and Bertha Solomon (1938-1958), both from the United Party. Helen Suzman was first elected to Parliament in 1953 as a member of the United Party, but in 1959 founded the Progressive Party, the first parliamentary organisation to offer white voters an alternative to apartheid policies (Lodge 1999). For many years Suzman was the sole Progressive Party representative, and from 1974 -1979 was the sole woman in Parliament.

While she won acclaim as a skilful and courageous fighter, Suzman acknowledged that she was not a staunch advocate of women's rights. She explained that 'I did not make gender discrimination a major priority, but I participated in every debate that affected women and women's rights in my years in Parliament' (Suzman 1993).

Suzman described Bertha Solomon of the United Party as the first real champion of women's rights in Parliament. Solomon spent many years arguing for the removal of women's legal disabilities and was largely responsible for the passage in 1953 of the Matrimonial Affairs Act, which removed some of the chief legal disabilities of married women (*Standard Encyclopaedia of Southern Africa* Vol 10 1974, 51).

As tables 1 and 2 below show, the parliamentary representation of women in South Africa prior to democratisation was low. From 1910 to 1994, only nineteen ('European') women held seats in the House of Assembly. In the Senate from 1910 to 1980, only six of 419 Senators (1.43%) were women. The first woman Senator was the Hon Mathilda Koster of the National Party, elected in 1955, and who remained until 1970. In the House of Delegates (representing the Indian electorate), only two women were indirectly elected by the National People's Party between1983 and 1990. In the eighty-seat House of Representatives (representing the coloured electorate) four women were elected during the same period. In the 1987 House of Assembly election, women were elected to five of the 166 seats (3.01%), and in the 1989 election six women were elected.[2] There was a total of eight women in the last Tricameral Parliament.

TABLE 1:
WOMEN ELECTED TO THE HOUSE OF ASSEMBLY IN THE 1987 GENERAL ELECTION[3]

GENERAL ELECTION: FEBRUARY 1987					
Party	**Votes**	**% Votes**	**Seats**	**Women**	**%**
National Party	1 790 291	52.4	123	3	2.44
Conservative Party	542 703	26.4	22	0	0
Progressive Federal Party	290 274	14.1	19	1	5.26
New Republic Party	39 587	2.0	1	0	0
Independents	27 149	1.3	1	0	0
Herstigte Nasionale Party	64 517	3.1	0	0	0
Total Seats			**166**	**4**	**2.41**

TABLE 2:
WOMEN ELECTED TO THE HOUSE OF ASSEMBLY IN THE 1989 GENERAL ELECTION

GENERAL ELECTION: SEPTEMBER 1989					
Party	**Votes**	**% Votes**	**Seats**	**Women**	**%**
National Party	1 039 704	48.0	93	4	4.30
Conservative Party	680 131	31.3	39	0	0
Democratic Party	431 444	20.0	33	2	6.06
HNP	5 416	0.2	0	0	0
Total Seats			**165**	**6**	**3.63**

The traditional and conservative norms of Afrikaner and English speaking political parties of the time, together with a constituency based electoral system (which often hampers women's electoral successes) ensured that women were principally relegated to the private sphere during this period.

The primary aim of the National Party (NP), which dominated South African politics for most of the twentieth century, was to enforce physical, social, and political separation of whites, blacks, Indians and coloureds by discriminating in favour of whites through apartheid policies (Seady 1999, 11). The NP had little regard for the position of women in society, or for their equal status with men. Whilst there were some outspoken voices on issues that affected women in the parliaments prior to 1994, such as Bertha Solomon, and later Sheila Camerer, gender equality between men and women was not high on the agenda of political parties. Nor was the representation of women and their interests a political issue for parties. It was outside the sphere of formal white parliamentary politics that the ANC, church groups, and women's organisations, struggled for women's political emancipation.

The ANC is the only political party in South Africa's past that has demonstrated an overt commitment to gender equality. Within the ANC and the national liberation movements, gender and race were linked with the demand for equal citizenship. The ANC was founded in 1912, essentially as a gathering of intellectuals. In the mid-1940s the leadership passed to men like Nelson Mandela, Oliver Tambo, and Walter Sisulu, pushing the movement into a more radical form of politics (Seady 1999, 8). The ANCWL was formed in 1943 and, while a feminist agenda did not dominate the ANC initially, the ANCWL raised issues of gender equality within the organisation. The work of the league throughout the 1940s was mostly confined to conventional 'women's work' such as fund-raising and catering, but in 1952 women started to participate in the ANC's defiance campaigns of civil disobedience, particularly against the pass laws (Geisler 1998, 5). In the 1950s, the League began to take up issues of formal discrimination against women in the law as well as broader issues of equality. This was reflected in the 1955 Women's Charter which claimed full gender equality, stating that the laws and customs that hinder women's progress hinder the whole nation, and warning that men would not be able to liberate themselves without extending equal rights to women (quoted in Geisler 1998, 5).

In 1954 the Federation of South African Women (FSAW) formed, uniting the ANC with white and Indian women's organisations and trade unions. One of the greatest victories for the FSAW and the ANC was the epic march of 20 000 women who gathered at the Union Buildings in

Pretoria in 1956 to demand an end to the pass laws. However, Geisler argues that the anti-pass protests did not question the patriarchal values that kept women in the home, but were a statement of outrage that gave them visibility in the public sphere. Furthermore, the needs often identified by the FSAW centred on the domestic role of women and resistance to Bantu education. '"Separationist feminist liberation" was not the focus of the movement's activities' (Geisler 1998). These examples highlight the largely conservative nature of the struggle waged by women during this period. Dubow argues that the FSAW was loyal to the ANC's liberation agenda, where women's concerns about issues such as the role of women in the domestic sphere or birth control were frequently secondary to the requirements of the national liberation movement (Dubow 2000, 56). Yet one of the most important features of the FSAW was that it was a women's organisation and 'managed to break new ground amongst women… ' by incorporating them into the political programme of the national liberation struggle (Geisler 1998, 7). Women were critical to the liberation struggle waged by the ANC, with thousands jailed, subjected to house arrest, killed, and exiled.[4]

With the banning of the ANC in 1960, and the closure of the FSAW in 1963, Geisler argues that a gap was left in political activism and the women's movement in the 1960s. In the 1970s trade union activism increased, and the heightened black consciousness militancy of students led to the Soweto uprising against Bantu education on 16 June 1976 (Geisler 1998, 7). In 1983, the United Democratic Front (UDF), consisting of nearly 400 anti-apartheid organisations, was formed. The UDF played a critical role in South Africa's transformation by mobilising people across the country to resist the state's institutions and policies. It promoted the profile of the ANC, and advocated a culture that emphasised democratic rights and claims indivisible by race (Seekings 2000, 3). Within the ANC a women's section was instituted which addressed the importance of women's liberation in the 1980s (the Women's League was re-launched in 1990). During this period many women were prepared to fight for liberation and were also drawn into the armed wing of the ANC, Umkhonto we Sizwe (MK). In 1989 women made up 20 per cent of MK cadres (Geisler 1998, 8).

In a Programme of Action adopted in 1986, the UDF stated that it was 'committed to the revival of the Federation of South African Women', and urged that 'women's organisations should be formed where none exist and should affiliate to regional structures which need to be built and strengthened to pave the way for a strong national structure' (Seekings 2000, 210). Branches of FEDSAW revived in 1987, but it was not for another five years that women's groupings in South Africa united as the Women's National Coalition. As Hassim argues, the demand for citizenship envisioned in the 1955 Women's Charter was not made again explicitly until the Women's National Coalition (WNC) drafted the Women's Charter for Effective Equality in 1993.

The motivation for forming the coalition arose from the broad understanding of the need for women to organise around specific issues. In mid-1991, the ANCWL called a meeting of political parties and women's organisations to debate how gender issues could be put on the agenda in the negotiation process. It was proposed that regional coalitions of women's organisations be established linking to national organisations in a broad coalition. The coalition engaged in a process of consulting with women throughout the country to draw up a document that would reflect their needs (Meintjes 1993, 9 and Albertyn, Hassim and Meintjes in this volume). The Charter moved equality beyond the formal terms of franchise rights and participation, where citizenship rights formed the basis of the right to equal participation in public office and in government.

The WNC, recognising the major challenge of demanding political rights for women amid the tough constitutional bargaining of twenty-six parties in the Negotiating Council, carried important issues into the national debate by linking the Women's Charter for Equality to multi-party debates about the Constitution (Funk-Bridgman 1994, 9).

> A tough demand now is to launch a fierce campaign to anchor the legal and social status of women as a central feature in any deliberations about the formation of a democratic South Africa. This is mainly a political question which would have to be embraced by all political formations and women's organisations for it to have any effect. (Wessels 1993, 3)

From the inception in 1991 of the negotiating process at the Conference for a Democratic South Africa (CODESA), there was a notable shortage of women negotiators. Proposals that mechanisms be adopted to ensure women's participation in the forum, led to the establishment of a Gender Advisory Council. However, when CODESA dissolved and the Multi-Party Negotiation Process (MPNP) started in 1993, there were again few women appointed. The WNC and political party representatives pressurised the MPNP and consensus was reached that there should be one woman delegate per political delegation and technical committee. Furthermore, a WNC monitoring group was established. Geisler (1998, 12) points out that this was the 'first ever *de facto* quota for women in South African history'. One of the critical successful interventions for women related to the status of customary law and traditional leadership, and whether customary law should be exempt from the equality clause in the Interim Constitution. In the end traditional leaders lost their bid to have it excluded. The lobbying and interventions of the WNC and the women political party representatives at the MPNP were crucial to the creation of a Constitution that secured and protected the political rights of women.

According to Caul, left-wing parties are more likely to support women's candidacies than right-wing ones because they are inclined to 'feel a need to be sensitive to groups traditionally excluded from circles of power'(Caul 1999, 82). Caul has also suggested that the number of women party activists can influence women's candidature. This argument is reiterated by Rai, who also argues that in transitional regimes the setting of strategic public priorities should involve all interest groups, as 'who plans and sets priorities, on what grounds and by what criteria, is critically important' (Rai 1996, 240). In Southern Africa there is a close correlation between levels of women's representation and political transformation. In South Africa, Mozambique, and Namibia, struggles for liberation raised debates about the representation of women (Lowe-Morna 2000, 40). Women activists fought for their concerns to be included on the agenda and as a result women are well represented in decision-making structures.

Along with the Interim Constitution, a new electoral system using proportional representation (PR) was adopted for South Africa's first democratic elections. A number of factors motivated the adoption of this system, including that fact that there was not enough time to register voters and produce a voters' roll, and the obvious need for the legislature to reflect as accurately as possible the number of votes cast for each party in the election (De Ville and Steytler 1996, 1). Fears that a constituency based system would result in the segregationist spatial arrangements of apartheid translating into ethnic bloc voting also prompted the use of the PR system. Another important consideration was that the legislature be representative of the people. In electoral terms, the general view of 'representation' is the relationship between a party's votes and its overall share of seats in the legislature. However, another important factor is the way in which the electoral system influences the degree to which the legislature 'mirrors' society and its different groups, in terms of race, gender or age. Representation is thus equated with an additional interpretation:

> [T]he electoral system should ensure an adequate representation of minorities, women and special interest groups in Parliament, as well as fair representation of parties according to their votes. (Krennerich 1999, 16)

Accordingly, representation can have a social dimension, where 'the composition of legislatures reflects the society from which they are drawn in terms of politically salient cleavages like gender, class, language and ethnicity' (Norris 1996, 184). In South Africa, the use of closed party lists provided political parties with the space to put up multi-racial, and multi-ethnic lists of candidates (Reynolds and Reilly 1997, 63). Although women are still somewhat under-represented in the National Assembly, the list-PR electoral system nevertheless provided the opportunity for a massive increase in the number of women representatives.

POLITICAL PARTIES AND GENDER EQUALITY IN LIST PR ELECTIONS: 1994-1999

In South Africa's national and provincial elections in 1994 and 1999 voters were given two ballot papers: one for the 400 seats in the National Assembly and one for the provincial legislatures. The allocation of seats to the legislatures was done according to a Droop quota and used the highest remainder principle (Lodge, Jones, and Ballington 1999, 100) with parties receiving seats in the legislatures in direct proportion to the votes cast for the party. Of the 400 National Assembly seats, 200 'regional' seats were allocated to provinces to ensure regional representation, and 200 were distributed according to the national vote. Political parties were required to present lists of candidates to the voters for election. It was up to the party to decide whether to submit both a national and a regional list, or a list for each region.[5] Nineteen parties contested the National Assembly elections in 1994 (of which seven achieved representation), and a further nine contested the provincial elections only. In 1999, sixteen parties contested the National Assembly elections (of which thirteen acheived representation) and a further ten contested at the provincial level only (IEC 1994, and Jones and Ballington 1999).

South Africa's PR system is based on the use of closed party lists, where electors vote solely for parties rather than for individual candidates.[6] Political parties determine the rank order of candidates on the lists and, unlike in a constituency election, voters are unable to influence, for example, the number of women elected to Parliament, by not selecting a woman candidate. The ANC 'balanced' its party ticket by ensuring representation of interest groups in society, including the largest group, women.[7]

While party organisational structure and ideology have a bearing on the number of women sent to Parliament by political parties, women party activists and gender related recruitment rules are the most direct mechanisms affecting women's parliamentary representation. Caul finds that the presence of large numbers of women activists within a party will enhance the likelihood that gender related candidate rules will be implemented (Caul 1999, 79). Rule notes that the nomination stage is crucial to a representative Parliament. Where women are politically active and form a large voting group, they are able to participate in the party nomination process (Rule 1994, 18). Parties are able to increase the proportion of nominated women candidates by creating formal rules that prescribe a certain proportion of women among the party's candidates. Such direct action may take the form of a gender quota or target, or a recommended percentage of women (Caul 1999, 83).

The concept of gender targets and quotas within parties first emerged in the late 1970s, and in advanced industrial societies the number of parties that establish quotas doubled between 1975 and 1985. The underlying assumption of a quota system is that its implementation will lead to a critical mass of women who will represent women's interests and be able to influence political decision-making to the betterment of women's status in society

(Ballington 1999, 9). No South African party other than the ANC has adopted the quota system.

1994 NATIONAL ELECTIONS, POLITICAL PARTIES, AND GENDER EQUALITY

The list-PR system gives political parties a certain amount of control over the composition of their parliamentary representatives. As parties determine the ranking of candidates on lists, they are able to plan in advance the composition of their caucuses (De Ville 1996, 24). Effectively this means that within political parties gender activists have to push for substantive roles for women or minority group representation.

As illustrated by Table 3, roughly 32 per cent of the ANC's candidates on the national list and regional list were women. The overall result was that 90 of the 252 ANC members of Parliament (35.7%) were women, a considerably higher figure than that of the representation of women in the other parties. The figure was also higher than the stipulated affirmative action principle pertaining to gender, suggesting that, overall, women were placed favourably on the list. An examination of the 1994 ANC lists reveals that the first woman, Albertina Sisulu, was tenth on the list, and was the only woman among the first twenty candidates. Of the first fifty names, only ten were women. Gevisser notes that the ANC list, even with its gender quota, bunched most of the women near the bottom, concluding that 'the top of the ANC remain[ed] a sea of testosterone' (Gevisser 1994, 5). This suggests that the high representation of women in Parliament rested quite substantially on the landslide victory of the ANC in 1994. In compiling representative candidate lists, it is therefore vital that women are placed near the top in 'winnable' and not merely ornamental positions.

The ANC quota system was heralded as a breakthrough by many. The *Mail & Guardian* concluded that 'those who consider the quota system patronising have underestimated the value of this achievement. The ANC appears to be the only party giving substantial attention to this issue. It is time others followed its lead' (*Mail & Guardian* 12 November 1993). They did not, and indeed some opposition candidates were vocal in their contempt for quotas as an instrument for increasing the representation of women. The National Party was opposed to affirmative action for women, and was

TABLE 3:
ESTIMATED PERCENTAGE OF WOMEN CANDIDATES ON NATIONAL AND REGIONAL PARTY LISTS AND NUMBER OF WOMEN IN PARLIAMENT PER PARTY IN 1994.[8]

1994 National Elections	Women National List %	Women Regional Lists %	No of MPs	No of Women MPs	Women as Proportion of MPs %
African Christian Democratic Party	12.9	9.6	2	0	0
African National Congress	32.2	32.6	252	90	35.7
Democratic Party	31.0	19.0	7	1	14.2
Inkatha Freedom Party	10.4	15.9	43	10	23.3
National Party	N/A	11.4	82	9	11.0
Pan Africanist Congress of Azania	11.8	12.0	5	1	20.0
Vyrheidsfront/Freedom Front	12.0	7.8	9	0	0
Total			**400**	**111**	**27.7**

reported to have found the quota offensive as 'it ends up humiliating the very people who are supposed to benefit from it. Merit alone should determine if a person gets a job' (Kooma 1994). The party's leader, F.W. de Klerk, was reported as saying that 'women's rights are not less or more important than those of men and children. The National Party stands for equality and equality to us means that rights of all must be balanced' (Kooma 1994). The removal of discriminatory laws and the introduction of development programmes supportive to women was reportedly the NP route to encouraging women's participation in politics (Gevisser 1994, 5).

As illustrated in Table One, the NP did not compile a national list of candidates for the National Assembly, but submitted regional lists with just over 11 per cent representation of women. An examination of the candidates lists reveals that women did not feature prominently. For example, on the list submitted for the Orange Free State, no more than three of thirty candidates were women, and in the Western Cape, women numbered five of the forty-two candidates. This had a significant impact on the number of women elected to Parliament. Of the eighty-two seats awarded to the National Party, only nine, a mere 11 per cent, were held by women. Nonetheless, this was twice the number in the last white Parliament in which only 4.3 per cent of NP seats were held by women.

For the Inkatha Freedom Party (IFP), the vision of a 'modern and liberal democratic society' meant a change in the status of women, particularly black women, in society (*Speak* May 1994, 2). The IFP Women's Brigade did not feel that a quota system was necessary, as Faith Gasa explained, 'because there is a tradition of participation' (*Sunday Times* 28 November 1993). But as the IFP committed itself to taking part in the elections one week before they were due to be held, there was little participation in the compilation of the party's lists. As Table 1 suggests, the IFP, without a quota, had few women overall on its candidate lists. However, ten of the forty-three IFP members of Parliament (just over 23%) were women, indicating that most of them were placed in 'electable' positions on regional lists. This was particularly the case in the regional list submitted from KwaZulu-Natal, from which seven of the ten female IFP MPs were elected.

The Preamble of the Democratic Party's regulations for nomination of candidates under a proportional representation system, adopted in December 1993, stated that:

> While no specific mechanisms for affirmative action on the basis of race or gender are contained in these regulations, the expected demands of the electorate for Party lists that are both non-racial and non-sexist are noted.

Although the DP was opposed to the implementation of a quota system, there was conscious recognition that women should be placed on the lists. Provincial candidate Anchen Dreyer stated in March 1994 that the DP believed equality should be achieved through legislation, noting that 'the DP believes that the ANC's quota system will serve to perpetuate the separate status of women' (Merton 1994). Dene Smuts, a staunch advocate of women's rights and a founder of the National Women's Coalition, opposed the quota system, arguing that 'when you send a person into public life under a quota system, you automatically send her with a question hanging over her head about her competence' (Gevisser 1994, 5). Although there was a high representation of women on the DP's lists overall there were only two women in the top twenty names on the national list. As a result, only one woman out of seven was elected to Parliament in 1994. While women constituted over 30 per cent of the names on the DP's national and regional lists, there was only 14 per cent representation of women at the national level.

The smaller opposition parties were equally cynical about the quota. The Freedom Front (FF) decided late in the process to take part in the elections and no elections or other wider discussion influenced the order of names on the national list As a result, there were only three women in the first thirty names on its national list. None of the nine Freedom Front parliamentarians elected in 1994 was a woman. The Pan Africanist Congress (PAC) did not have a specific policy on women because the PAC 'views women as equals' (*Speak* 1994, 2). However, women were not equally represented on party lists. Only Patricia de Lille appeared in the top fifteen names on the national list, and she was the only PAC woman to be elected to Parliament (on the regional list). The African Christian Democratic Party (ACDP) had a low representation nationally, nearly 13 per cent, and regionally, less than 10 per cent of women on its party lists in 1994. As the party only won two seats in the legislature, no women were elected on its ticket.

Partly in response to the low representation of women on party lists, the Women's Rights and Peace Party (WRPP) was formed in early 1994 to contest the elections so as to increase women's participation in politics (Vutela 1994). The WRPP wanted women's rights and issues to be considered in every decision made in Parliament, and argued that women's issues should not be ignored or left to a section of government dealing with those issues. The party's manifesto stated that 'it is time for the presence of a women's party in government in which the leaders are women and the majority of candidates are women', and 'it is time for women to have equal decision making powers with men'. The WRPP received insufficient votes to be represented in the National Assembly. This is perhaps not surprising, as Kelley illustrates by reviewing the experiences of women's political parties in other western democracies, where they have had a minimal effect. The impact of women's issues is apparently insufficient to generate and maintain a viable women's political party and obtain the broad based support needed to obtain power (Kelley 1992 7-8). These findings confirm the view that women do not conceive of politics simply in terms of gender, but that politics is issue based and these issues are linked to gender within the party.

The 27.7 per cent figure of women in the National Assembly in 1994 was not quite reached at provincial level where 102 of the 425 (24%) members of provincial legislatures (MPLs) were women. The representation of women was low in the Senate (which has since been replaced by the National Council of Provinces). Women comprised 17 of the 90 members (18.8%). Both the Speaker and the Deputy Speaker of Parliament were women, as were eight chairpersons of select committees (CEDAW report).

Between 19 May 1994 and 23 April 1999, there were 122 resignations from the National Assembly. Only eighteen of these (14.8%) were women – twelve from the ANC, three from the NP, two from the IFP and one from the DP. However, thirty-two replacements were women twenty-three ANC, six NP, two IFP, and one DP, increasing the number of women in the National Assembly to 115 (28.8%) at the end of 1998.[9]

1999 NATIONAL ELECTIONS

In the 1999 national and provincial elections little changed in the positioning of political parties with regard to the compilation of party lists, and their stance toward a gender quota.

In May 1999, approximately half the ANC's membership, and twenty-one of seventy-three members of the National Executive Committee (NEC) were women (EISA questionnaire 1999).[10] A commitment to gender equality filtered through many ANC documents, including its election manifesto and conference resolutions. The party again expressed its commitment to gender equality by implementing a gender quota guaranteeing at least a 30 per cent representation of women on party lists but in1999 it went one step further by not only increasing the representation of women to 39 per cent on the national list, but also placing them in 'electable' positions (one in three) throughout most of the list. Three women featured among the top ten names on the national list, ten among the top thirty, and eighteen among the top fifty, compared to one woman in the top ten and ten in the first fifty in 1994. The ANC boasted the highest representation of women on both national and regional lists, with an average of 36.5 per cent. As a result, 96 of the party's 266 seats in the National Assembly were held by women after the election.

Former Health Minister Nkosazana Zuma was the first woman on the national list, in position three (up from 51st position in 1994), followed by Geraldine Fraser-Moloketi and Winnie Madikizela Mandela in sixth and ninth places (*Government Gazette* 1999).[11] Sixty-two women who had sat in the previous Parliament were returned, indicating that nearly two-thirds of ANC women were re-elected in 1999. There were thirty-five new women's faces in Parliament, and twenty-five women (27.7%) chose not to return to the National Assembly in 1999.[12]

Among the opposition parties, twenty-three of 134 (17%) seats in 1999 were held by women. This figure was higher than the total in 1994 when women occupied twenty-one of the 148 opposition seats (14.19%). Included were twelve new faces, and eleven MPs who had sat in the 1994 Parliament. All seven IFP women elected had held seats in the previous Parliament. Most of the new faces appeared in the DP, where Dene Smuts had been the only representative in 1994. Sheila Camerer and Anna van Wyk of the NNP returned in 1999. As in 1994, none of the opposition parties contesting the elections implemented a gender quota. Consequently, women were low on party lists.

Before the 1999 elections, the ACDP estimated its female membership as 51 per cent, and six out of the fifteen members (40%) of its national executive were women (Response to EISA questionnaire 1999). The party's position on gender equality is that 'neither man nor women [is] more equal than the other', and the biggest problem women face is marginalisation. 'Issues such as rape, domestic violence etc [are] a consequence of this dilemma.' With regard to the representation of women on party lists, the ACDP believed that women enjoy equal access within the party to develop and contribute to the balance of abilities and gifts within the ACDP. As such, the party, in compiling lists, used no official affirming mechanism. Next to the ANC, the ACDP boasted the highest representation of women on its national list, with 29 per cent, and second highest on the regional lists, with 24 per cent. This was a notable improvement on its 1994 average of about 11 per cent. Both MPs elected to the National Assembly in 1994 were male. In 1999 women held two of the party's six seats.

While the gender composition of the Democratic Party is unknown, twenty-eight of ninety-two (30%) members of the DP's Federal Council in 1999 were women. The party's position on gender equality was that 'women's rights are part and parcel of human rights, and any form of discrimination constitutes an infringement of the principles of equality and dignity'. The party was still 'opposed to quotas because they actually disadvantage people entering public life (Response to EISA questionnaire 1999)' and preferred to raise awareness of representivity. In 1994 an average of 25 per cent of women were represented on national and regional party lists. In 1999, the figure on the regional lists decreased to 21 per cent. As a result, women held only seven of the party's thirty-eight seats (18.4%).

Before the elections in 1994, the IFP had taken the position that a quota system for increasing women's representation was not necessary. In 1998, its leader, Mangosuthu Buthelezi, was quoted as saying: 'I would really like to see that our lists of candidates for the 1999 provincial and national elections reflect the notion of comparable, if not equal participation of women in politics' (Commission on Gender Equality 1998).

In 1994 only 13 per cent of candidates on the national and regional lists were women. In 1999 that percentage had increased to 22 per cent on the national list and 28.6 per cent on the regional lists, still shy of the party leader's wish to see equal participation. Women hold seven of the party's thirty-four seats in the National Assembly.

In March 1999 women formed approximately 58 per cent of the NNP's support base, and three of its twenty-member national executive were women. The NNP developed a Women's Policy document which acknowledged the important social, economic and political role women play in South Africa and committed the party to full equality for all women of South Africa as guaranteed by the Constitution (NNP 1999, 1). Tersia Wessels explained that the NNP was not in favour of implementing a quota system for its party lists for the 1999 elections. The Federal Women's Action of the NNP highlighted a number of aims with regard to the 1999 elections, including 'the empowerment of women (skills training) to move into decision-making positions in the party' and the education of 'women about the need for female representatives at the decision-making positions in politics and parties' (NNP 1999, 1). Like the DP, the NNP opted to submit only regional party lists to contest seats in the National Assembly rather than to submit both regional lists and a national list. In 1994, only 11.4 per cent of its regional lists comprised women, and 11 per cent of the elected MPs were women. In 1999, the number of women on the lists increased to just over 18 per cent. Only three of the party's 28 seats (10.7%) were held by women in 1999.

Approximately 25 per cent of PAC members in early 1999 were women. The party claimed to support 'African womanhood' as well as equal opportunities for all. But while the PAC was aware 'that women face numerous problems positioning themselves within the Party due to male attitudes, culture and traditions', it did not confront these problems by implementing a quota system guaranteeing women positions on party lists, stating that women were free 'to take up any position whatsoever' (EISA questionnaire 1999). In 1994, only 12 per cent of candidates on the PAC's national and regional lists were women. In 1999 22 per cent of the national and 19 per cent of the regional lists consisted of women. Patricia de Lille was the only woman to be elected on the PAC ticket in 1999.

Approximately 42 per cent of the Freedom Front's members were women, and, before the 1994 elections, six out of 75 (8%) members of the national executive were women. The party's official position on gender equality was that 'we believe in gender equality in all spheres of life, but that merit should play a decisive role'. While 'the issue of representation is [borne] in mind' merit was of prime importance, and 'quotas will not be considered' (EISA questionnaire 1999). None of the nine elected MPs in 1994 was a woman. In 1999 the party increased its representation of women on lists to 16 per cent nationally and 17.7 per cent regionally, but women were not placed in 'electable' positions and hold none of the party's three seats in Parliament.

Before the 1999 June elections, approximately half the United Democratic Movement (UDM)'s membership and support base consisted of women. The party subscribed to the constitutional right to gender equality, where the full participation of women in economic, social and political activities must be encouraged. While it did not implement a quota system, it applied an affirming mechanism in its list procedure to promote women.

TABLE 4:
ESTIMATED PERCENTAGE OF WOMEN CANDIDATES ON NATIONAL AND REGIONAL PARTY LISTS, AND NUMBER OF WOMEN IN PARLIAMENT PER PARTY IN 1999.[13] BETWEEN 10 JUNE AND 1 SEPTEMBER 1999, THE NUMBER OF WOMEN REPRESENTED IN PARLIAMENT INCREASED TO 120 WITH THE ADDITION OF ANOTHER WOMAN TO THE ANC, BRINGING THE ANC TOTAL TO 97.

1999 NATIONAL ELECTIONS

Party	Women National List %	Women Regional Lists %	No of of MPs	No of Women MPs	Women as Proportion of MPs %
African Christian Democratic Party	29.0	24.0	6	2	33.3
African National Congress	39.0	34.0	266	96	36.1
Afrikaner Eenheids Beweging	14.5	18.5	1	0	0
Azanian People's Organisation	18.0	15.6	1	0	0
Democratic Party	N/A	21.0	38	7	18.4
Federal Alliance	13.0	13.6	2	0	0
Inkatha Freedom Party	22.0	28.6	34	7	20.6
Minority Front	14.0	1.6	1	1	100
New National Party	N/A	18.4	28	3	10.7
Pan Africanist Congress of Azania	22.0	19.0	3	1	33.3
United Christian Democratic Party	26.0	24.7	3	0	0
United Democratic Movement	23.0	19.0	14	2	14.3
Vryheidsfront/Freedom Front	16.0	17.7	3	0	0
Total			**400**	**119**	**29.75**

This took into account the merit, abilities, experience, and capacity of each candidate. The UDM was the only party apart from the ANC to specify the gender of candidates on the national list but after 1999 only two of the party's fourteen seats (14.3%) were held by women.

Five other small parties gained representation in the 1999 Parliament, retaining a total of eight seats between them. Of these, only one was held by a woman, indicating that the presence of many parties in Parliament may hinder women's chances of election. While the only seat gained by the Minority Front was held by a woman, Sally Rajbally, the party was not strictly committed to a policy of gender equality. As Table 4 demonstrates, only 14 per cent of the party's national list and a mere 1.6 per cent of the regional lists consisted of women. The other minority parties are right of centre on the ideological spectrum, confirming the oft-touted thesis that more women are likely to be elected from centre-left parties.

As Table 5 shows, 27.6 per cent (an increase over the 24 per cent in 1994) of Members of Provincial Legislatures (MPLs) in 1999 were women, most of them elected on the ANC ticket. The National Council of Provinces (NCOP), which is the second legislative chamber at the national level, consists of 90 members, of which 54 are permanent and 36 are special (rotating) delegates. Each of the nine provincial parliaments sends six permanent members to the NCOP. In 1999, seventeen of the fifty-four permanent delegates (31.4%) were women. This figure excludes special delegates as they are continually subject to change.

After the 1994 elections, three of twenty-seven ministers (11%) and three of twelve deputy ministers (25%) appointed by President Mandela were women. In the last white Parliament only one minister and one deputy minister were women. In a Cabinet reshuffle in March 1996, Mandela increased the number of women ministers to four out of twenty-five, and appointed three new woman deputy ministers, making a total of eight out of thirteen (CEDAW report). In June 1999, newly elected President Mbeki increased the number of women Cabinet ministers from four to eight out of twenty-nine (27.6%), and included eight women deputy ministers out of thirteen (61.5%) in his team. This new Cabinet was heralded as 'revolutionary for its high number of female candidates (Inter Press Service 18 June 1999)'. This total compared favourably with the rest of Africa, where, in 1999, roughly 7.8 per cent of ministers were women. The global average is 8.7 per cent, with Western Europe recording the highest proportion 20 per cent (Reynolds 1997, 19).

In terms of women party leaders South Africa falls behind the world average. In 1994, the only one of nineteen parties (5.3%) contesting the national elections headed by a woman was the WRPP (the Women's Rights Peace Party). The South African Women's Party was also headed by a woman, but the party only contested the provincial elections in the Western Cape. In 1999, the Green Party was the only one of sixteen parties (6.3%) contesting at the national level to be headed by a woman. The Mass United Movement, also headed by a woman, contested the provincial election in KwaZulu-Natal. None of the political parties represented in Parliament to date has had a woman at its head. Reynolds notes that aside from Ruth Sando Perry's eleven-month period as Liberia's transitional head of state (1996-97), no woman has ever led a party or been head of state in Africa.

TABLE 5:
WOMEN MEMBERS OF EXECUTIVE COUNCILS AND MEMBERS OF PROVINCIAL LEGISLATURES

Province	MPLs	Women	Proportion of women %	MECs	Women	Proportion of women %
Eastern Cape	63	15	23.8	10	2	20.0
Free State	30	7	23.3	11	3	27.3
Gauteng	73	25	34.2	11	3	27.3
Kwa-Zulu Natal	80	21	26.2	11	1	9.1
Mpumalanga	30	8	26.7	10	2	20.0
Northern Cape	30	8	26.7	11	3	27.3
Northern Province	49	15	30.6	11	1	9.1
North West	33	10	30.3	11	3	27.3
Western Cape	42	10	23.8	13	2	15.4
Total	**430**	**119**	**27.6**	**99**	**20**	**20.2**

(compiled from lists received from Provincial Parliaments on 1 September 1999)

Internationally, less than 11 per cent of the world's party leaders are women, and the number of women leading their nations as Prime Ministers or Presidents at any one time has never reached double figures (Reynolds 1997, 20).[14]

CONCLUSION

South Africa's chequered electoral history demonstrates the compounding effect of the electoral system and political parties on the representation of women in Parliament. From unification in 1910 to the establishment of democratic institutions in 1994, no more than thirty women held seats in the House of Assembly and the Tricameral Parliaments. Elections during this period were contested under FPTP in what was essentially a two-party system. While whites were enfranchised throughout most of this period, South Africans of all races were only enfranchised in 1994. The FPTP electoral system, together with the conservative nature of traditional 'white-right' political parties, gave women little visibility in the public political realm prior to 1994.

During the liberation struggle, and primarily through the structures of the ANCWL, FEDSAW, the UDF, and the WNC, issues of gender equality gained prominence on the national agenda. The contributions of the WNC, together with those of committed gender activists, ensured that South Africa's Interim Constitution reflected a democratic dispensation that secured the political and citizenship rights of women. The adoption of the list PR electoral system in the 1994 elections provided the opportunity for an increase in the number of women legislators. Largely thanks to the ANC's quota policy, the number of women legislators increased nine-fold from a mere 3.63 per cent in 1989 to 27 per cent in 1994.

In the five years between 1994 and 1999, 230 women were elected in national elections, contrasting with the mere thirty women elected in the eighty-four years between Union and democratisation. Favourable electoral procedures offer women the best opportunity for representation but do not ensure their election to office or the existence of a representative Parliament that can only result from representative party lists and the placing of women in electable positions on those lists.

NOTES

1. As Lodge explains, African voters were removed from the roll in 1936 and instead qualified voters could vote for three white 'Native Representatives' in the Cape. Indirect elections were also established to send four white native senators to the Upper House, and Africans could elect twelve African representatives to an advisory Native Representative Council. These arrangements were abolished in 1959, and until 1994, the only elected bodies that represented Africans were those that existed in 'homeland' areas established by the apartheid government. Indians and coloureds were removed from the municipal rolls in Natal in 1964 and the Cape in 1968, but were re-enfranchised in 1984 with the establishment of the Tricameral Parliament.
2. Unofficial list received from Parliamentary Library, 25 November 1999.
3. The National Party MPs were Sheila Camerer, Tersia King, and Joanna Hunter. Esmé Chait was indirectly elected as a National Party member in May 1987. The Progressive Federal Party representative was Helen Suzman.
4. Pressure of space does not allow me to expand on this point but it is a subject worthy of detailed analysis in its own right. My intention here is to highlight the many and varied roles that women played in liberation politics in South Africa. I refer readers to Saul Dubow for further reading.
5. In 1994 the National Party submitted regional lists only. In 1999, the NNP and DP submitted regional lists only.
6. A closed list system can be distinguished from an open list system by the fact that under the latter voters are able to express a preference for a particular candidate on a party list. Under a closed list system political parties determine the order of candidates.
7. The composition of the ANC lists also represents the party's alliance partners including the Youth League, Women's League, the South African Communist Party, and the Congress of South Africa Trade Unions (Cosatu).

8. It is important to note that the number of women on candidate lists is approximate. As candidates' names, and not title or gender, appear on official published lists, the possibility of minimal error in determining women candidates does exist. Information is taken from final consolidated lists of candidates published in the *Government Gazette* Notice 409 of 1994.
9. These figures are calculated from unofficial data received from Parliament, 28 April 1999. As a result, the numbers are subject to correction.
10. Information taken from responses to a questionnaire compiled and circulated by EISA, May 1999.
11. Information is deduced from lists of candidates submitted to the IEC for election of the National Assembly and Provincial Legislatures, published in *Government Gazette* Notice 921 of 1999. Pretoria, 11 May.
12. Number of women in Parliament is calculated from a list published in *Government Gazette*, 10 June 1999.
13. As gender is not specified on party lists, percentages are approximate. N/A= not applicable as only regional lists were submitted. Number of women in Parliament calculated from list published in *Government Gazette*, 10 June 1999.
14. In 1998 only five nations were headed by women: Guyana, Sri Lanka, New Zealand, Bermuda, and Bangladesh.

5

THE DUAL POLITICS OF REPRESENTATION: WOMEN AND ELECTORAL POLITICS IN SOUTH AFRICA

Shireen Hassim *

ARGUMENTS IN WESTERN FEMINISM

Women's electoral politics in South Africa in 1994 and 1999 was marked by the collective demands of women for participation and representation. In both elections, arguments for the increased representation of women in elected offices and for greater visibility of 'women's concerns' in national political debates marked the substance of the engagement of women's organisations' in electoral debates. By the 1999 election debate had shifted from a concern with numbers to a concern with the nature and quality of representation and participation. The interventions of women's organisations in electoral politics reflected a concern with specific policy issues and party manifestos, and with the relationship between elected women representatives and women voters. These shifts suggest a maturing of women's electoral politics and a consolidation of women as an electoral constituency. The balance of this chapter charts this process of constituency building among women in the 1999 election, examines the electoral outcomes in terms of their implications for increasing women's political leverage in the representative sphere, and considers the challenges that continue to face women in political parties and women's organisations with regard to consolidating their constituencies.

* The author thanks Rupert Taylor, Stephen Gelb, and Adila Hassim for comments on this chapter.

The idea that women, as a group, constituted an electoral constituency entered South African politics in the early 1990s.[1] The interests that were seen to hold this constituency together, however, were narrowly defined in terms of a common exclusion from the processes and forums of public decision making. Indeed, inclusivity had been the prime focus of the Women's National Coalition since its formation in 1992. The concentration on 'getting women in', to a large extent regardless of political ideology, provided the glue which held together a diverse range of women's organisations and gender ideologies in the run-up to the 1994 elections. Debate focused on mechanisms to achieve women's representation – most notably the quota – rather than on the particular interests of different groups of women.

Accompanying the drive to 'get women in' was an emphasis on 'getting women's vote out'. Women's organisations (and, to a lesser extent, political parties) were concerned that higher levels of illiteracy, poverty, and spatial marginalisation would prejudice women's right to exercise their vote. In addition, it was feared that a combination of political violence and patriarchal control would keep women out of the electoral process. A significant proportion of the efforts of women's organisations was therefore devoted to voter education campaigns directed at women which constituted the ambit of gender politics in the April 1994 election.

Within these terms, the strategic approach of the women's movement was successful. Women constituted a record 27.7 per cent of all parliamentarians elected, placing South Africa in the ranks of advanced democracies on this indicator. This statistic was widely used locally and internationally to signal the extent to which the new democracy was inclusive. Furthermore, for the 1999 election, just over 1.5 million more women than men registered to vote. This figure suggests that women are informed citizens and that, at least at the procedural level, they are not disadvantaged.

In the June 1999 election, the conception of constituency among women's organisations advanced significantly beyond broad formulations. While representation and participation remained key concerns, there has been a much deeper consideration of the strategic uses of political leverage. This has been facilitated by a dense network of organisational initiatives to pressurise political parties to consider both the quality and the extent of women's representation on their party lists, to challenge parties on the gender implications of their manifestos, and to engage in interest group politics around specific policy initiatives.

CONSTITUENCIES, INTERESTS, AND WOMEN'S POLITICS

A central feature of South African women's politics in the 1990s was the notion of difference – of race, age, location, and ethnicity (Cock 1997; Fester 1997; Hassim and Gouws 1998; Meintjes 1998). This view differs from 'conventional' feminist arguments which seek to treat women as a single political group and focus on justice (the exclusion of women from politics is unfair), different values (women bring a specific set of values, experiences and expertise to politics, whether because of biology or social relations) or different interests (between women and men in society).[2] When transposed to debates about representation, these attempts to construct women as a coherent group tend to lead to the replacement of electoral politics – party contestation over policies with debates about the premises of various arguments. This may be both misplaced and unnecessary in current South African politics. The glaring disparity between the numbers of women voters and of women representatives, even where formal equality is the norm, underlines the salience of women as an electoral category (Phillips 1989).

With this disparity in mind a useful starting point from which to argue for a greater numerical representation of women is a strategic perspective suggesting that the likelihood of gender inequality becoming a policy issue is in direct proportion to the number of women representatives. Thirty per cent is seen as the critical mass in national legislatures – achieving this makes women's participation effective (Dahlerup 1998; Ballington 1998). Though some women representatives may have neither the ability nor the inclination to address gender inequalities, this 'scatter shot' strategy suggests their cumulative weight will impact on Parliament.

This argument is valuable because it sidesteps the controversial areas of normative judgements about fairness, as well as the essentialist arguments about women's difference. It does not assume that women are best able to represent women's interests, or that women's interests are coherent across race, class or age. Rather, it is an argument posed at the most general and pragmatic level, and is relatively detached from assumptions about what kinds of policies are best for women, or what kinds of substantive changes are needed to empower women. For this reason, it is an argument that can be made strategically within any political party or non-governmental organisation (NGO) that claims to be supportive of gender equality.[3]

Interest in representation *per se is* common to all women, regardless of class, race and ideological differences. The demand for greater representation in its broadest formulation does not pre-judge the ways in which gender inequalities will be taken up by representatives once they are in the legislature. The issue is rather one of access to arenas of public decision making so that the *various* interests of women can be debated and acted upon (Karam and Lovenduski 1998). Without broad representation it is unlikely in fact that the complexities of gender inequalities can be fully appreciated in policy terms. It is a significant gain for the widespread debate over the quota in 1994 that virtually all political parties in South Africa have formally accepted the need for greater women's representation.[4]

THE 1994 AND 1999 ELECTIONS

There are many reasons why possession of the franchise will not in itself immediately result in substantial numbers of women being elected to Parliament. There is no social consensus in South Africa as to the political significance of women's interests relative to other issues of empowerment.[5] The attempt by the Women's Party to mobilise the women's vote separately was singularly unsuccessful.[6] While a number of gains have been made at the formal level[7], these gains were won as a result of elite persuasion rather than by a mass movement of women. The fact that this 'negotiated revolution' has not yet developed deep social legitimacy has implications for the process of building an electoral constituency, as the broad population of women voters is not convinced of the need to elect women to positions of power.

An associated tendency is for stereotypes of women's supposed inabilities as leaders to continue to hold, despite the greater visibility of women in politics. Anecdotal evidence of this abounds among women in political parties women are regarded, even by other women, as incompetent, weak leaders.[8] Party political processes also create obstacles which prevent women's election to national office. Fewer women candidates are available because of internal party obstacles such as the operation of 'locker-room' networks. Social constraints on women's entry into politics make fewer candidates available for selection. Women's multiple social roles, in particular their child care responsibilities, create a 'time poverty' which keeps them out of formal politics (or at least keeps out women with young children or elderly relatives who need care).

In South Africa, the formal commitment in the Constitution to equality has been used by gender activists to argue that the under-representation of women in Parliament is undesirable.[9] However, there is no consensus among women activists in political parties as to how better representation could be achieved, and there are major differences over the use of quotas. One argument is that the blockages to women's political participation will be removed in the long term as women are economically and socially empowered. This gradualist argument is most fully articulated by the Democratic Party (DP), and supported by the New National Party (NNP) and the Inkatha Freedom Party (IFP). It assumes that as more women enter the workforce, as discriminatory practices such as job stereotyping are removed, and as educational opportunities are spread evenly between the sexes, women will move into the public political realm in greater numbers. For this reason, the DP has opposed the use of quotas to increase women's representation, seeing these mechanisms as an unnecessary incursion into civil liberties (see also Ballington in this volume).[10]

The DP has adopted a consistently liberal position on gender equality, whether in terms of representation or policy manifesto. By contrast, the NNP has tended to be more reactive to the way in which gender issues are articulated by the ANC, which has allowed some room for gender activists within the party to make inroads into leadership despite the absence of a clear policy on gender equality. While the NNP also officially rejects quotas, there is some support for quotas among women activists at lower levels of the party. Tersia Wessels, Gauteng Member of the Executive Council for the party, has acknowledged that the ANC's use of a quota had a positive impact on the NNP's party list, and the party has been making more active efforts to include women in leadership positions.[11]

The implication of a non-interventionist approach is that the attainment of gender equality is seen as a slow, gradualist process. Embedded in the gradualist position is a wariness of special status being granted to specific groups, stemming from a concern that it reduces the choices of individual voters. A counter argument is that party pre-selection exists in most electoral systems as candidates are selected before they are put to the public vote, and there is no particular reason why the criteria for pre-selection should not include gender. This is particularly true with a Proportional Representiaton (PR) list system. Moreover, studies of more established democracies reveal that there is no guarantee that equality will extend beyond the formal level despite the reduction of opportunity disparities between the sexes.

In the 1999 elections in South Africa women benefited from the creation of a range of mechanisms to advance democracy, including a constitutional provision on gender equality. These mechanisms provided a legitimising framework for the advancement of gender claims in policy debates. The constitutional clause on equality establishes gender equality as a core principle and value of South African democracy. This provision has had far-reaching formal impact, in that both political parties and the Independent Electoral Commission (IEC) must ensure that women's participation is not prejudiced in any way by the nature of electoral campaigns or by the procedural aspects of the elections.[12] The presence of gender activists among IEC commissioners has facilitated attention to gender issues in the work of the Commission.

Two prominent studies of women in European legislatures have found that there is a distinct gender pattern in the allocation of ministerial portfolios (Lovenduski 1986; Randall 1987). Lovenduski argues that women are generally allocated the 'soft' ministries of family, welfare, and culture. She regards this as a further aspect of gatekeeping.

South Africa does not fit into this pattern. After the 1994 election, 15 per cent (4 of 27) of ministers were women and 56 per cent (8 of 14) of deputy ministers. This significant representation of women at the highest levels contrasts with the proportion of women MPs. The 'social' portfolios (Health, Welfare, Housing) assigned to women were key areas that formed the cornerstone of the ANC's electionl manifestos in both elections. Moreover, the deputy ministers of the 'hard' portfolios of Finance, and Trade and Industry in the 1994-1998 Parliament were also women.

A more significant gender pattern can be found in the membership of parliamentary portfolio committees. Women's representation ranged from 0 per cent (Public Accounts) to 73 per cent (Health) (Mtintso 1999, 64). Committees in which women dominated include Welfare (60%), and Communications (66%). Women are notably under-represented in Land Affairs (18%), Mineral and Energy Affairs (12%), Transport (12%), Foreign Affairs (12%) and Labour (19%) (Mtintso 1999,64).

After the 1999 elections the new President, Thabo Mbeki, consolidated women's position in the Cabinet (see Ballington, Chapter 4 in this volume), appointing eight women ministers (of twenty-nine). In addition eight (of thirteen) deputy ministers are women. Among the portfolios occupied by the latter are Defence and Mineral and Energy Affairs, both traditionally considered 'hard' portfolios. The Minister of Mineral and Energy Affairs is also a woman.

Comparative research on women who have entered the representational sphere suggests that entry does not usually translate into upward mobility within the hierarchy of Parliament. In a wide-ranging comparison of women parliamentarians in European democracies, Joni Lovenduski found that:

> When gatekeepers are forced to admit women, they may still manage to keep them at the bottom of hierarchies once admitted. This, it appears, is what has happened in Europe. A generally higher proportion of women in legislatures, which has failed to be reproduced in executive bodies, is an indicator of such a pattern. (Lovenduski 1986, 241)

This was found to be true even in Scandinavian countries, which have a long history of quotas for women in various forms. Vicky Randall (1987, 109) reaches a similar conclusion after studying women in formal politics. She notes, 'At the apex of the representational hierarchy within national governments, women often virtually disappear.'

The opposite is the case in South Africa as it is in Australia and Uganda. In Australia, Moon and Fountain found that 'Australian women's political fortunes improve as they move from the party to the parliamentary arena' (Moon and Fountain 1997, 458). Their explanation for the counter-trend is twofold. Firstly, they argue that in 'parties of the left' party 'gatekeepers' are responsive to the notion that the selection of women is good for the party. They are therefore prepared to circumvent, through the use of the party list, traditional cultural and structural obstacles to women's political mobility. Secondly, they maintain, once women are in Parliament they are more likely to be judged on merit rather than on their gender. Given that women have to be 'twice as good' as men to overcome intra-party obstacles to their selection, those who are elected to Parliament are likely to be better qualified.

It is too early to offer definitive explanations analogous to those of Moon and Fountain for the high representation of women in the South African Cabinet. A democratic parliament would have to be in operation for many terms before it would be possible to determine whether a trend could be discerned in the relationship between women MPs and different party hierarchies. It is possible to note that the ANC, the majority party in the first two governments, was highly responsive to claims of gender representation and that this has underpinned many party policies.[13]

The establishment of a climate in which gender representation was part of the democratic discourse of 1994 was largely due to the successful mobilisation of the Women's National Coalition. With the decline of the organisation, and the increasing power of political parties, the women's sections within parties will have to exert pressure to keep gender issues on party manifestos and programmes. As Anne Phillips (1989) has shown, within representative democracies it is political parties that offer the most substantial vehicles for advancing group claims to representation. The capacity of internal women's structures will therefore become the crucial link to the long-term success of women's demand for access to decision-making forums.

THE INTERNAL POLITICS OF CONSTITUENCY BUILDING

Apart from successfully making women's representation a multiparty concern, women's organisations ensured that the majority of political parties expressed a commitment to gender equality in their election manifestos. For the most part, though, these were rhetorical commitments, thin on policy detail (Ballington 1999). The response of women's organisations was to intensify their demands at public forums that parties detail their policies gender issues.[14]

This was most evident in the debate on the provision of the HIV/Aids drug AZT to rape survivors. The focus on policy issues signalled a shift of focus from numerical representation to interest representation.

Apart from the central role played by the Commission for Gender Equality (CGE), a number of NGO initiatives, including the Gender Advocacy Project (GAP) in the Western Cape, the Electoral Institute of Southern Africa (EISA), the Women's Development Foundation (WDF) and Nisaa, the Institute for Women's Development in Gauteng, tracked party positions on gender. The WDF and GAP launched a two-pronged national campaign aimed at increasing women's representation and at ensuring that women voters considered party positions on gender issues when voting. A considerable media effort was launched. This included contributions to the mainstream media[15] as well as the development of an *Elections Bulletin* produced in both tabloid and electronic form by Women'sNet, on behalf of a range of women's organisations. Almost all election programmes on national radio and television devoted time to gender issues.[17] These forums were used to debate how parties were taking up key issues such as violence against women, unemployment, housing, and health care.

Not surprisingly, this shift to concerns about the quality of women's representation and about accountability to women's interests resulted in contestation between women in political parties over policy issues. Although women activists in all parties had been united about maintaining the pressure for greater political representation, within the domain of women's forums there has been a painstaking reiteration of the limits of common interests. Beneath the surface of collective action simmered discontent about the relative power of certain women's organisations over others, and mistrust about the extent to which particular political parties could be trusted to advance the agendas of the women's movement. Within Parliament, early attempts to create a multiparty forum such as the Parliamentary Women's Group for women MPs have foundered as a result of tensions between the DP, ANC and NNP.

Women are not a homogeneous constituency. Even where women MPs are committed to broad principles of gender equality, their definitions of what this means, their strategies for achieving equality, and the constituencies of women they represent, may be vastly different. It is significant that the driving force behind legislative reform to eliminate gender discrimination has been the ANC Women's Caucus rather than the multiparty forum, reflecting the different weight given to gender equality by different political parties. Differences in party ideologies could not be overcome by broad commitments to gender equality.

By the 1999 elections, women's organisations were much more sceptical of the extent to which women MPs represented women's interests rather than party or even personal political interests. The issue of accountability emerged very forcefully in various electoral forums.[17] Although accountability remains an elusive notion in women's politics accountability to parties? to women within parties? to all women? the South African debates have focused on both the formal (accountable to political parties) and moral (accountable to the cause of gender equality) aspects of accountability (Hassim 1999). In both cases, the consolidation of women's constituencies is vital.[18]

To ensure formal accountability, women within political parties have to become significantly more organised – both so that women MPs may be even more effective within the legislative arena and so that there are internal party mechanisms to hold them accountable to women members and not just to party leadership.[19] There has been a tendency among women's organisations to conflate the tasks of building constituencies and of representing them. Women's sections of political parties (of which women MPs should ideally be active members) need to articulate the interests of women supporters of their parties, and ensure that these are addressed within the party's broad political platforms and electoral manifestos. In other words, they need to build a constituency of women in the party and of party supporters.

Their ability to claim constituencies is crucial to their success within the party, as electoral politics favours vote-catchers. In addition, they have to groom women leaders, and support them for internal party election. They also have to function as one among many conduits between women in Parliament and grassroots women. Without active women's sections within parties, women MPs can be left adrift, overburdened with the multiple tasks of committee work, party responsibilities, and gender activism, and with no clear political direction (*vis-à-vis* gender) to their work. The primary task of women MPs should be to define areas of intervention in the legislature and to support and report to women in the party: to represent, not to build, constituencies. The failure to separate these tasks has led to tensions between women in political parties and women's organisations in civil society.[20]

There is also an expectation of moral accountability within the women's movement. The first cohort of women in Parliament was very aware of this responsibility, as it was argued that their election was the product of collective struggles. Many women MPs made enormous efforts to consult with civil society, and to share information and build strategies collectively, despite the pressures of being pioneers.[21] However, the relative demobilisation of the women's movement since 1994 will result in fewer women on party lists who have long and deep connections to women's organisations. Without the moral and political pressure from outside Parliament, there is always the danger that women MPs will be unable (or increasingly unwilling) adequately to represent the various interests of women. Women's gains in and through parliamentary representation are an important facet of the long-term battle to recognise women as agents in political processes, and to provide voices for them in the various arenas of public decision-making. It is important, however, to maintain a critical tension between MPs and government bureaucrats (male and female) who claim to be speaking on behalf of women, and the constituencies in whose name these claims are made. Without strong mechanisms for upholding accountability, the danger always exists that representation carries little power to advance the agenda of gender equality.

CONCLUSION

The apparent paradox between the demands of women as an identifiable constituency in electoral politics and the internal debates about different interests within that constituency suggests that women's politics is conducted simultaneously at two levels. At an external level, a narrow terrain of common purpose is mapped out, articulated, and defended, while at an internal level there is vigorous contestation over specific policies and party political manifestos. This tendency seems counter-productive: it may be argued that women might do better in terms of increasing their political leverage if their external (in this case electoral) politics was directed at articulating their interests within the framework of party-political contestation, rather than a non-partisan, 'common front' approach. However, this dual politics is the outcome of the need for women simultaneously to build a constituency that will have political leverage – to present the illusion of a united constituency, if you will - and to articulate the diverse interests of women arising from the intersections of race, class and gender inequalities. If the current trends in women's politics continue, it can be expected that future elections will see even more sophisticated positioning of the policy demands of different groups of women. There will consequently be greater pressure on political parties to move beyond platitudes in their party manifestos as they seek to capture women's votes.

NOTES

1. The ANC Women's League took an especially strong stance over women's representation in constitutional negotiations, threatening to boycott the first non-racial elections with the slogan 'no women, no vote'. Although it is unlikely that it would have been able successfully to organise a women's boycott of the elections, the threat exposed the limitations of claims to democracy by progressive political organisations.
2. While these are distinct theoretical positions, in practice a combination of arguments is more likely to be found. For example, see Lowe-Morna 1999.
3. Of course, substantive content will have to be given to the roles of women candidates once in Parliament, but this can be determined by the particular ideological and organisational orientations of each party.
4. A notable exception is the African Christian Democratic Party, whose representative argued against gender equality at a Nisaa Forum on Women and the Elections in May 1999.
5. No significant differences between women and men on electoral issues or party preferences have been found by any of the electoral surveys, suggesting that the connection between gender inequalities and the position of women is either not recognised or is considered unimportant by women voters in South Africa. For further discussion of voting behaviour and gender in South Africa, see Gouws 1999.

6. The Women's Party, led by feminist artist Nina Romm, was unable to secure a single seat in Parliament, despite the relatively low cut-off threshold.
7. For example, the provision for equality in the Constitution, the establishment of national machinery for women, and the creation of a statutory body (the Commission on Gender Equality – CGE).
8. Comments made by women representatives of political parties at the CGE 'Dialogue on Women, Politics and the Elections' (henceforth the Gender Dialogue), held on 29 June 1998. A summary report is available from the CGE.
9. Although gender inequalities should be a matter of concern to both men and women, it has generally been women who have politicised gender issues and who, because of their subordinate position, are most likely to raise issues of unequal power.
10. Indeed, a common argument is that there are more than enough enabling mechanisms for women at the moment, including the Constitution, the Office on the Status of Women, and the CGE.
11. Comments at Gender Dialogue .
12. The Electoral Act requires that all registered political parties and candidates subscribe to an Electoral Code of Conduct designed to promote conditions that are conducive to free and fair elections. These include tolerance of democratic political activity, and free political campaigning and open public debate. Item 6 of the Code specifically requires political parties to give effect to the rights of women.
13. At the Gender Dialogue, ANC spokesperson Melissa Levin argued that giving women access to key offices was a deliberate ANC policy.
14. In a notable example, at the Gender Dialogue the CGE expressed its discontent with the quality of party presentations. Echoing this, Deputy Speaker of the Gauteng Legislature, Lindiwe Zulu, commented that 'there was nothing earth shattering about the presentations 'This is not acceptable. It is an insult and disservice to women'. The report (*Gender Dialogue: Women, Politics and the Election*) was sent to all political parties.
15. Culminating in a front-page lead in the Johannesburg daily, *The Star*, entitled 'One woman, one vote is the key to power: Majority of voters are female – and they mean business' (5 May 1999).

16. Both public and private media were concerned about the gender representivity (along with race) of election commentators.
17. These included the CGE Gender Dialogue in June 1998; the AWEPA/GAP conference 'Women at the Crossroads: Women and Governance' in October 1998; and the EISA Round table 'Putting Women into Power' in February 1999.
18. This analysis is based on observation at a number of election-related events, but most notably at the AWEPA/GAP Conference, op cit., and the EISA Round table, op cit.
19. These include, for example, structures such as the Women's League within the ANC and the Women's Brigade within the Inkatha Freedom Party.
20. Comments by Barbara Watson, Director of the Women's Development Foundation, at the AWEPA/ GAP Conference.
21. Comments by Baleka Mbete-Kgositsile, Deputy Speaker in the National Assembly, AWEPA/GAP Conference, op cit. See also Govender 1998.

6

WOMEN AS POLITICAL PARTICIPANTS: THE GENDER GAP IN VOTING BEHAVIOUR

Amanda Gouws

INTRODUCTION

The study of electoral behaviour in South Africa became interesting at the time of the 1994 elections because it was the first time that the South African electorate could be studied in its entirety. Since then a huge body of literature has been developed that tries to piece together motivations for party support, possible future party dealignment, the development of a one-party dominant system, and ways in which electoral engineering could achieve the best possible results for democracy. Some scholars have tried to determine whether South African elections are, in fact, merely a form of racial census. In most of this literature the electorate is dealt with as a single entity, or is broken down into racial or ethnic groups. Very seldom is a differentiation made between men and women as voters.

As the Commission on Gender Equality (CGE) *Review of the 1999 Election* (1999, 31) correctly states: 'Little documented information on women as voters – much less as registrees – is available and this demonstrates how women in these roles remain unacknowledged within political processes.' But women are the majority of voters in South Africa and can therefore determine if a party comes to power or stays in power. The women's vote in South Africa is a crucial element of democratic electoral competition.

When we look at women as a political constituency we need to ask whether they are different from men and if so, how? Where men and women's political attitudes and voting behaviour differ we can talk about a 'gender gap'. This gap can be a significant difference between men and women with regard to political issues as well as political beliefs. But it is very often most pronounced in voting behaviour – where men and women get the chance to act on their political beliefs. Conover (1988) mentions four types of gender gap: electoral – the differing vote choices of women and men; partisan – the difference between the party identification of men and women; policy preference and ideology – how men and women differ with regard to these issues; and attitudinal – the difference between the political attitudes of men and women[1]. An electoral gender gap exists when women vote for a specific party in proportionally larger numbers than men; or when women vote in proportionally larger numbers for candidates who campaign for women's issues.

The gender gap is often very difficult to determine because it is necessary to know not only how the attitudes of men and women differ but also if these attitudes inform actual political behaviour and policy preferences. Differences in political attitudes can be tested through opinion surveys, but it is much more difficult to determine a gender gap in voting behaviour. One common way to do so is to include a question in exit polls about which party or candidate the respondent voted for. Exit polls in South Africa are new, and this particular question was not asked in any of those held during the 1999 elections because of the sensitive nature of the question as well as the secrecy of the ballot. Since even the Independent Electoral Commission is not allowed to keep such statistics, there is no access to this information. Another way to determine the gender gap in voting is by means of regular omnibus surveys that include the question 'which party did you vote for?'. In the United States this is done through the National Election Survey, which is regularly administered to a representative sample of Americans and makes it possible to trace change over time. Omnibus surveys are fairly new in South Africa.

In more mature democracies gender gaps seem to appear and disappear around policy issues or candidates who specifically pursue women's issues. They appear to result from a certain level of gender consciousness and an understanding of women's issues. It is also important for women's groups to organise around important policy issues in order to raise awareness that women have options.

More recent evidence has shown that gender gaps can appear because of the behaviour of men. In the United States, for example, a growing conservatism among men has resulted in a shift in their support away from the Democratic Party towards the Republican Party (Kaufman and Petrocik 1999).[2]

The aim of this chapter is to situate women's voting behaviour in South Africa within a larger body of theory and to try to determine whether there is, in fact, a gender gap. Data about general political beliefs will be analysed in an attempt to make a link between women's political attitudes and their voting behaviour.

EXPLAINING WOMEN'S VOTING BEHAVIOUR

The conventional wisdom about women's political behaviour is that they are less active in party membership, in attending political meetings, and in involvement in election campaigns (Randall 1987, 54). Cross-cultural data have shown that women's political participation, when it is conventionally defined, is overall less than that of men.

Conventional politics includes behaviour such as voting, campaign activity, communal activity, and contacting officials on personal issues. These activities require different degrees of initiative and co-operation with others, involve different amounts of conflict, and exert different amounts of influence. Voting, for example, requires little initiative and co-operation but can be very influential because it determines which party will come to power. Contacting officials, on the other hand, requires a lot of initiative and some co-operation but may be low in influence (Dalton 1988, 37). Women are usually characterised as showing a lack of initiative and as shying away from conflict.

Views of women's political participation are based on assumptions about the political attitudes of women that may not be rooted in reality. These are:

- Women are conservative – they tend to vote for more conservative parties;
- They are apolitical – they do not show an interest in politics and are not knowledgeable about politics;

- They are moralistic – they moralise about politics because they tend to disapprove, for example, of nuclear war and defence spending;
- They personalise politics – they vote for candidates on grounds of personal attributes;
- Political behaviour is male dominated – women tend to follow the decisions of husbands or partners.

(Randall 1987, 70-82)

On closer analysis, as Randall (1987) has shown, it becomes clear that these assertions can only be made with many qualifications. More recent evidence has also shown that this gender differential, if it existed, has decreased or nearly disappeared as women have entered the labour market and the division between the public and the private has been challenged. Gender has to be analysed in relation to other predictors of political behaviour such as levels of education and urbanisation.

When politics is redefined to include the notion that the 'personal is political' (issues of the home and family are also political issues) evidence shows that women are very often involved in unconventional political behaviour such as protest politics, demonstrations, and even revolutionary politics. Women may get involved in short-lived campaigns on issues related to children, health, and violence. They also prefer to exercise personal influence in women's organisations (Randall 1987, 58-68).

But even with regard to conventional political participation more recent evidence based on information in the World Values Survey, which analyses between sixteen and eighteen countries in Europe on different issues, has shown that there is no gender differential. Klingeman and Fuchs (1998, 46) have found no evidence that women are less involved in politics than men, and in some cases evidence has shown that women participate more than men.

What is needed is a more systematic testing of hypotheses regarding women's electoral behaviour. In the context of the USA Sapiro and Conover and (1997) have done sophisticated analyses, testing the positional as well as the structural approach, involving different assumptions about how women make electoral choices. According to the positional approach the beliefs, values, and issue positions of men and women differ, resulting in different electoral choices. In this regard men and women have the same considerations but take different positions. For example, public opinion surveys in the USA have shown that women and men have different positions on welfare spending and on war.

The structural approach, on the other hand, is based on the assumption that men and women have different considerations and use different criteria to reach electoral judgements. Women are concerned with the private sphere and with care, which is why their views on welfare spending, for example, differ from those of men (Sapiro and Conover 1997, 498).

Evidence has been found to substantiate both approaches, but what Sapiro and Conover have added is the role of context. They argue that the election context can make a gender gap appear or disappear because it cues gender relevance. For example, if an election campaign focuses on women's rights both women and men may pay more attention to it but may have different opinions about it (Sapiro and Conover 1997, 499). However, as they also point out, not all people use gender as a framework to interpret the world around them, and those most sensitive to gender cues are people with a gender consciousness.

They conclude that:

> Our theory of the gender basis of electoral behaviour points to a complicated and changing interaction of voters' socialisation, experiences and predispositions; the context of the election, and the cues offered by the candidates, parties and other opinion leaders in creating a political mosaic in which gender matters differently and to different degrees in different elections. (1997, 522)

Different models are used in the attempt to explain voting behaviour. According to the sociological model, socio-economic status, religion, location (rural or urban), ethnicity, and race, as well as gender, may determine how a person will vote. Gender is included in the list of sociological variables that help to explain the vote, but is seldom used as a dependant variable (one that needs explanation in and of itself).

The social-psychological model explains more as it takes into account the political dimension of an election. This dimension includes personal loyalty to a party (also called party identification), orientation towards issues, and evaluation of the candidates (Niemi and Weissberg 1984, 12-13).

The issue of political socialisation has been a significant one in the study of voting behaviour because it underlies theories of party identification. Identification with a specific party is often the most important reason why people vote and is a psychological attachment socialised over time. It is a long-term factor in the stability of party support and is difficult to change. Party identification is used as a filter through which candidates and political issues are evaluated.

Given the existence of sexist attitudes in most societies it is no wonder that women are socialised to be passive and to shun politics. These attitudes, coupled with women's roles in the private sphere as mothers and caregivers, very often leave little time for active participation in politics. Women are also over represented in disadvantaged categories in society such as the poor, the undereducated, and the illiterate, which prevents them from participating actively in politics. This is especially true in Third World countries.

While party identification is a long term factor short term influences such as issues specific to the election and candidate performance may sway a voter during one specific election to vote for another party. People who vote according to party identification are less willing to make judgements about their party's performance and more willing to vote for the party out of loyalty. Issue voters, on the other hand, seem to be more willing to evaluate a party's performance and to calculate the costs and benefits of voting for a specific party. This 'retrospective voting' occurs when voters attempt to determine how parties have benefited them personally during a specific period. Such voters, also called 'rational choice voters', anticipate the expected benefits that will be derived from voting to outweigh the costs (Niemi and Weisberg 1984, 14). It is easier for rational choice voters to switch parties.

Short-term influences include the campaign, previous performances of a party, and high profile political events, such as scandals, that emerge immediately before an election. The length of an election campaign and the exposure of voters to speeches and media coverage of issues and candidates can also contribute to changes in party loyalty. A voter may thus be influenced by his or her sociological characteristics, such as gender, class, and area of location, but the actual vote is a consequence of a more complex set of influences.

Women voters may therefore be motivated to vote on grounds of loyalty to a specific party, but they may also be influenced to change their vote by campaign issues and candidate evaluations. During the struggle against apartheid, for example, many women supported the ANC without insisting that gender be made a priority. Loyalty towards the party in its fight for liberation outweighed gender concerns. Similarly, many Afrikaner women supported the National Party and uncritically accepted its gender blind policies for many years.

We may not have data on how women voted but we do have data on how they registered, on the political opinion that may inform voting behaviour, and on poll data from opinion polls taken during the 1999 national and provincial elections.

WOMEN AS A CONSTITUENCY IN SOUTH AFRICA

General attitudes

Not much is known about the political attitudes of South African women. One reliable way to gauge them and to ascertain whether a gender gap really exists is to analyse the results of broad based opinion surveys. From a large sample it is possible both to generalise to the general population and to do a breakdown of the different population groups to see how they differ. Gender analysis of survey data of large samples of the South African population is very uncommon. The data used for the following analysis is drawn from a 1996 public opinion survey conducted by Decision Surveys International for a study of democratic values in South Africa[3]. The sample is large (3 031) and the smaller population groups have been over sampled so that reliable generalisations can be made. The response rate was 94 per cent.

The composition of the sample is:

Women 1 377 (53.7%)
Men 1 185 (46.2%)

African 1 933 (75.4%)
White 361 (14.1%)
Coloured 193 (7.5%)
Asian 76 (3.0 %)

It is important to ascertain the extent to which women and men participate in conventional political activities and which activities these are. Of 2 509 respondents who were active in organisations, 0.9 per cent of women versus 3.5 per cent of men were active in trade unions; 1.7 per cent of women versus 6.3 per cent of men in political organisations; 3.4 per cent of women versus 7.3 per cent of men in youth organisations; 1.1 per cent of women versus 2.4 per cent of men in street committees; 0.9 per cent of women versus 2.6 per cent of men in civic organisations; 3.4 per cent of women versus 6.6 per cent of men in social groups. Women were more active in religious organisations and groups – 12.7 per cent of women versus 11 per cent of men in religious organisations; 9.7 per cent of women versus 6.8 per cent of men in religious groups.[4] Women were less active in political parties – 2.1 per cent versus 7.3 per cent of men.

The results reveal that most people are politically inactive but men are more involved in political activities, while women are more involved in religious organisations.

When we shift our focus to unconventional political activities we find that a negligible percentage of the sample has participated but that men's participation far outstrips that of women – 41.8 per cent of women (N=254) versus 58.2 per cent of men (N=354) had joined a boycott; 38.6 per cent (N=314) of women versus 61.4 per cent of men (N=500) had attended a rally; 34 per cent of women (N=107) versus 66 per cent of men (N=208) had joined an illegal strike. Even fewer people – 25.2 per cent of women (N=27) versus 74.8 per cent of men (N=80) – had delivered a speech criticising the authorities. Only 20.7 per cent of women (N=17) versus 79.3 per cent of men (N=65) had organised rallies to criticise the authorities. The results reveal that women are in general less willing to participate in unconventional politics.

Women and men differ in their belief in the importance of rights. The findings for the category 'very important' are reflected in Table 1. The only right in which women expressed a stronger belief than men (and that only by 1 per cent) was the 'right to a job'. The biggest gender differences relate to civil liberties – freedom of expression and freedom to join and participate in social and political groups are more important to men.

TABLE 1: SUPPORT FOR RIGHTS

	WOMEN	MEN
Freedom of expression		
Important	25.3 (N=348)	26.8 (N=317)
Very important	46.3 (N=636)	53.8 (N=637)
Freedom to join and participate in social and political groups and unions		
Important	27.8 (N=383)	30.4 (N=359)
Very important	38.8 (N=534)	47.2 (N=558)
Equal treatment under the law		
Important	22.7 (N=313)	23.4 (N=227)
Very important	67.2 (N=925)	70.0 (N=829)
Right to a job		
Important	19.2 (N=265)	20.3 (N=240)
Very important	75.5 (N=1039)	74.5 (N=882)
Right to own land		
Important	19.8 (N=273)	19.3 (N=229)
Very important	66.4 (N=914)	70.5 (N=835)
Right to a clean and safe environment		
Important	20.3 (N=279)	21.4 (N=254)
Very important	72.7 (N=1001)	72.2 (N=857)

There are no statistically significant differences between men and women with regard to important political attitudes such as support for the rule of law, political tolerance, and liberty, which underlie democratic values and help to bolster the stability of the political system. See tables 2, 3 and 4.

TABLE 2: SUPPORT FOR THE RULE OF LAW

	WOMEN	MEN
Sometimes it might be better to ignore the law and solve problems immediately		
Disagree	35.4 (N=486)	37.5 (N=444)
Agree	46.3 (N=636)	47.0 (N=557)
It is all right to get around the law as long as you don't actually break it		
Disagree	46.3 (N=636)	50.9 (N=604)
Agree	35.4 (N=486)	34.1 (N=405)
In times of emergency the government ought to be able to suspend law in order to solve political and social problems		
Disagree	49.8 (N=685)	52.8 (N=624)
Agree	22.5 (N=310)	25.5 (N=302)
It is not necessary to obey the law of a government that I did not vote for		
Disagree	29.4 (N=404)	31.0 (N=368)
Agree	56.4 (N=775)	57.3 (N=680)

TABLE 3: POLITICAL TOLERANCE

	WOMEN	MEN
Least liked party should be banned in your community		
Disagree	20.7 (N=280)	25.0 (N=289)
Agree	64.7 (N=876)	66.0 (N=764)
Members of least liked group should be prohibited from standing as a candidate for an elected position		
Disagree	26.7 (N=362)	28.3 (N=327)
Agree	61.1 (N=827)	62.8 (N=727)
Members of the least liked group should be allowed to hold street demonstrations in your community		
Disagree	74.0 (N=1011)	74.0 (N=857)
Agree	13.1 (N=177)	17.8 (N=206)

TABLE 4: ATTITUDES TO FREEDOM

	WOMEN	MEN
Better to live in an orderly society than allow disruption		
Disagree	74.8 (N=1027)	75.5 (N=891)
Agree	9.5 (N=131)	11.7 (N=138)
Free speech not worth it if I have to put up with radical political views		
Disagree	18.5 (N=253)	22.2 (N=262)
Agree	55.1 (N=755)	54.9 (N=648)

Society should not put up with views that differ radically from the majority		
Disagree	47.1 (N=645)	45.1 (N=532)
Agree	23.7 (N=325)	29.6 (N=348)
Because demonstrations become disorderly, radical groups should not be allowed to demonstrate		
Disagree	58.0 (N=796)	58.3 (N=687)
Agree	17.7 (N=243)	19.2 (N=227)

However, there is a significant difference between men and women in regard to political attitudes that reflect how voters feel about their own political competence and the way they view their own capacity to influence the political system (also called political efficacy). There are two kinds of efficacy – external, which is caused by factors outside the control of the individual, and internal, caused by the individual's own belief in the extent to which he or she can influence the political system. The results reveal a great deal about women's lack of political competence and feelings of disempowerment.

EXTERNAL EFFICACY

The attitudes of men and women to the different items that make up the 'external efficacy index' are remarkably similar. The results reflect feelings of a lack of competence.

The findings report the combined percentages for 'strongly agree' and 'agree':

- 49.1 per cent of women (N=655) and 49.5 per cent of men (N=573) agreed that 'the people who run the country are not really concerned with what happens to people like me'.

- 49 per cent of women (N=664) and 47.2 per cent of men (N=546) agreed that 'If public officials are not interested in hearing what people like me think, there is really no way to make them listen'.

- 38.7 per cent of women (N=525) and 37.3 per cent of men (N=447) agreed that 'In our country all political power is concentrated in the hands of a small group of people and it is impossible for the rest of us to influence what the government does'.

The 'disagree percentages' decrease if those who were 'uncertain' are taken into account.

INTERNAL EFFICACY

There is a definite gender gap in relation to feelings of internal efficacy. The results reveal the following:

- 46.8 per cent of women (N=633) and 65.2 per cent of men (N=755) agreed with the statement 'I feel that I have a pretty good understanding of the important political issues facing our country'.

- Only 29.6 per cent of women (N=399) but 45.4 per cent of men (N=524) agreed that 'I feel well prepared for participating in political life'.

- 68.3 per cent of women (N=923) but only 56.7 per cent of men (N=657) agreed that 'Sometimes politics seems so complicated that a person like me can't really understand what is going on'.

The Levene test of equality of variances (a variation of the t-test) with regard to two independent groups (men and women) reveals significant differences on the items regarding internal efficacy.[5]

While these findings tell us that there is a gender gap in relation to internal efficacy it is important to disaggregate the sample into the constituting population groups to determine whether women differ among themselves about their political participation and feelings of internal efficacy.

In general, African men and women are politically inactive, and among those who are active there is a considerable difference between the participation of women (2.2%) and men (8.7%) in political parties.

Coloured people are also politically inactive and no coloured woman indicated participation in political organisations. Even fewer women than men participate in religious organisations.

Indian women participate in equal numbers with men in political parties and seem to be as active politically as men. It has to be borne in mind that this sub-sample is very small and it is difficult to generalise from the findings.

White people are in general also politically inactive, with white women apparently the most inactive of all the political groups. No women participated in trade unions or political organisations, and only one man reported activity in political organisations. Fewer women than men are active in social groups.

DISAGGREGATED FINDINGS ON POLITICAL EFFICACY

With regard to external efficacy the findings for women and men of all population groups are similar. But results for internal efficacy are quite revealing for the different sub-samples. (All results report the categories 'strongly agree' and 'agree' combined.)

Only 42.4 per cent of African women versus 60.8 per cent of men agreed with the statement 'I have a pretty good understanding of the important political issues facing our country'. It is, however, generally believed that women in rural areas are the most disempowered politically, and if we control statistically for location our findings lend support to this belief.

In metropolitan areas 61.5 per cent of women agreed with the statement: 'I feel that I have a pretty good understanding of the important political issues facing our country', while 14.2 per cent disagreed (76.4 per cent of men in metropolitan areas agreed with the statement). By contrast, 39.7 per cent of rural women agreed with the statement while 33.8 per cent disagreed, indicating that there is a small difference between women who feel efficacious and those who don't. The percentages are still smaller than those of men (54.7 per cent of men agreed).

On this item 66.5 per cent of white women agreed, versus 79.2 per cent of white men; 51.1 per cent of coloured women agreed, versus 70.4 per cent of coloured men; and 81.1 per cent of Indian women agreed, versus 82.1 per cent of Indian men. The findings reveal that Indian women feel the most efficacious, followed by white and urban African women, while coloured women feel less efficacious, but rural African women are the least efficacious on this item. Women of all population groups feel less efficacious than men. Only 30.9 per cent of African women versus 46.3 per cent of men agreed that 'I feel well prepared for participation in political life'. When location is taken into consideration 45.8 per cent of women in metropolitan areas compared to only 26.9 per cent of rural women agreed. There is little difference between African women and African men (51.45%) in metropolitan areas but a larger one in rural areas (48.1 % of men agreed).

Only 26.1 per cent of white women versus 40.5 per cent of men felt well prepared for participation in politics; only 18 per cent of coloured women versus 42.3 per cent of coloured men agreed. Among Indian respondents 31.6 per cent of Indian women and 51 per cent of men agreed. From these findings it is clear that urban African women feel most prepared to participate in politics while women of the other population groups do not feel well prepared. Percentages are much smaller than those for men.

Responding to the statement 'Sometimes politics seems so complicated that a person like me can't really understand what is going on' 69.3 per cent of African women versus 58.9 per cent of African men agreed.

In metropolitan areas the percentage of African women was 66.2 and of men 52.8, and in rural areas 68.5 per cent of African women agreed and 52.4 per cent of men; 61 per cent of white women agreed compared with 47.2 per cent of men; 76.6 per cent of coloured women versus 59.8 per cent of men; and 55.3 per cent of Indian women versus 47.3 per cent of men agreed. It is clear that people from all population groups find politics complicated but women find it more so than men of all population groups and Indian women feel more efficacious than women from other groups.

INTERPRETATION

The above results reveal the importance of disaggregating data when doing statistical analyses. Women are not a homogeneous group. The profiles of urban African women and of Indian women show differences between them and women of other population groups. The results lend support to theories about the disempowerment of rural women and also show that rural African men feel more disempowered than men from other population groups and coloured women feel least efficacious. The results show that there is a gender gap on internal efficacy but they also show the differential impact of patriarchy and religion on different groups of women.

What the general attitudinal data show is that women and men have similar beliefs about politics but that women feel less empowered when it comes to understanding them. One interpretation is that these perceptions may prevent women from voting, yet attitudinal data from the 1999 elections show that women are aware of the issues, and the registration data belie the feelings of disempowerment, especially of rural women.

ATTITUDES TO ELECTIONS

A survey done by the Commission on Gender Equality (CGE) before the 1999 election showed that women believe voting will improve their socio-economic conditions as well as those of their children. Some believed the vote would lead to the provision of a job, housing, and education. Others thought that it would result in an improvement in the provision of basic needs such as running water, reparation of roads, and the building of bridges (GCE 1999, 21–22).

Some women felt that as citizens they were obliged to vote, but most believed it was necessary to do so to improve their quality of life. Women wanted to vote for a party that was responsive to their needs because they felt that the needs of their families were not being met (CGE 1999, 26).

The Human Sciences Research Council's survey of 2 200 respondents (random cluster sample) – *Public Opinion on National Priority Issues – Election '99* – shows that men and women prioritise different issues. More women than men thought that government did not give sufficient priority to women's needs and that party manifestos should take gender differences into account. A much larger proportion of women than men thought there should be a law to force political parties to adopt a quota system for women's representation and that because of past discrimination employers should give women preference over men (HSRC 1999, 45). The findings of the survey also show that women have different priorities from men when they vote, giving more weight to equality, family welfare, education, women's rights, more work and crime prevention (HSRC 1999, 47).

More women than men believed that it was important to have women in Parliament to present their needs, and 51 per cent of women versus 33 per cent of men supported affirmative action.

An opinion poll conducted by the Institute for Democracy in South Africa (IDASA) in April 1999 revealed the existence of a gender gap with regard to policy preferences – 12.9 per cent of women versus 9.3 per cent of men saw water provision as the most pressing problem; 8.6 per cent of women but only 4.9 per cent of men mentioned electricity provision; 5.3 per cent of women but only 4.8 per cent of men mentioned street construction; and poverty reduction was mentioned by 9.8 per cent of women versus 8.6 per cent of men (Gouws 1999, 165).

WOMEN IN THE 1994 AND 1999 ELECTIONS

Women turned out in large numbers to vote in the 1994 and 1999 elections. Motivated by party loyalty or party identification, they helped put the ANC in power and free South Africa from apartheid. However, the 1999 elections put another hurdle in their way with the establishment of a voters' roll, which required them to register. In order to do so many women had to arrange for childcare, to travel, and to stand in long lines. The gender neutral registration process disadvantaged women (CGE 1999, 27). Yet, most surprisingly, 1 589 690 more women than men registered for the 1999 national and provincial elections, a gender gap that shows women's commitment to voting.

Registration

In each province, with the exception of Gauteng, more women than men registered. The following data obtained from the Independent Electoral Commission (IEC)[6] shows the difference in numbers:

	Women	Men
Eastern Cape	1 450 633	1 058 088
Free State	666 831	580 224
Gauteng	2 108 086	2 123 138
Kwazulu/Natal	1 979 264	1 511 117
Mpumalanga	682 598	614 960
North West	806 104	741 492
Northern Cape	199 758	181 932
Northern Province	1 137 289	754 028
Western Cape	997 950	882 311

In four provinces – Eastern Cape, KwaZulu-Natal, the Northern Province, and the North West Province – more rural than urban women registered. In the Northern Province 383 261 more women than men registered, and 720 255 more rural women than urban women registered. If women showed the same commitment to voting as they did to registering, clearly more women than men voted in the 1999 elections.

Party political commitment to gender equality

While there is clearly a women's vote that could be canvassed by different political parties, little was done to woo this vote. Party manifestos paid lip service to gender issues, but women's issues were rarely used as drawcards to political meetings.

Although some parties referred to women's equality in an attempt to win votes, they lack a true commitment to gender equality. Their gender policies read like a shopping list, including every possible issue without a real focus. Prior to the 1999 elections parties were not forthcoming with information on gender and the way in which it is integrated into their party manifestos. Only four parties – the ANC, Azanian People's Organisation (AZAPO), Pan Africanist Congress (PAC) and New National Party (NNP) – responded to a survey on these issues conducted by the Commission on Gender Equality.

Parties seldom accounted for their policies on gender and women did not feature as sources of election related news. They were also rarely used as spokespeople for political parties (CGE 1999, 47). The basic needs that women had singled out as important were not used as campaign issues. Yet it was the women's vote that was instrumental in affording power to parties.

One reason why parties do not have to take the women's vote seriously relates, ironically, to the electoral system. The same system that was designed *inter alia* to enhance women's representation is also silencing the voices of ordinary women. Because of the party list system women could not vote for candidates but only for parties, so they could not register their support for gender sensitive candidates. They therefore had to vote for the party with the best track record on gender issues or service delivery, which happened to be the party in power, the ANC. Women therefore in a sense are a captive audience and parties (specifically the ANC) do not have to do much to attract their votes.

CONCLUSION

This analysis shows that women form a separate and powerful constituency in South Africa, yet they are not treated as one by the different political parties. The only gender gap that exists in relation to general political attitudes is that in the sphere of internal political efficacy, and this will change as women become politically more involved, educated and empowered. There is, however, a clear gender gap in relation to priorities and issues that identified the women's vote very clearly. Yet women had very limited options, and therefore their party identification seems to have been the greatest motivating factor in their choice.

The gender gap reflects women's lived experiences. Their priorities reflect their lack of basic needs such as housing, education and the necessary infrastructure to improve their quality of life. Although the 1999 election cued gender issues, it did not make them central to the election.

While women were a captive audience in 1999 and may continue to be one in the next few elections, there may come a time when the existence of viable alternative parties or candidates may enable them to swing elections. Women are already showing signs of becoming 'rational choice' voters, evaluating the issues and looking retrospectively at party performance.

Much more research is needed to understand how women's political attitudes and party identification are related to policy preferences and how the attitudes of women with feminist beliefs differ from those of non-feminist women. But it is safe to argue that there is in South Africa a women's vote that women can use strategically to empower themselves.

NOTES

1. I am not looking at the gender gap in relation to men and women's representation or in terms of constituency building. These arguments can be read in Shireen Hassim's chapter.
2. Research in the United States has also shown that there is a gap between feminist women (and men) and non-feminist women (and men) based on first mentioned greater concern for disadvantaged groups and the well-being of society as well as caring (see Conover 1988; and Shapiro and Mahajan 1986).
3. The data of a joint project of Professor Jim Gibson of the Department of Government at Washington University, St Louis, Missouri USA and the author. The author acknowledges the support of the Law and Social Science Program of the US NSF (SBR 9424287) for the funding for this project
4. Religious organisations are more institutionalised than religious groups.
5. With regard to the item 'Sometimes politics seems so complicated that a person like me can't really understand what's going on' there is no significant difference, although on the face of it there should be. The fact that the means on this item for the two samples are close indicates that both men and women feel that they do not understand politics.
6. Data obtained from Mr Brian Heuvel of the Pretoria Offices of the Independent Electoral Commission.

7

ENCOURAGING WOMEN'S PARTICIPATION THROUGH VOTER EDUCATION

Julie Ballington

INTRODUCTION

South Africa's liberation struggle and democratisation process culminated in the 1994 national and provincial elections in which the majority of the electorate was finally liberated from white colonial rule under apartheid. These elections have often been referred to as the 'liberation elections' in which the African National Congress (ANC) was democratically elected to lead the Government of National Unity (GNU) which led the country in the transition from apartheid to democracy. The elections signified a new political order in which blacks gained the full citizenship that had previously been reserved exclusively for whites. Indeed, the 1994 elections, together with the 1995/96 local government elections, marked the first voting experience for roughly 80 per cent of the South African population. One of the most significant democratic exercises has therefore been the education of first-time voters, many of them illiterate, about the mechanics of voting in democratic elections (Ballington and Fick 1999, 91).

More than 19 million newly enfranchised citizens voted in the April 1994 election. As 400 newly elected Members of Parliament took their seats in the National Assembly in May 1994, South Africa's new democracy emerged victorious. A significant achievement was the number of women who took up their seats alongside their male counterparts. However, equally impressive was the high number of women (thought to be more than the number of men) who turned out to vote on polling day. Gouws argues in chapter 6 that a gender gap can exist in the form of a significant difference between men and women with regard to political issues, but is often most pronounced in voting behaviour. It is traditionally argued, in relation to the gender gap, that men often take more of an interest in politics than women. However, the high turnout of women in the 1994 election challenges this thesis. While the significance of the liberation election accounted largely for the enthusiasm and interest, the enormous efforts of voter educators arguably also contributed to the high turnout.

Voter educators worked throughout the country in what has been described as a 'large scale pedagogical undertaking that was probably the most massive national educational communications campaign of all time' (Rebehn 1999). In both the 1994 national elections, and the 1995 local government elections, a large part of state expenditure (and donor funding) was devoted to voter education. Comparatively this is not unusual when states move towards democratisation, voter education is a necessary expenditure as the electorate is often unfamiliar with the process of multi-party elections (CORE 1994, 12). Within the education drive in 1994, various programmes were developed for different target groups, including programmes that focused on educating women for democracy and electoral participation.

This chapter aims to show what was needed, and the factors that determined the successful democratic process of mobilising and educating all South Africans, despite substantive differences in race, gender and class. It will examine the efforts and effects of the voter education drive, with a particular emphasis on the education directed at women voters.

WHY VOTER EDUCATION?

The freedom of citizens to choose their elected representatives is a critical feature of democratic governance. During an election citizens need to be informed of their rights and the voting process, as Dundas argues: 'Political consciousness and informed choices are key factors in an electoral democracy' (Dundas 1996, 168). For voters to participate effectively in the electoral process, they need to be familiar with the requirements of registration and voting and balloting procedures as well as aspects such as party choice and preference.

The apartheid policies of the National Party, which divided the country into a number of self-governing territories, ensured that South Africans of different race and ethnic groupings were separated. White men and women had been accustomed to voting in national elections since 1910 and 1930 respectively, although in a constituency based 'winner takes all' system. A minority of coloureds and Indians had had some limited experience in voting for the Tricameral Parliament since 1983, also in a constituency based system. The list proportional representation (PR) system used in 1994, as well as the new structure of national and provincial government, was therefore new to white, coloured and Indian voters. However, even more critical was the fact that the majority of black voters, many of them illiterate, had had no previous experience in voting, with the exception of the small number of Africans who voted in 'homeland' elections. The election was therefore the first time that all South Africans could take part in a unifying democratic process. Voter education therefore became a key task. Singh explains the importance of voter education succinctly:

> The intensive and extensive work amongst voters was the real building of democracy. For the first time, all South Africans were informed of their choices and given the opportunity to go out and make their choice. Mass voter education was instrumental in setting the climate for democratic participation. (Singh, 1996, 7)

South Africa's liberation struggle had been characterised by cycles of violence and conflict that inevitably caused fears and scepticism about the electoral process. Establishing a culture of non-violence and conflict resolution through the ballot box was pivotal to the process of democratic consolidation and nation building. Rebehn argues that the voter education campaign prior to the election therefore contained trust building measures as well as teaching the basics of democracy and electoral procedure. He describes the period that led up to the election as 'a social education process that had as its aim on the one hand the electoral participation and electoral competence of all South Africa, and on the other attempted to create trust in the system as such' (Rebehn 1999, 17).

Opinion polls conducted and research undertaken prior to the election indicated that a number of factors influenced voter participation, including voter literacy, fear of intimidation and political violence, ignorance of the electoral process, and scepticism about the secrecy of the vote. A nationwide survey conducted by the Human Sciences Research Council (HSRC) revealed that the two major obstacles confronting black voters were low levels of voter literacy and violence and intimidation (De Kock and Ehlers 1994, 71). Explaining the secrecy of the ballot proved to be a critical area of focus for voter educators, as large numbers of people thought that 'the community will know how I vote' (Johnson and Schlemmer 1996, 98). Schlemmer argued that perhaps the most discouraging find of a pre-election poll conducted by Markdata in 1993 was that only 'some one-quarter of African, Indian and coloured voters ha[d] faith in the secret ballot. Among whites, only about one-half of voters seem[ed] to feel certain that their choices will remain a secret' (Giliomee, Schlemmer and Hauptfleisch 1994, 155). It was therefore apparent that voter education had to achieve a number of key tasks, including educating the electorate about the electoral process, motivating them to participate, and convincing them of the secrecy of the vote (Gilder 1994, 211).

ADVANCING GENDER EQUALITY

Ahead of the 1994 elections, the status of women was a central concern to political parties and voter education organisations. The elections were an important step in consolidating the gains South African women had secured in the multiparty negotiation process leading to the finalisation of the Interim Constitution under which the elections were contested. Because the structures and institutions of apartheid had subjected women to unequal opportunities with men, it was critical that they should participate in the new government structures, most notably the GNU. A successful transition to democratic rule required the participation of all South Africans eligible to vote, regardless of gender, race or ethnicity.

As women constituted more than half the estimated 22.7 million voters used by the Independent Electoral Commission (IEC) in its planning it was critical that they participate in the first democratic elections. They were not aware of their political rights, nor that their vote could make a difference. According to former Women's National Coalition convenor, Frene Ginwala, 'it is important for women to vote because it will not be enough for us if the only change we get after the election is black men replacing white men in government. Political parties should start spelling out what they have to offer women, why women should vote for them ... We will still have to push, but voting is a major step' (Mojola 1994). ANC candidate Nozizwe Madlala reiterated this point when she stated that: 'When choósing their party, women should not only look at the party election manifestos.... We should ask how many women are on the party's list and how committed the party is to upholding women's interests' (Madlala 1994, 8).

However, being granted the right to vote meant different things to different people, and it did not necessarily guarantee the majority of women effective political representation. 'Indeed, many women themselves [did] not believe that the mere fact of having a vote will make them effective democratic citizens of the new South Africa' (Levy 1993, 40). Women who are continually subordinated to men or are financially dependent on their husbands will possibly view voting as a largely ineffectual activity. Therefore, one important challenge was for voter educators to explain the individual rights of men and women, and convey the message that elections are a vital way of moving towards gender equality. By providing voter education to women the process of women's empowerment was advanced. Voter education was a valuable means of explaining that 'the process of exercising citizenship – and accompanying empowerment – only starts with the acquisition of an effective right to vote' (Levy 1993, 42).

This was particularly so for rural women, who were among the most ignored and oppressed sector of society. For ANC candidate Mamlydia Kompe, the 1994 elections brought with them new hopes for changing the position of women (Ballington 1999, 3). Voter educators also needed to take cognisance of the fact that women were often less accessible and less educated than men:

> Especially in rural areas they (women) often cannot make use of written voting instructions and are more likely to respond to verbal political appeals. Many will be subject to the authority not only of husband or father, but also of boss, farmer

> and traditional leader. They will also be bound to the home and the workplace by daily duties and responsibilities of domestic service, the needs of their own children and homes, and the demands of factory or farm labour. (Ballington 1999, 40)

CONDUCTING VOTER EDUCATION

In the early 1990s, a number of organisations representing civil society were committed to democracy and education initiatives. Key among these was the Matla Trust, formed in 1991 to support organisations such as churches and civic councils, and to undertake developmental and educational projects. It developed a Community and Citizen Education Programme which ran voter education initiatives through various means including theatre groups performing voter education plays (Rebehn 1999, 91). Other organisations that conducted voter education were the South African Council of Churches, the Institute for Multi-Party Democracy, Project Vote, Institute for a Democratic Alternative in South Africa (IDASA), and the Black Sash, as well as smaller organisations working in specific areas.

In an attempt to avoid duplication of programmes, the Independent Forum for Electoral Education (IFEE) was founded in early 1993 and run by Barry Gilder. The organisation integrated nearly half the non-governmental organisations (NGOs) active in public voter education. It represented a merger between 33 NGOs, churches, and civil society organisations, and aimed to implement a 'co-ordinated and nationwide electoral preparation programme' (Rebehn 1999, 94) by sharing resources to cover areas lacking in voter education. Membership of the forum was voluntary and members were required to commit themselves to a code of conduct which stressed support for genuine democracy and non-partisan electoral education (Gilder, 1994, 214). Similarly, the Democracy Education Broadcast Initiative (DEBI), also formed in 1993, co-ordinated voter education programmes on radio and television. DEBI consisted of 51 NGOs, as well as two-thirds of the membership of IFEE. The main tasks of IFEE were to educate voters about democracy; explain the secrecy of the ballot, appeal for political tolerance, and motivate citizens to vote (Rebehn

1999, 111). Ultimately it aimed to 'capture the attention of the South African electorate though serious voter education mixed with entertainment' (Rebehn 1999, 118).

Two months before the elections enormous effort was made to inform citizens about the mechanics of voting and about their democratic rights and responsibilities. Most NGOs, political parties, and civil society organisations developed their own creative approaches to education depending on their target audiences. A 'great variety of material was produced of a standard that could never have been achieved by a government or single party' (Rebehn 1999, 89). A survey undertaken in 1993 and 1994 highlighted the needs of the African electorate with regard to voter education. It found that 'the concerns of potential voters in South Africa fall into three main areas: The broad needs of voters, such as the need for voting literacy, ID documents, etc; the broad fears of voters including the fear of violence, lack of secrecy etc; and the specific needs of those who say they are unsure whether they will vote or not, or who won't vote' (Rebehn 1999, 104-105). There were two main areas of voter education activity, namely training and a media strategy.

The secrecy of the vote was perhaps the most important voter education message, followed by freedom to vote for the party of one's choice. All voter education programmes stressed this. For example, the *Let's Vote!* Education manual stated 'Remember: Your vote is a secret. Nobody will know who you vote for. Nobody can see who you vote for. You can vote for any party you want. If people ask you who you are going to vote for, you do not have to tell them' (Moller & Hanf 1995, 25). IDASA also identified four messages that needed to be conveyed to the electorate: 'Your vote is important – Your vote is secret – You can vote – You can trust and accept the result' (Gilder 1994, 210). This emphasis on the privacy and secrecy of the ballot as an individual act ran counter in many ways to the practices of African political processes such as the *kgotla*, where decisions are made by consensus and in public. For people in rural areas, or members of trade unions, voting by show of hands was a familiar experience.

IDASA also identified as critical the need for a clear understanding of the relationship between voting and the elected government. Voters were instructed about which identity documents were valid for voting, how to put a mark next to the party of their choice on the ballot paper, and about the difference between the ballot papers for the National Assembly and the provincial legislatures. In violence-torn regions like KwaZulu-Natal and the Western Cape it was also important to emphasise the security and safety of the ballot. Fears of rigging were widespread, and there was little confidence in the neutrality of the police. The presence of a large contingent of international and domestic observers was necessary for the credibility of a free and fair election.

The Independent Electoral Commission (IEC) was also involved in electoral education, but somewhat later in the process than other organisations. By the time the IEC started work in January 1994 more that 120 organisations, most of them considered well developed and non-partisan, were already conducting education,. Rather than duplicate these efforts the IEC opted to strengthen the organisations logistically and financially (Smith 1997, 88). It assumed the task of accrediting voter education programmes and invited organisations to apply for accreditation. Education programmes were required to be non-partisan and support democratic principles and values; to cover the mechanisms and structures of the voting process; to emphasise the secrecy of the ballot; to address post-election expectations; and to have clear objectives and be simple to comprehend (IEC 1994, 46). In all 108 education programmes were accredited. Another ten leading organisations were contracted and funded by the IEC to close gaps identified in voter education.

The IEC expected voter education programmes to ensure that historically disadvantaged groups were informed of their political rights, with the aim of efficient participation in the polling station and a reduction of spoilt ballot papers.

> Naturally, a programme of this nature should be apolitical, professional, simple, affordable, but also one which integrates voter information with civic education. It should satisfy various audience groups: from the first time hesitant voter, to the cynical voter to the disadvantaged voter, rural voters, members of the security forces, reluctant employers such a farmers who may not provide time off to their staff or allow them to stand for elections. A clear strategy of how to begin the educative process, assessing absorption of messages and

> peaking the campaign at various stages, should be devised. (CORE, 12-13)

The IEC acknowledged the huge challenge presented by a country the size of South Africa and was aware that NGOs would not be able to reach all corners of the country. Gilder noted that as the majority of voters in rural areas were illiterate or semi-literate, the 'logistics of reaching a significant percentage of these people with a substantial education campaign [was] daunting and extremely expensive' (Gilder 1994, 210). As a result, the IEC's voter education division became increasingly involved in training voter education trainers, and special projects were launched to reach target groups not adequately covered (IEC 1994, 89).

Weeks before the election it became apparent to the IEC and to voter education organisations that concerted efforts needed to be made to significantly increase the voting skills of certain target groups. Among the special projects the IEC implemented was a schools project where a number of students of voting age received voter education aimed at increasing their motivation to vote. A campaign, entitled Operation Access, was designed to counteract the effects of 'no-go areas' and promote an atmosphere of open debate in areas afflicted with conflict and violence (IEC 1994, 89).

If voter education was to have maximum impact, necessary information had to be packaged and directed to different target groups. One of these was women. No nation-wide co-ordinated campaign targeted women voters, rather education initiatives were dependent on the individual efforts of organisations that identified women as a constituency with special needs. These organisations included the IEC, the Independent Mediation Service of South Africa (IMSSA), whose Elections and Balloting Project department played a major role, and the Black Sash. An important initiative was the establishment by the IEC of a Women's Desk which worked together with a number of organisations (IEC 1994, 90). IMSSA's Elections and Balloting project developed a programme aimed primarily at training educators from rural areas to work in their own areas. The organisation emphasised the inclusion of women trainers in its programmes. It is reported that a number of women were empowered by the training they received, and it was encouraging to have women imparting information which had historically fallen into the male domain (IMSSA 1994, 27).

The IEC also worked in co-operation with DEBI as part of a publicity drive that employed print and electronic media, enabling a large number of citizens to receive voter information. Both radio and television were critical, with radio reaching a larger proportion of black voters and television reaching a larger number of coloured, Indian, and white voters. An important focus of DEBI was to reach women in rural communities. As Shirley Smith explained:

> DEBI gave priority to previously disenfranchised citizens and *in particular targeted women, young people and rural communities* ... Programmes on voter education were carried on seventeen radio stations in each of the country's eleven languages ... In all, approximately seventeen million pamphlets, leaflets and posters were distributed, including seven million sample ballot papers in full colour, as were videos, newspaper advertisements, teaching guides and manuals. (Smith, 90, emphasis added)

Further, as part of DEBI's media strategy, various documentary films were produced to target groups that required special motivation and information ahead of the election. A film was produced portraying women in rural areas and highlighting the problems they faced and ways in which they could organise voter education workshops in their areas. The film included interviews with leading figures in rural women's movements, and focused on the fears, hopes, and expectations of rural women. As many rural women did not have access to television, the documentary was widely disseminated by means of mobile video units (Rebehn 1999, 128).

While most of the content and focus areas of the programmes that targeted women voters were similar to the others used by IFEE affiliated organisations (most IFEE programmes stressed that women should vote), there were often problems in terms of access that necessitated targeting women as a separate constituency. This was particularly so for women in rural areas as many had traditionally played a minimal role in community meetings and their participation was limited either by formal prohibitions or by male domination. Wixley explained that 'their excessive work burden – including collecting firewood and water, childcare and ... tending to livestock – seldom [left] women any time to attend workshops or meetings.

Even if a woman is willing and able to participate, the chief retains a power of veto: if he does not give the go ahead for voter education, it does not happen' (Wixley 1994, 13). Illiteracy was a further complicating factor for rural women, which often meant that they were ill informed about the electoral process, political parties and structures like the Government of National Unity. 'Voter educators find themselves hard-pressed to convince women who have experienced homeland elections that the April 27 vote will be different' (Wixley 1994, 13).

The Black Sash was another organisation that aimed to reach women voters, particularly in rural areas. While the organisation was formed in 1955 to give humanitarian and legal aid to those oppressed by apartheid, the rights of women was one of its major aims. 'After decades of support for human rights and democracy, the organisation entered the voter education campaign with workshops and materials aimed especially at women in rural areas and townships' (Rebehn 1999, 90). National co-ordinator of voter education, Gille de Vlieg, acknowledged that it was extremely difficult to break down the barrier 'between men who see they have the right to ask the questions, and women who feel they have to take a backseat in politics' (Wixley 1994, 13). Black Sash therefore trained women from the Rural Women's Movement (which was a community based organisation tackling issues of land, gender and development) and university students to run voter education programmes in their own communities, as this encouraged women to take part in the training sessions. De Vlieg noted the importance of women trainers in rural areas:

> The patriarchal structure of our society makes women feel intimidated. Feedback from our trainers is that the biggest problem to be overcome is male domination, which sometimes results in women being denied access to some areas. Chiefs are suspicious of women entering their areas and educating women about voting. A lot of voter education is done by males and we believe that it is very important for women to be educated by other women. (Mojola 1994)

As men were also often disruptive, the Black Sash ran separate workshops for women which encouraged them to speak up and discuss what they wanted. The workshops concentrated on 'dispelling the widespread fears about the voting process, by staging voting exercises ... We speak a lot about intimidation – not only about political intimidation but intimidation of women by men. We emphasise that women must vote for whoever they want, not just who their husband, father, uncle or brother tells them' (Wixley 1994, 13). While the efforts of the Black Sash were not large scale compared with those of other organisations, they nevertheless represented the recognition of the special needs of rural women in the run-up to their first voting experience.

Ntomb'futhi Zondo, organiser for the Education for Democracy campaign, argued that only a limited effort had been made to reach out to women in rural areas. For Zondo, a critical task when educating women in rural areas was to develop a way of dealing with intimidation and to create an understanding that when it comes to elections women must make their own decisions about who to vote for:

> The reality is that most women, especially in rural areas (where the majority are) are not aware of their legal rights. Further, in some cases, discrimination seems to be officially sanctioned ... When speaking to women about women's participation in political affairs, they can't understand what you're talking about. (Zondo 1995, 58)

In her voter education programmes she emphasised that voting was both a right and a responsibility. Other issues she considered important included explaining to women that their husbands and employers would not know how they had voted; convincing women that they had a leadership role to play; and teaching them how to pressurise government to ensure it initiates an enabling atmosphere for women to establish themselves (Zondo 1995, 60).

The Women's Development Foundation (WDF) moved beyond other voter education programmes by acknowledging from the outset that women were encouraged to vote in elections, but with no guarantee that they would be included in leadership. WDF programmes therefore encouraged women to read party manifestos and policies on gender equality and vote for a party with policies that addressed their special needs. As part of its strategy,

WDF produced pamphlets in all eleven official languages, conducted radio and television interviews, and developed cassette messages to be played in taxis – a common form of transport for the black population. Videos were also produced to accompany training materials at voter education workshops (Watson 2000, 3). A similar message was to be found in *Speak*, a publication which produced election and education supplements. One message carried by *Speak* stated: 'If women stand up and clearly state their demands, they can force parties to adopt policies which will meet some of their needs ... Women have the advantage of being one of the biggest groups of voters in the country. As long as women are well organised and united, they stand a good chance of realising some of their goals' ('Voter Education'. *Speak*, May 1994, 24).

The large number of education programmes meant that millions of voters were reached. Separate workshops for women proved to be useful and necessary although few programmes identified the correlation between the women's vote and an improvement in the lives of women, or what democracy means to women in the broader sense beyond the exercise of the franchise. Overall, a mammoth effort went into preparing South Africa's electorate for the polls, but unsystematic attention was paid to the position of women in the emerging democratic order.

POLITICAL PARTY ACTIVITIES

It was in the interest of political parties to conduct voter education to ensure that their supporters went to the polls on election day and voted correctly. Therefore the voter education conducted by political parties was clearly partisan as the majority of the twenty-six parties that appeared on the 1994 ballot paper had never contested an election. The National Party and Democratic Party, with their history of participation in previous elections, had election machinery and the skills to run an effective campaign. However, the ANC and Pan Africanist Congress (PAC) had never taken part in elections. This proved a major challenge for parties, as Roshene Singh explains:

> The ANC and PAC had previously operated as liberation movements with the capacity to mobilise around specific issues

> but their support had never been tested though the ballot box. Their experience of mass organising was limited to mass action in the form of boycotts, marches, demonstrations and public rallies which did not reach more than ten per cent of the population. They did not have the organisational capacity to reach all voters. There, they had a massive task ahead to build their capacity and effectively reach millions of voters. (Singh 1996, 3-4)

Training was therefore necessary to transform the organisational culture of liberation movements to that of political parties ready to contest elections. The massive amount of training required by the ANC could not be conducted by one NGO. As a result, four NGOs formed a consortium called the Voter Education and Election Training Unit (VEETU) to conduct electoral training for a range of organisations involved in the electoral process.[1] The members of the consortium worked in partnership around the country, and received donor funding. VEETU produced client specific manuals, general training and information manuals, and mass voter education materials (Singh, 1996, 44).

In line with its aim to increase the capacity of the ANC to fight an election campaign and provide voter education, it combined training for election management together with the training of voter educators (Singh, 1996, 5).

VEETU's ANC voter education campaign had to take into account the attitudes of voters, their lack of information, and the inaccessibility of voters in certain areas (Singh, 31). Voter education training focused on informing voters how to vote and stressed the necessary documents that were needed in order to do so. It also aimed to mobilise voters on election day to ensure a high turnout (Singh, 34). Training was usually conducted in the language commonly spoken by participants, although most of the training manuals were in English. VEETU also used mock elections, which proved to be the most effective way to reach large numbers of people, and were effective in demonstrating the voting process. The constituency groups targeted were in rural villages, squatter settlements, hostels, farms, and rural towns and urban townships (Singh, 38). In the year leading up to April 1994 VEETU reached 50 000 people (Singh, 5).

In the middle of the campaigning phase it became evident that women were not participating as actively in election training and campaigns as men. Singh explains that the average attendance of women at VEETU workshops was between 30 and 40 per cent, which was a cause for concern (Singh, 41). As a result, a course for women activists was planned after discussions between the ANC Women's League (ANCWL) and the ANC. Included in the course content was:

> ... an understanding of the position of women in South Africa and where women are organised. The participants planned special programmes to empower women to become involved in the elections and discussed women's issues that needed to be put on the election agenda of political parties. (Singh, 41)

The ANCWL conducted voter education workshops in rural communities and townships where women were concentrated to 'help get out the women's vote' (Oliver 1994, 8). It was recognised that if it was effectively to reach women across the political spectrum VEETU would have to move beyond the base of the ANC.

The need to develop a separate training programme for women was confirmed by the responses from the workshops which reported that women 'felt more comfortable in a workshop not dominated by the input of men' (Singh, 41). As ANC activist, Bongiwe Njobe commented: 'Voter education is extremely important. We have to tell the women that your vote is independent of your husband's ... We tell them ... your decision is yours. You are a person in your own right' (Oliver 1994, 8).

Voter education not only informed women of the mechanics of voting but aided in confidence building in a land where the majority of women had been denied education. Njobe stressed that voter education for women triggered an awareness and confidence, thereby aiding in the empowerment of women seen as critical for the country's future. As 'women constitute the majority of the people in the rural areas ... we want women to acquire skills so that when women get land, they know what to do with it' (Oliver 1994, 8). Furthermore, the workshops gave women the opportunity to interact constructively with other organisations and groupings, creating a support network.

The ANC, with VEETU, was not the only party to target women. For Faith Gaza, then Chairperson of the Women's League of the Inkatha Freedom Party (IFP), the issue of safety for women was a critical issue. The KwaZulu-Natal province, where IFP support was concentrated, was racked by pre-election violence and intimidation which resulted in the declaration of a state of emergency weeks before the election. In the months prior to the elections, the IFP resisted participation, and only decided to take part on 19 April, a week before the election date. The uncertainty of IFP participation left little time for the party to launch an election campaign or for voter education (Rebehn 1999, 115). However, between December 1993 and April 1994 IMSSA trained 1 350 IFP trainers to conduct voter education in a number of rural areas. In the time available IFP trainers held regular workshops and provided voter education to hundreds of IFP supporters (IMSSA report 1994, 19).

According to Moller and Hanf the ANC was viewed as the most active voter education organisation in most areas. Responses to a survey conducted after the elections indicate that 43 per cent of respondents had received voter information from a party, and of these 78 per cent were reached by the ANC, 10 per cent by the National Party, 5 per cent by the IFP, and 2 per cent by the Democratic Party. The other parties reached only a fraction of voters (Moller and Hanf, 13).

The ANC was also the only party effectively to identify women as a constituency. But Wixley states that despite 'the ANC's slick newspaper ads publicising their plan to improve the lives of women by "guaranteeing women the right to home and land ownership", their American style roadshow has not been adapted for rural voters' (Wixley 1994, 12). She argues that the 'people's forum' (aimed at increasing grassroots participation) did not reach the people who were traditionally left at home while their men made decisions under the *kgotla* tree. This argument was reiterated by Mamlydia Kompe:

> Very little is really happening ... no political party is really taking the initiative to organise rural women and show them how to vote. We've heard about a mobile education van; we haven't seen it. (Wixley 1994, 12)

Watson believes that political parties focused on women merely as a vote bank. 'An overall conclusion around the extent to which special attention was given to women as voters during the elections is that, to a large extent, women were encouraged to vote so that a party could win. There was very little time and attention given to women's rights through voting. Women's rights [and] interests were subsumed by the national interest' (Watson 2000, 3-4). For gender activists, South Africa's first democratic election was pivotal to the liberation of women. The fact that political parties did not to take this into account in their electioneering and education strategies created a critical issue around which women could mobilise. The lack of gender awareness of many political parties even prompted the formation of two women's parties ahead of the 1994 elections.

Overall, voter education was regarded as a huge success. The low number of spoilt ballot papers – less than 1% – indicated that most voters had mastered the voting process. According to Moller and Hanf, results of a post-election survey indicated that as many as nine in ten voters were reached by the media and a wide range of face-to-face voter education programmes before the election. Younger and better educated first time voters gained easier access to all programmes, and information in the form of comic books was popular. Nearly half of first time voters received education, most notably from the IEC and the ANC, along with other political parties, organisations, and trade unions. Smith of the IEC maintains that: 'There can be no doubt that, without voter education, the majority of South African citizens would have effectively been disempowered from exercising an informed choice in the election process' (Smith, 88).

The Moller and Hanf surveys also indicated that black voters were adamant that voter education was essential: '87 per cent stated that without this information they would not have voted correctly' (Moller and Hanf, 20). It is reported that up to three-quarters of voters received education in their home language. Voter education messages were perceived to be both salient and easy to understand, and messages concerning democratic principles were regarded as being as important as those concerning voting skills. The Moller and Hanf survey suggests that 'the majority [of voters] felt confident of their new voting skills and that their vote was in secret. Most voters indicated that they had voted of their own free will for the party of their choice' (Moller and Hanf, Synopsis).

Notwithstanding the importance of the high turnout and low number of spoilt ballots, problems hampered voter education in some areas. The sheer number of first time voters made it impossible to provide direct education, and it appeared that most voters relied on other sources for information. One analysis suggested that only about 20 per cent had received direct voter education, with most voters relying on the mass media (Friedman and Stack, 319). Singh points out that ANC education efforts were sometimes hampered because remote rural areas were difficult to reach, and in some areas chiefs prevented free political activity. This often had a direct impact on the education of women in remote areas. Illiteracy was a further problem, with up to 50 per cent of the black population estimated to be illiterate (Singh 28-29). Some voter education programmes were criticised for 'the stereotyping of women in their classic roles as teachers, nurses and domestic servants' (Moller and Hanf, 265).

LOCAL GOVERNMENT ELECTIONS: 1995 AND 1996

South Africans went to the polls again just over a year after the 1994 elections, this time to vote for an 'interim' phase of local government with democratically elected councils. The apartheid regime had created exclusionary black and white councils at the local level, which came to an end with first phase of the transition in 1994, creating temporary municipal councils consisting of representatives from black and white communities. In 1995-96 differentiated categories of elected local government were created for metropolitan, urban and rural areas, with different power structures and functions depending on the area in question. The interim phase of local government was based on elected councillors occupying positions in this range of structures (Pottie 1999). These elected structures remained in place until the 2000 local elections when non-racial and democratic local councils were elected. Most provinces held elections on 1 November 1995, but the KwaZulu-Natal Province and metropolitan Cape Town elections were delayed until May 1996 because of disputes over demarcation and irregularities in the registration process.

As the sphere of government directly responsive to communities and responsible for the provision of services, local government is the area of government closest to the people and is fundamental to the consolidation of democracy. Central to effective local government is 'an electorate that brings out its vote in an informed manner [which] must be kept alive by citizens who hold their representatives accountable ...' (Bam 2000, 4). Local government is of special importance to the lives of women as they are primarily responsible for family well-being and community care. Effective municipal service delivery not only makes women's lives easier (particularly in rural areas) it can also contribute to greater gender equality in the community (Van Donk 2000, 13). It was therefore important that women should be elected to local government structures. As one candidate stated ahead of the election:

> ... women are better equipped than men for leadership of local authorities. Local government deals with local issues ... I believe it is women out there who know exactly what they want. Women know what childcare facilities are needed ... [and] stand in long queues for hospitals and for paying rates ... All these services affect women more than any other person.
> (Badat 1995, 22)

Voter education was again an important task in the run up to the local elections. While there were some similarities to the 1994 elections, there were numerous differences that needed to be communicated to the electorate. Among the issues which needed explanation was the need for second elections so soon after the national and provincial elections. Voters also had to be acquainted with the roles and functions of local government structures: 'Developing voters' understanding of local government models, powers and responsibilities in 1995/6 was a more complex task than that required regarding national and provincial governments in 1994' (Camay and Gordon 1996,108). At a practical level, the 1995/96 elections were far more complicated than the 1994 elections. Voters were required to register, a new concept for the majority of the population. Balloting and electoral systems were different, with voters required to vote for a candidate of their choice (ward vote) as well as for the party of their choice (proportional vote). After the 1994 elections many of the organisations that had provided voter education were forced by a lack of funding to abandon their education initiatives. The momentum created by the national elections, therefore, did not carry over to the local elections. Ongoing education about the rights and responsibilities of South Africans was not prioritised, and it was as though '...the April 1994 election was seen by many as completion of the political transformation, rather than the beginning of a new era in which democracy had to be truly entrenched in South African society' (Camay and Gordon 1996, 105). As a consequence, the education infrastructure developed for the 1994 elections had largely disappeared and a shortage of funding hampered education efforts.

While the 1994 elections were centrally administered through the IEC, the administration of the local government elections was decentralised, with local authorities carrying the responsibility for conducting them. As a result, voter education was also decentralised and not as well organised or co-ordinated as it had been in 1994 (Camay and Gordon 1996, 108). Although the national Elections Task Group's (ETG) Communication and Voter Education Task Team had a mandate to co-ordinate voter education activities, it did not develop an effective detailed national strategy. As a result, some areas received no voter education, while in others several programmes ran concurrently (Camay and Gordon 1996, 127).

Most programmes only began in early 1995 when voter registration started. A number of organisations, including local authorities and the NGO community, were involved in providing education. Among the NGOs were Idasa, IMSSA, the Matla Trust, Project Vote, and the South African Council of Churches. The content of the programmes varied greatly and included information on registration, the importance of the vote, the significance of local government, demarcation, the voting process, and ways of holding councillors accountable. As election regulations changed throughout the process, voter education materials had to be changed accordingly.

Many of those who worked as educators believe the process began too late, and the electorate did not receive much of the election information and education in time to absorb and utilise it effectively. One reason for this was that provincial personnel were appointed late, another that there was a delay in the receipt of funding allocations. Despite the range of organisations involved, few programmes were directed at women or identified women as a category with certain needs. Julie Oyegun believes voter education before the local elections would have benefited women if it had recognised:

> ... the unequal reality of women's gender experience of the state and should suggest strategies to re-design programmes in order to enhance actual programme delivery for women. Women must be well equipped to actively participate in the ... elections and to fully recognise the power of their votes. Women should also be informed on which candidates will represent their interests within the structures of local government... Women must not be instructed just to vote. They must gain a fresh appreciation of the power of their voters as a force for change in the gender status quo. (Oyegun 1995, 4)

Camay and Gordon, note that 'Women's organisations felt that election education should have been targeted to women's needs, including training women educators and involving women's organisations in the development of materials' (Camay and Gordon 1996, 134). The impact of this absence of training was seen in the fact that women appear to have participated less in the local elections than in the previous national and provincial elections (Camay and Gordon 1996, 248). It also emerged that many women faced similar obstacles to those they had faced in 1994. For example, there was similar stereotyping of women in politics, particularly in the media, and many women felt pressured not to cast their votes:

> Rural women, in particular, feared intimidation which caused some not to cast their votes, and certainly not to contest the elections as candidates. Some awaited consultation with their migrant worker husbands. Given the known high rates of female illiteracy, not enough provision was made for oral transmission of important election information. (Camay and Gordon 1996, 248)

Furthermore, Camay and Gordon note that the majority of participants at empowerment workshops prior to the elections were men; that women were often marginalised and had family responsibilities; and that many women felt threatened if they demanded their rightful role in politics (Camay and Gordon 1996, 248). Zondo also noted that rural women were often confused about the local elections, some viewing them as 'another step towards getting more men in government or reaffirming their ... positions in rural communities'. Given that similar obstacles were prevalent in the 1994 elections, lessons learnt would have pointed to the need for gender-specific training. Because of the limited funding available, together with the short time frames and absence of co-ordination of education activities on a par with 1994, it appears that gender-specific training was not prioritised.

It was not only the participation of women as voters that was limited by a lack of education, the participation of women as elected representatives was too. Many women who were actively involved in politics did not receive support from their families and communities or from other women. This clearly impacted on their role:

> There was some evidence that the leadership of many women's organisations were ill-informed and uninvolved, with little detailed knowledge of the election management structures and processes. Their disappointing participation in those structures pointed to a general absence of gender awareness in the way the election was planned and executed. (Camay and Gordon 1996, 248)

In order for women to participate effectively at the local level in the future, there is clearly a need for voter education that targets women as a particular constituency with special needs. As local government is the sphere of government that potentially has the greatest impact on the daily lives of women, particularly in rural areas, women need to be encouraged to participate in local government elections. Not only should education seek to encourage effective participation during elections, it should also seek to raise awareness about the benefits of continued interest in local issues between elections.

DWINDLING VOTER EDUCATION IN ELECTORAL PREPARATION

The enormous effort and money committed to voter education in 1994 has been absent from subsequent elections. This was particularly apparent during the 1999 national and provincial elections when, although a number of organisations were involved in voter education, there was clearly a decline in funding, co-ordination and international interest. There was limited funding available to NGOs for voter education, particularly from foreign donors who had contributed significantly in the 1994 elections. The late announcement of the 1999 election date and new requirements for voting created new challenges (Watson, 8). It was also apparent that women's organisations and educators were not well prepared or co-ordinated.

The main difference between the 1994 and 1999 national and provincial elections was that in 1999 a national common voters' roll, different from that prepared for the local elections in 1995/6, had to be compiled. The franchise was confined to South African citizens in possession of an identity document or temporary certificate, who had to apply for registration in the voting district in which they ordinarily resided. The result was that the task of informing citizens of the requirements and venues for registration proved to be a critical challenge in the administration of the 1999 elections. Of the 22.8 million estimated voters, more than 18.3 million (80.4%) registered. Women constituted 53 per cent of the voters' register.

The IEC and NGOs embarked on a number of public awareness campaigns to inform voters of registration and polling processes. After the compilation of the voters' roll, it became apparent that voter educators had to focus not only on providing information on the mechanics of balloting, but also had to encourage citizens to vote after opinion polls pointed to an increasing apathy towards the election. The Election Act of 1998 stipulates that voter education is one of the responsibilities of the Electoral Commission. However, the responsibility is not confined to the IEC, as historically NGOs have played an important role in this regard (EISA 1999, 13).

The limited financial resources of the IEC ahead of the elections meant the allocation to voter education was much less that had originally been intended. The IEC therefore made provision to assist NGOs involved in voter education on condition that they met with its accreditation requirements. The prerequisites included non-partisan course content and adherence to a Code of Conduct publicised by the Commission in 1998 (EISA 1999, 13).

A number of NGOs were involved in providing voter education nationally. EISA was one of them. It initiated a voter registration and information campaign, distributing 100 000 voter education posters, mainly through the IEC, and published a voter education pamphlet, as well as providing extensive voter education training (EISA 1999). Other organisations included the Institute for Democracy in South Africa (IDASA), Co-operative for Research and Education (CORE), and other NGOs working at the provincial level, as well as community outreach programmes. Voter education courses typically focused on the registration process, the mechanics of polling, the secrecy of the ballot, and the importance of voting as a key component of exercising one's democratic rights and consolidating democracy. Another important message was that only voters who had registered would be able to vote. Political parties also compiled their own voter education programmes.

Few NGOs targeted women in their campaigns. However, the Women's Development Foundation embarked on a voter education for registration campaign, aimed particularly at women in rural areas (Watson, 9). The programme was designed to encourage women to acquire the requisite identity document, register, and vote on polling day. EISA also targeted its voter education campaign at women in rural areas.

After the 1999 elections, the Commission on Gender Equality (CGE) conducted a gender analysis of five sets of material used for voter education (EISA, IDASA, CORE, IEC and SACSOC). The analysis included an examination of how awareness was raised about the right to vote, the voting process, whether there was a specific focus on the unequal power relations between women and men, and the extent to which materials used examples of gender sensitive problems (Mbere 1999, 34). While the courses were found to be wanting in gender sensitivity in some areas, most of the activities targeted women. The IEC booklet raised gender awareness in a chapter on 'Women in Society'.

It is estimated that more than 7 000 women were reached through these five programmes. However, an important finding of the analysis is that most organisations commenced their education in 1999, which hampered efforts to reach rural voters – the group that requires the most information about aspects of the electoral system, registration, and voting. 'A majority of women live in rural areas, and even though statistics indicate that 65%-70% of women have registered, many of those not reached may [have been] rural dwellers' (Mbere 1999, 38).

While there was a decline in the scope of voter education compared with previous elections, there were a number of important initiatives aimed at raising voter awareness of the election. EISA produced a bi-monthly publication, *Election Talk*, which provided up-to-date information on a range of issues including political party developments, the progress of the IEC, and registration trends. It also sought to raise gender issues by providing articles on the political party manifestos and the number of women forwarded by political parties for election. Another important initiative was the *Election Bulletin* newsletter produced by Women'sNet, an information-clearing house that seeks to empower women through the use of information communication technology. The newsletter contained a wide range of articles on issues related to women's participation in the electoral process, and encouraged women to vote and have their say in the democratic process.

CONCLUSION

South Africa's successful transition from white minority domination to an inclusive democracy culminated in the first all race elections in May 1994. Key to the success of the elections was the ability of South Africans, most whom had previously been denied the franchise, to participate confidently in the electoral process. Voter education was fundamental in ensuring democratic participation and in transmitting key messages.

The status and participation of women was a central issue ahead of the 1994 elections. Women had made some gains in the negotiation process leading up to the elections and it was critical that these gains be consolidated by their participation and representation in the new democratic dispensation. It is evident that the enormous voter education ahead of the election was a huge success, and was central to ensuring a high turnout at the polls and creating an environment for the participation of all South Africans in the new democratic dispensation.

The decline in turnout in both the 1995-6 local elections and the 1999 national and provincial elections demonstrates the need for continued education. Women must be equipped with the knowledge to ensure their full participation in democratic and electoral processes and to appreciate the force of their votes as a means of improving their present position. Until all women are electorally and politically aware, intimidation, stereotyping and marginalisation, particularly among rural women, may continue to cloud their participation in the process. In order for all women to participate effectively, voter education that targets them as a particular constituency with special needs, should be considered.

NOTES

1. As Singh explains, the four NGOs were the Education and Information Project, HAP Organisational Development Services, the Centre for Community and Labour Studies, and Co-operative Planning.

8

WHY ELECTORAL SYSTEMS MATTER TO WOMEN

Sheila Meintjes and Mary Simons

In this chapter, we explore electoral models from a gender perspective. We do not examine the different systems other than where they are relevant to gender politics. In South Africa, the achievement of democracy was the outcome of a protracted struggle against apartheid, which ended in a negotiated settlement. This found expression first in the Interim Constitution in 1993 and ultimately in the Constitution, Act 108 of 1996, which emphasised non-sexism alongside non-racialism as foundational principles.

While the composition of Parliament was generally specified in the Constitution, the choice of electoral system was left fairly open, with the proviso that the election outcome 'results, in general, in proportional representation' (ch 4 s 46:1(d)) and with a provision allowing for a revision of the system.[1] The electoral system is only as good as the commitment of the parties to diversity.

The different parties involved in negotiating the Constitution readily agreed that if there was to be a fully representative legislature it would be necessary to move away from the old Westminster model of political representation, epitomised by majoritarianism. In its place, proportional representation (PR) was acknowledged as the fairest way of representing the diversity of political parties and political interests in the country. The parties would decide on their representatives by means of a party list system. The system allows South Africa to fulfil its constitutional obligations and avoids the tendency to view women as second class members of Parliament (De Ville and Steytler1996, 1).

At the national level, the closed list PR system together with the African National Congress's (ANC's) 30 per cent quota of women) has been successful in bringing a critical mass of women representatives to Parliament. At the local government level, the mixed system combining constituency and PR based representation gives a useful comparative basis for an evaluation of which system might be most conducive to the representation of women in South Africa. We recognise that there are hard choices to be made in selecting an electoral system, in defining constituency boundaries, and in identifying and selecting representative candidates.

As earlier chapters have shown, our concern is not merely with numerical representation, we are also interested in the relationship between the electoral system and the variables of political culture, commitment to women's representation in Parliament, the existence of politically organised women's movements, and state institutional commitment and support. All of these provide a framework within which we are able to evaluate the importance for women of the electoral system adopted in South Africa.

South African political parties identify problems in the relationship between elected representatives and the voter under the PR system. The lack of a direct link between representatives and constituencies raises the spectre of parties ignoring the will of 'the people', except at election time.

After the experience of two elections, political parties demanded a revision of the system to ensure more direct lines of constituency accountability. At the time of writing, a review of the electoral system is being considered. Among suggestions for change are a return to the constituency system and the introduction of the mixed proportional and constituency model used in local government elections.

POLITICAL CULTURE, POLITICAL PARTIES AND ELECTORAL SYSTEMS

The relationship between political culture, gender, and the electoral system is significant in relation to the presence, participation, and representation of women in politics. Although all societies are marked by forms of patriarchy that have, historically, produced 'androcentric' political cultures, male domination is not the same everywhere, nor is it uncontested. Perhaps the most useful way of viewing male domination is as an expression of the social relations between men and women. This view emphasises the relational aspect of how the social is constituted, and that male domination is intertwined with other forms of inequality. This is not a constant, but can vary with time and in different contexts. Struggles against different forms of domination have led to significant changes in society that have restructured social relations.

The struggle against racial domination in South Africa saw the mobilisation of all sectors of society, including large numbers of women. Alliances across race and class were formed to combat the apartheid system. However, despite the achievement of democracy, equal citizenship on a formal level, and the presence of large numbers of women in Parliament and in government, the power of patriarchy continues to block effective equality. In older democracies, like Britain, the presence of women has also been fairly limited in terms of numbers. Part of the explanation lies in the fact that society as a whole does not support the participation of women as party representatives. There is considerable evidence that in elections the voters prefer to vote for men rather than women candidates. Therefore in systems where party structures play a significant role in selecting candidates there is a greater likelihood of fewer women being nominated. Thus, the nature of the electoral system becomes an important variable in facilitating the presence of women in Parliament.

Evidence that the presence of women in the political system changes the norms of the electorate is ambiguous too. It would appear in Scandinavian countries that women's presence in the political system over time has led to their acceptance and to change in the political culture. The evidence from Africa is, however, less sanguine, suggesting that despite the significant increase in the last ten years in the number of women parliamentarians, and even of women cabinet ministers in African parliaments, the political culture remains opposed to the presence of women. African societies in general are very conservative (Reynolds 1999b, 4).

Religious attitudes are a useful barometer of broad social and cultural approaches to gender equality. South Africa is a highly religious society, with some 76 per cent of the population active members of a religious organisation. Many of these religions hold conservative views on the place of women in public life. In order for religious and other socio-cultural barriers to be overcome, considerable commitment to gender equality and women's emancipation is needed. In particular, citizens, both men and women, must be re-educated to accept the legitimacy of women in decision-making positions including positions as political representatives in Parliament.

In South Africa, this process has been hastened by the manner in which women engaged in the struggle for equality during the period of negotiations, and the fact that the ANC, as the governing party, integrated women and women's issues into its leadership and policies. This was not a simple matter. It involved, and continues to involve, women and men in a struggle within the ANC for women's ongoing integration.

The position of women in politics is affected, too, by whether a political regime is progressive or conservative. In more traditional societies, governed by religious fundamentalism or by traditional authorities such as chiefs and kings, culture is often inimical to the social advancement of women, but not necessarily to their presence or even participation in politics. These women need not necessarily be elected as representatives in the same manner as men. They could be placed in office through a variety of mechanisms – through the president, the parliament, or the dominant party.

In the first case, the appointment of women may boost the presidential office without necessarily having any beneficial effect on the status of women generally.

The second process – parliament making the selection – is more democratic as opposition parties join the ruling party in nominating representatives. The consequence of this process, however, is to make such women nominees dependent on parties.

Even in democratic societies in the North, where women struggled for the vote, formal rights did not lead to their greater representation. The advancement of women had to wait until the mobilisation of social movements in the second half of the twentieth century. The claims of Northern feminist movements for more than mere formal equality linked women's advancement to an emancipatory and transformative project. Once this evolved into an engagement with the state, as was the case in many western countries, women's issues became matters of policy. In some cases states developed specialised institutions to improve the status of women in society. In South Africa the mobilisation of opposition to apartheid wove a complex pattern of different ideological perspectives and practices. The fight against apartheid brought many strands together – African nationalism, liberalism, socialism, radical feminism, social feminism, and social democracy – not all of them wedded to the emancipation of women. The experience of the Left in South Africa, including the ANC in its liberation phase, conscientised these movements on gender issues, and politicised the status of women. The outcome of this experience led to the quota on the national list of the ANC and to the appointment of women to the Cabinet. Political liberalisation enabled women to mobilise within the public sphere as bureaucrats or as representatives in legislatures.

Political parties in modern states act as gatekeepers for representatives, both women and men. The first assumption we make is that parties are concerned with democracy and the representivity of all citizens. In order to grasp why the electoral system matters in this process, we need to remember that the more women representatives there are in Parliament, the more likely it will be that a proportion of those representatives will be committed to non-sexism and will actively attempt to erase gender inequalities and improve the status of women.

South Africa is unlike many other countries where politicians tend to come from a pool of citizens who are highly educated and have professional jobs and access to the resources of public life. It is a society in which the bulk of the population is denied access to education or to higher education or employment and is not socialised into a world close to public decision-making. The result of this is that the 'democratic' pool is substantially reduced. In addition, women-unfriendly cultural norms have retarded the prospects of women entering politics as a matter of course (Reynolds 1999a). What is particularly fascinating about the way in which the South African transition to democracy unfolded was the high level of organisation and lobbying to ensure that women's issues were made part of the agenda of change. The South African case subverts conventional explanations and suggests the importance in democratic transitions of women's political mobilisation and organisation as a constituency. It also suggests the importance of pushing for recognition of the gender dimensions of discrimination and political interests.

It is noteworthy that once political parties commit themselves to incorporating women in a variety of roles, the door opens for the admission of other historically and traditionally excluded groups (gay, disabled, ethnic).

On the whole, though, political parties have coalesced around broader ideological, class, and economic interests, taking on along with these, the particular interests of identity groups, including gender, disability, and even ethnicity. Women party members and representatives and women voters are pivotal in this process, and their presence in government and in the electorate is key to ensuring democracy for all. In the light of the discussion so far, it is clear that women's presence in politics remains dependent on political party commitment, because constituencies are unlikely to share that commitment (Reynolds 1999a, 2).

The electoral system acts as the gateway to women's presence as representatives in Parliament and other legislative bodies. The choice of a particular model (PR or majoritarian) maximises or minimises the ability of political parties to manipulate the slate of candidates and representatives. Stephen Rule argues that favourable social conditions will not substitute for unfavourable electoral systems in order for women to reach their optimal representation in Parliament and local legislatures. But unfavourable contextual conditions – including cultural biases and discriminatory practices – can be overcome to a great extent by the selection of an appropriate electoral system (Rule 1994b, 689).

In its purest form, the First-Past-The-Post (FPTP) system is older than the PR system and is strictly majoritarian. It is characterised by constituencies, in which the winner of the parliamentary seat is the candidate with a fifty per cent-plus-one majority of votes in a two-way contest, and a third-plus-one vote in a three-way contest, in a philosophy of 'winner takes all'. A simple majority wins a seat. The votes cast for the losing candidate are lost and therefore a vote for a losing candidate has no value (De Ville and Steytler 1996, 5). Sometimes the system allows for candidates to be chosen by local party officials and members of the party. Increasingly, the world-wide tendency in majoritarian systems is for power to reside in the central party, among party leaders (De Ville and Steytler 1996, 7).Generally in the West, voter turnouts show a decline in participation so the simple majority forms an increasingly low percentage of the potential voter population.

In the purest form of PR system every vote counts, and the number of seats allocated to parties is proportional to the number of votes cast for each party. The formulae for arriving at the proportional ratio vary (De

Ville and Steytler 1996, 19-28). The entire country is often treated as a single district, but this too may vary. However, it is possible for a district to have several representatives, resulting in a high magnitude of district seats to party candidates and providing parties with considerable choice in balancing their representatives in each district.

Under a PR system representatives are chosen from either closed or open lists which are created in a variety of ways involving varying levels of party membership participation. The level of choice given to the electorate varies according to whether the list is open or closed. The open list refers to the voter's ability to choose both the parties and the candidates on the list. In the closed list, the voter may only vote for the party. Women friendly voters can influence the party by voting for women on the open list. This may be beneficial to women in countries that are more gender emancipated. In countries where the electorate is hostile to women, a closed list gives women greater opportunities for electoral success.

The absence of constituencies means the party tends to dominate more in the PR system than in the majoritarian system.

In contrast to FPTP, the PR system may have thresholds of greater or lesser significance. High thresholds may lead to the dominance of fewer parties, whilst low thresholds provide opportunities for a wider range of parties, and thus for a broader range of interests to be represented. In effect the fact that this system allows smaller parties to function forces bigger parties to diversify their lists. PR systems in practice allow for the incorporation of a variety of approaches in combination with elements of FPTP (Reynolds1999b, 5).

Systems that combine single-member districts and lists fall somewhere between list PR and FPTP. Ballington has shown that these are less favourable to women. In her analysis of South African local government and national government elections, she notes that the ANC was the only party to adopt a voluntary party quota and in fact the number of women who got into Parliament exceeded the quota. However, if this figure is broken down, a more complex picture emerges (Ballington 1999).

At national level in 1999 every third candidate was a woman. At local government level, the combination of list and ward systems resulted in women being elected to19 per cent of the available positions. Of these only 11 per cent came from wards, while 28 per cent were from the lists.

This appears to indicate a party bias towards male candidates in ward or constituency seats. In the absence of a quota, women's representation drops dramatically (Pottie 2000, 2). The mixed system is not only less favourable to women than the PR system, there is also a tendency to view people on the party list as second-class legislators. In societies where there is a resistance to women in positions of power this is likely to be detrimental to women.

Like all political institutions, electoral systems have different functions some of which are directly contradictory and in conflict. Nohlen suggests that electoral systems have to fulfil five functions in a democracy – representation, participation, concentration, legitimacy, and simplicity (De Ville and Steytler 1999, 16). Representation refers to an insurance that all members of the electorate have a voice, including women, minorities, and special interest groups. It also means fair representation of political parties. Nohlen argues that participation requires that voters be able to choose both candidates and parties. In theory, in systems where there was a limited franchise and small constituencies, levels of participation were high because there was much greater direct involvement of the electorate.

The complexity of modern society and modern politics encourages concentration of power in the party and the elevation of the importance of political leaders. Concentration refers to the political aggregation of social interests into a limited number of political parties so 'that the political institutions are able to act decisively' (De Ville and Steytler 1999, 16). Concentration is desirable if stable and effective government is to be achieved. Legitimacy derives, firstly, from the population's acceptance of the electoral system; secondly from acquiescence in election results; and thirdly, from the recognition of the right to rule of the representatives chosen through the electoral process. The final necessary requirement for an electoral system is simplicity, the level of which depends upon the context within which the system has to operate. In highly literate and modern societies the electoral system and the administration of the election can be more complex, without in any way affecting the legitimacy of the system. In societies with high levels of illiteracy both the electoral system and the administration of the election must be easy to understand and to operate.

South Africa's PR system contains four of Nohlens's variables. While representation is wide and diverse, one of the aspects not always understood is that there is an urban bias in the way parties draw up their lists. In our view, it falls short on rural representation, particularly of women and the poor. In terms of participation, at national level the electorate can only vote for a party, not for particular candidates. It should be noted that party members' participation in the composition of the lists appears also to be restricted. In the election of specific members, the ANC, the Democratic Party, and the New National Party had a system in place to nominate branch candidates for the party lists. But this process had less weight than the intervention of the party leadership in determining where candidates were placed on the lists.

In South Africa, the leadership of all parties plays a major role in composing lists and placing candidates in the sequence of their choice. There is thus a high level of interference which, although it does not fulfil Nohlens's stipulation for participation, has actually had beneficial consequences for women. In the early phase of developing a non-racial, non-sexist democracy, it is in the interests of parties to provide a balanced list. Because the lists were closed, the electorate could only choose between parties, not between candidates. This may be a feature of the early stages of the democratic process, and certainly legitimates it (de Ville and Steytler 1996, 26), but it may serve the interests of political parties in future to involve their own members more in the choice of candidates and in the composition of the party lists. This might lead to an increase in the participation of party membership in political parties, thus improving the levels of commitment to democracy, but as we suggested above, it endangers the representivity of women candidates, for whom there may be little support because of the hostile political culture.

The new democratic order in South Africa enjoys a high degree of legitimacy. In the first election there was no voters' roll, and it was impossible to assess turnout, but it was estimated at 86 per cent. The high turnout was not simply a case of support for the electoral system, as is usual in long-standing democracies, but was a measure of how much the society valued the idea of the vote as an indicator of freedom from oppression. The support for electoral politics was sustained in the second election, before which a voters' roll was drawn up.

IMPACT OF ELECTORAL SYSTEMS ON WOMEN'S PARTICIPATION, PRESENCE, REPRESENTATION, AND POWER

Andrew Reynolds, in a careful survey, identified the variables that facilitate or block the integration of women into public electoral politics through a multivariate regression analysis (Reynolds 1999a, 2). He confirmed that 'certain electoral systems were more "woman friendly" than others'. But he also suggested that ideology and religion were significant in determining whether or not women obtained office. Another significant variable was the degree of party fragmentation. Interestingly, neither the degree of democracy nor the length of experience of elections was a good predictor of women's success in parliamentary politics. The level of socio-economic development in a country does not appear to be a reliable indicator either. The presence of large numbers of professional women in a society will not necessarily translate into more women in decision making positions in government.

Re-democratisation of Africa in the 1990s is marked by the presence of women in political office. More than 650 African women are members of their national parliaments. Eighty-five women hold cabinet office in Africa. But Europe, particularly the Nordic countries, still has the most women in its parliaments. New Zealand, the first country to grant a universal franchise to all adults (in 1893), was eighth in the world in terms of women's representation, with 30.8 per cent of its seats held by women. But even in countries with high levels of women's representation, the cultural negativity towards women in high political office often remains. Indeed, nowhere can there be said to be a gender neutral political sphere.

As Albertyn, Hassim and Meintjes argue in this volume, the broadest representation of the electorate is necessary in order to meet women's special interests and needs. It is also a recipe for the most democratic form of governance. Diversity secures a better democracy and the quality of legislation improves the conditions of women and children in society at large. We do not mean by this, though, that women alone can represent the interests of women, for such interests are too diverse, cross-cut by class position, racial, ethnic, and cultural identities for there to be a single identifiable set of 'women's gender interests'.

The argument in favour of constituency representation relies on the idea that a constituency representative in parliament is committed to the constituency and represents the interests of constituents. This is not borne out by research either in Germany, with its mixed system, or in Britain, which has a pure constituency system (Matland 1998, 84). The more centralised a governmental system, the less constituencies count, and, in both Germany and Britain, the party, party leadership, and party interests are served before the constituency. By contrast, the American system, for a number of reasons, shows a high level of accountability and representative loyalty to the constituency. One significant reason for this is that party discipline in the United States is much weaker than that in Britain. Historically, electoral candidates have retained a strong sense of individual independence, with party control seen as a corrupting influence. This is simply strengthened by the nature of the Presidential system and the history of civic republicanism. Representatives are able to vote according to their consciences.

Other systems between list PR and single member district, plurality-majority systems combine attributes of both proportionality and candidate centred majority voting. Block voting or 'at large voting', where voters have as many votes as there are seats to be filled in the district, is more favourable to women than FPTP (Rule and Zimmerman 1997).

The question of the accountability of women representatives is complex because they are affected not only by the party or by the constituency but also by an imagined community of other women. There are several aspects to this assumed relationship. One is essentialist – a belief that all women have the same interests regardless of any differences between them. Another emphasises women's diversity while arguing that the later entry of women into the political system and their ongoing subordination creates common objectives.

The tension embedded in the question of accountability is not readily resolved where women's political caucuses or women's movements do not exist. Even where such caucuses and movements do exist, the key is how political parties address the diversity of women's political interests, and which electoral system assists or hinders women's participation and representation in political life (Hassim, in this volume). Studies assessing women's performance in parliament, their contribution to parliamentary committees, and the extent to which their presence influences the direction of policy, legislation and the issues debated, frequently adopt an essentialist view (see Britton 1996).

ARGUING THE CASE FOR SOUTH AFRICA

Andrew Reynolds has argued convincingly for both continuity in and change to certain aspects of the PR system. In order to meet the demand for accountability, he suggests that the number of districts be increased. His view of the closed list PR system is that there is a problem with the fact that in large districts representatives are detached from the citizens they are supposed to represent. Instead, they are accountable to party bosses. To counter this problem, he suggests that voter districts for the National Assembly should be smaller, with between three and twelve representatives each. Voters could be given a choice between candidates as well as between parties. In addition, the system could be changed to a mixture of single-member constituencies and PR lists (i.e. MMP – mixed member proportional system) without affecting the constitutionally prescribed overall proportionality of the system.Reynolds proposes two possible alternatives, a 50-50 split between constituency members and list members, or more district than list seats.

The difficulty with this proposal is that few comparative systems elsewhere help in making an informed decision. No countries in Africa use the MMP, and district size varies greatly among the sixteen African countries that use the PR system. Germany and Russia use the MMP system and more women are elected from the list than in the district constituencies. In Japan, where the lower house uses the Single Non-Transferable Vote (SNTV) and the upper house uses PR, there are more women in the upper house.

The implications are that the smaller the district, the fewer the safe seats and the more contested by party candidates, the more likely is the nomination process to favour men. Irrespective of size of district a switch to open lists will reduce chances of women being elected. In the current South African PR system, compared to the previous constituency-based system, from a mere 3 per cent under apartheid, we now have a critical mass of nearly 30 per cent of women representatives.

Quotas, which are covered in other chapters in this volume, compensate for the absence of women in office and for the inability of 'androcentric' political systems to adequately represent women's interests. The existence of quotas will increase the number of women in the legislature, as has been evident in other countries with quota mechanisms both compulsory and voluntary.

Compulsory quotas for women MPs have dramatically increased their presence in representative institutions in Argentina, Belgium, Brazil, North Korea, and Nepal. Reserved seats have been established in Bangladesh, Burkina Faso, Uganda, and Tanzania. The danger is that women representatives occupying these special seats are considered secondary representatives, whose participation in general debates about national politics is not seen as legitimate. Reserved seats are seen as tokenism and as unhelpful to the ultimate development of a gender neutral political sphere. In thirty-six countries reviewed by the Inter-Parliamentary Union (IPU), many of the political parties had quotas for women's candidatures for legislative elections. The IPU argues that quotas should be considered temporary measures to be employed only while gender discrimination in parties and society restricts the prospects for election of women candidates (IPU 1997, 61).

CONCLUSION

The selection of an electoral system is a political choice influenced by history, the current political and socio-cultural configurations in society, and finally by the political parties themselves, depending on what they consider to be in their best interests. Individuals and parties across the board in South Africa are concerned about the lack of connection between parties and their constituencies because of the PR system. Theoretically, for a PR system to be effective parties must exercise considerable discipline over their MPs. This is in contrast to a FPTP majoritarian system, where the constituency holds the MPs accountable.

This lack of accountability means the party political system in South Africa has failed to meet voters' needs. The introduction of a mixed system of PR and ward representation in the local sphere of government has been an attempt to compensate for this lack of direct accountability. The mixed system will permit much greater political diversity, and possibly break the dominance of the majority party at the local level. At the same time, constituency representatives will be held much more accountable for developmental delivery by local government, strengthening the relationship between the local state and the citizen. The consequence will be that the local sphere will become of greater significance to citizens than the national.

Although no system can guarantee gender equality there can be little doubt that women in South Africa have done relatively well in terms of representation, thanks to the PR process, and should thus be cautious about advocating any change to the electoral system. Given the patriarchal and segregated nature of South African society, the retention of the PR system, using a single list with a low threshold, is the best way of ensuring the widest representation. In our view the critical debate should be about the existence and size of a quota for women in the electoral system.

NOTE

1. The Constitution specifies (Ch 2, s 19:2) that there should be free and fair elections on the basis of universal adult suffrage, a national common voters' roll and regular elections within a multiparty system of democratic government (Ch 1, s (d)). It also specifies the value of ensuring 'accountability, responsiveness and openness' (ibid).

9

LOCAL GOVERNMENT

Alice Coetzee and Subethri Naidoo

INTRODUCTION

As part of the development of an informal settlement in Soshanguve, north of Pretoria, the local council decided to install toilets on each stand. The toilets were placed on the street side of the stand with the door facing the street. The engineers reasoned that this would make the toilets accessible. For the women the toilets were a disaster. Firstly, they were far from the houses so they were afraid to use them at night. Secondly they felt afraid because they could not see the toilet door from their houses and wouldn't be able to monitor who went in or out or who might be lying in wait for them. 'If only they had asked us before they installed the toilets, we could have told them what we needed,' remarked one of the women.

This story has become something of an urban legend in Pretoria. Irrespective of how fact and fable merge, it captures how women are overlooked in the delivery of local government services that impact directly on their daily lives.

This chapter seeks to explore how gender determines the involvement of women within local representative government. It provides a background to South African local politics and the nature and impact of women's participation since 1995. Local government is at the coalface of issues facing ordinary people in their daily lives. Given that women's role in the community has been determined in gendered (often patriarchal) terms, there are clear economic and consequent social imperatives to secure their active participation in politics at this level. To ensure economic and social stability, growth and development, it is vital that women's participation is understood as central to the development and growth of a democratic culture in South Africa. We argue that to achieve equity, financial stability, and sustainable development in local government, it is imperative that the relationship between women's practical and strategic needs is understood and used to inform the manner in which local government fulfils its constitutional obligations. Without this focus, local government will not be able to deliver according to its mandate.

BACKGROUND

To understand how and why development fails (as in the example above) despite the context of a new democracy, it is important to understand the historical development of local government in South Africa.

The shaping of the apartheid city began long before apartheid came into being. The 1913 Land Act gave 87 per cent of fertile, productive land to whites and the remaining 13 per cent to Africans in the form of tribal reserves. Effectively this policy created a large, landless population, which drifted to the cities in search of employment.

With the advent of the Native Urban Areas Act in 1923, a system of municipally controlled passes was created and was managed by local municipalities. This system 'allowed' black labour into a municipality (which was understood to be for white people only) to provide services, and then leave. Black labour was seen as supplying a temporary need and family migration was actively discouraged.

This resulted in a number of informal, unserviced settlements being established at the fringes of the city. When the National Party came into power in 1948 it attempted to address this 'problem' by introducing the homelands policy that allowed African people to have rights only in areas identified as 'theirs' and determined by language and tribal differences. Africans were seen as temporary labourers who would return to 'their' homeland once they had completed their work. But numbers kept growing and the apartheid government realised it could not keep up with this new urban spread. The best it could do was to keep these areas separate from the urban white city centres (Planact Handbook 1997, 10).

The resulting Group Areas Act (41 of 1950), which instituted strict residential segregation along racial lines, further entrenched and limited the extent to which affluent white municipalities would bear the burden of servicing disadvantaged black areas (*White Paper* 1998, introduction). Since service provision within traditionally white communities was adequately financed, the interaction of local communities with their councillors was, at best, minimal. This sphere of government was seen as dealing with 'bread and butter' issues, and satisfaction with the levels and adequacy of service determined how communities engaged with their local authorities. Local authorities were seen often as institutions with which very little active engagement was necessary.

Within predominantly black communities however, there was a very different scenario. Black Local Authorities (BLAs) established by the National Party government in 1982 consisted of nominated individuals who had no significant revenue base to manage and who were regarded by those under their jurisdiction as politically illegitimate. The result was that this sphere of politics became an important arena of mass mobilisation in the 1980s. At the time communities were effectively organised by the United Democratic Front (UDF) to boycott rent and service charges and to protest the introduction of the Tricameral Parliament. The UDF also succeeded in uniting communities in all black (including 'Indian' and 'coloured') areas behind what became known as the 'rolling mass action campaign'.

The role of women during this time of civic politics was extremely significant. They became involved in organising a whole range of social services for communities through autonomous civil society organisations. For example, women were crucial to the successful operation and functioning of advice offices which had been set up throughout the country to deal with community-related issues and also served as an important means of political mobilisation and organisation. There is a direct link between the gendered implications of women's responsibilities in their social context and their responsibilities within community structures. Because many women were not in full-time 'employment', as commonly defined, they were freer to manage and work in these structures. They managed a range of activities from administration to providing legal advice to those who were experiencing difficulties with their family, the municipality, or the state.

When negotiations began in the early 1990s, few of these women were included in the political delegations set up to negotiate the future dispensation. Women's roles were defined as local and community orientated. The hard political negotiations were seen mainly as the prerogative of their male comrades. No conscious effort was made to include women in the strategic processes that ultimately determined the focus and pace of negotiations. In the past, women had mainly fulfilled a supportive role such as catering for workshops, conferences, and funerals; mobilising supporters for mass rallies; or assisting families who had lost their breadwinners in the struggle. While important, these activities did not lead to the next level of political struggle: negotiating new local representation. In many ways this lack of visibility resulted in fewer women candidates being nominated by their parties for the first fully democratic local government elections on 1 November 1995. Despite attempts by political parties, in particular the ANC, to ensure sufficient numbers of women on their party lists women occupied only 19,04 per cent of local government seats in seven provinces surveyed by the Institute for a Democratic South Africa (Idasa Logic 1997,1). It could be argued that this was the result of existing gendered perceptions of the work done by women in the community who were more often seen as supporters than as leaders and were defined in gendered 'nurturing' terms rather than as tough negotiators.

The impact of those struggles admittedly led to a situation in which there was legislative recognition of the role of women in developing a democratic culture. The legislative framework that determined the interim phase of local government and ended with the promulgation of new municipal structures and the second local government elections in 2000 was provided by the Local Government Transition Act (1994) and the Local Government Amendment Act (1995). Both the Constitution and the Local Government: Municipal Structures Act 117 of 1998 governed the 2000 local government electoral process. While women were largely absent from negotiations for the pre-interim and interim forms of local government, their presence as elected councillors during the interim phase enabled them to make a more coherent, collective contribution. Through gender structures at national and provincial levels of organised local government they were able to participate in and influence policy debates during the 1998 *White Paper* process on restructuring local government. The results can be seen in the strong focus on 'developmental' local government in the *White Paper* (which emphasised that community participation was critical). This meant that communities would in future have the opportunity to participate through 'the rolling up of sleeves, our acting like citizens, as opposed to mere atomised consumers…' (*White Paper* 1998, viii).

The legislation recognised that previously marginalised groups (like women) had an important contribution to make to the development of a democratic culture. The legislative responsibility to restructure local government was recognised as vital to the process of social and economic stability and growth in South Africa. The restructuring process attempted to redistribute resources equitably so that communities in historically under-developed and under-resourced areas would have access to acceptable levels of service. The problem was to retain the levels and quality of service provision in those areas that already had them while extending adequate services in others. This disjuncture between geographic areas separated by pockets of wealth and extreme poverty needed to be addressed and the demarcation process emanating from the *White Paper* and culminating in the Local Government: Demarcation Act 27 of 1998 attempted to deal with these inequities.

THE DEMARCATION PROCESS

Demarcation proposed 'redrawing' the outer and inner boundaries of urban and rural areas created by the Group Areas Act to ensure that resources were used more effectively and efficiently to achieve equitable service provision and maintain or create sustainable tax bases. Much of this re-managing and re-planning understandably created serious difficulties for both communities and government. For example, linking prosperous Sandton with the neighbouring Alexandra township with its developmental and financial needs, or the needs of the wealthy suburbs of the City of Cape Town with the demands of the Cape Flats, posed enormous problems. Different interest groups challenged the agenda of the Demarcation Board. The bottom line, however, remained concern about development, and the ultimate object of the process was to ensure equitable and financially stable planning and service provision. Extensive work was done to ensure ongoing community participation and transparency. The demarcation process engaged interested stakeholders in a consistent and participative manner.

But the next question is whether or not the demarcation process considered the gender implications of its work in a substantive way. Given the fact that women made up 52 per cent of the population and that more than 70 per cent of women in the rural areas existed in a poverty-stricken situation (Budlender 1998), the obvious issue is whether and how gender impacted on the deliberations of the Demarcation Board. Women are the main users of water and energy (in fact, most local services), and women feel the impact of service provision more directly because of their domestic responsibilities. The lack of adequate sewerage systems and refuse removal or the under-provision of clinics, therefore, has health implications for the community broadly, but the consequences are ultimately borne by the women. In the circumstances, it would make sense for the success of government's legislative initiatives to be measured by the effectiveness with which it was able to address the issues of women's participation and representation at the community level.

Dr Mike Sutcliffe, Chairperson of the Demarcation Board, had this to say about the gender dimension of demarcation:

> For us it is about dividing the country into financially viable, sustainable economic parts. Gender has not been dealt with in an explicit way, but rather arises out of the work we've done. So, for example, poverty indices and their implications have been seriously considered even though that hasn't necessarily entailed a detailed gender analyses. We have tried to address those issues within the context of poverty. Given the tight timeframes around this process though, the nature of our work has determined the depth of focus on these specific target groups. (Telephone interview May 2000)

CONTEXTUAL ANALYSES

It is against this background that we now examine how gender determines women's involvement in local electoral politics. In terms of the Constitution, local government – in the form of metropolitan, local, district or rural councils – is responsible for the provision of basic services such as electricity, water, sewerage, refuse removal, roads, clinics and municipal planning. These services affect every person's quality of life and have an impact on people's realities in very practical ways.

Whether or not women are 'household heads', their lives and those of the community (especially children, the aged, and the disabled) are dependent on adequate service provision. For example, the connection of water to houses rather than to a communal tap, as is the case in many informal settlements, affects the health of households while easing the domestic duties of women. The health of the community is also improved by the provision of waterborne sewerage as opposed to long drops, or by the connection of electricity to replace wood and coal burning fires. The health implications of the absence of such services are almost immediate – pollution and disease – and the effects are most directly borne by women as the caregivers.

Adequate rubbish collection, street cleaning, and even lighting, impact on the safety and security of women and children. Even a service not directly paid for, such as town planning, determines the supply and location of clinics, schools and libraries, and creates an enabling environment for economic development and job creation through the provision of necessary infrastructure. The paucity of these resources not only affects those in the immediate environment, it has cost implications for planning. The debates about economic sustainability and poverty alleviation at national level must be informed by an understanding and acceptance of the need for adequate planning at the local level. And 'effective, efficient' planning at local government level cannot be conceived of apart from the realities that face women and families on a daily basis.

A closer analysis of the consumption of services shows that in both rural and urban areas women are the biggest consumers of local government services. According to the Central Statistical Services survey on women and men in South Africa, proportionately more women live in the urban areas of the Western Cape and Gauteng. This is significant because the metropolitan authorities of Gauteng and the Western Cape control huge budgets, in some cases larger than the budgets of provinces like North West and Northern Cape.

The metropolitan authorities are the main developers and deliverers of services to their residents. The question therefore is, given their significance to the work of local government, whether and to what extent women are able to impact on how they determine their budget allocations. While, at a practical level, this economic imperative is clear, there are two other reasons to promote the strategic and political empowerment of women.

One is to fulfil the obligations imposed by the Constitution, the other, more important one is to realise the significance of the relationship between political power and the decisions which shape and are shaped by the social and economic imperatives of citizens and voters. Planning at local government level must recognise that effective community participation will encourage productivity and financial sustainability in all its functions (Parnell and Pieterse, in Naidoo 1999a). If participation and democratisation are to be meaningful, the interests of those in need of services have to be reflected in the planning process.

The Constitution emphasises the importance of the full and equal participation of all citizens in political institutions and executive decision-making (Madonsela, in Naidoo 1999a, 7). The *White Paper* (1998), largely in spirit but also in content, echoed these sentiments by acknowledging the importance of improving the quality of life of previously 'marginalised' groups (which included women). These policy and legislative imperatives highlight effective participation as a means of enhancing a democratic and credible system of local governance. Elected representatives (at national, provincial, and local levels) often lacked the political will to focus on women's interests. Indeed very little attention was given to the mechanisms needed to ensure the implementation of the local government developmental agenda. Similarly, officials were often insensitive to the specificity of women's needs and were never neutral arbiters of government policy. The interests of women depended on the interventions of particular individuals, who drove the 'women's agenda'. The problem was not merely one of the institutional mechanisms for implementation, but resided also in the commitment of political leadership.

A survey commissioned by the National Housing Forum Trust and the Friedrich Ebert Stiftung in 1998 to evaluate the experience of recipients of government housing subsidies found that for women and women-headed households in particular, hardship was increased if certain infrastructure and community services did not accompany housing development (Gear 1999). Most new houses were on the periphery of urban centres, which meant women had to travel long distances to work, to clinics, and to shops. Public transport was often not available, and the lack of street lighting made them vulnerable to rape. Many reported a loss of income and found it harder to fulfil their multiple responsibilities.

This example is one of many that demonstrate that local municipalities during the first democratic phase had very few of the skills and competencies required to translate legislation into practical planning approaches. While municipalities were best placed to implement legislative equity policies, they were often ill-prepared to transform the institutions' bureaucratic processes, procedures, policies and budget priorities (Albertyn, in Naidoo 1999a,15). The traditionally gender-blind approach to development does not benefit everyone equally and often impacts negatively on women because the unequal access has the effect of reinforcing unequal gender power relations.

While the 1998 *White Paper* placed the emphasis firmly on developmental local government, it was not able to integrate its references to gender equity in any way that made a substantive difference to the manner in which municipalities worked. It did not spell out how councils should draw gender in nor did it provide the mechanisms for them to do so.

Submissions from gender activists, including the Commission on Gender Equality (CGE), the Gender Advocacy Project (GAP), and the South African Local Government Association (Salga) Gender Working Group, supported three main proposals. First, they suggested that gender structures be established to mainstream gender in councils and make them more 'gender-friendly'. Secondly, they proposed that the political parties should comply with a 30 per cent mandatory gender quota to increase the representation of women in councils, and thirdly, they advocated that training and mentoring be provided so gender issues would be aligned to council budgets and women councillors empowered with the necessary skills.

These proposals were not included in the *White Paper*, presumably because of opposition from political parties who felt they were too far reaching. Tactically too, this would not have been a strategic move since there was no effective enforcement process by which the Minister of Provincial and Local Government could have ensured compliance by political parties. The recommendation from then Minister Valli Moosa attempted to draw in some of these views, and they were expressed in the *White Paper* as a need to 'encourage' political parties to increase their quota of women candidates to 30 per cent.

In 1996 Salga's Executive Committee supported the establishment of gender structures within municipalities and called on individual councils to ensure that this happened. These efforts however, were limited in that there was no compulsion upon municipalities to do anything about them. While councils operated within the framework of the *White Paper*, each administration still made its own policy, decided on its delegation of powers, established its own standing committees, and drafted its own budgets. A chief executive officer or town clerk would decide whether or not sufficient funds were available to carry out this agenda – in most cases deciding that gender issues did not warrant the expense and that more pressing issues needed to be addressed. Again, this illustrates the failure of many within the administration who held authority to see gender as central and critical to the transformation of municipalities.

Research carried out in 1998 by GAP in ten urban local councils and two metropolitan local councils in the Western Cape served to reinforce this view. It indicated that most municipalities lacked an understanding of the structural nature of gender inequalities and how they played themselves out in the workplace. As a result, the councils were unable to develop appropriate strategies to enhance the representation of women (Van Donk 1998). In spite of international frameworks, constitutional commitments to gender equality, and national gender machinery, the achievement of gender equality within local government was limited. The under-representation of women had serious consequences for the transformation of local government as an institution and for the advancement of women within all levels of society.

PROGRAMME OF ACTION

At a groundbreaking symposium in May 1996, organised by the Commonwealth Local Government Forum and the interim body of organised local government, gender activists from local government within Southern Africa came up with a programme of action to transform gender relations in local government. This included the formation of machinery within local councils and organised local government bodies to promote the effective participation of women in local government, networking with gender organisations, and developing policy guidelines. Part of the programme of action for South Africa was an undertaking to work more closely with the CGE and the Office of the Status of Women (OSW).

The South African representatives, who formed themselves into an interim group, realised that, because of the autonomous nature of the 850 local councils, the best way of establishing gender mechanisms within local government was through the formation of gender working groups at national and provincial levels of organised local government. This, they hoped, would set a precedent for local councils who were members of the organised local government associations. Unfortunately, at the time of the meeting, the OSW was not yet adequately constituted and staffed and there was very little interface between these two initiatives. By about 1997-1998 the links between the provincial OSW representatives and provincial gender working groups in Salga were better established, allowing for a more co-ordinated approach to many gender issues and events.

The principle of gender equality enshrined in the South African Constitution and the government's commitment to The Convention on the Elimination of All Forms of Discrimination Against Women (CEDAW) were used to lobby the executive committee of the interim local government association over a period of months. There was much in-principle support from the executive committee which was keen to see concrete plans and programmes. Unfortunately, it was also involved in a number of other initiatives related to the establishment and recognition of Salga, and its support therefore remained ad hoc and unrelated to broader developments within the association. Its support did, however, result in a principled agreement to establish a gender working group, and in a commitment to enshrining gender equality in Salga's constitution. The Gender Working Group was formally instituted at the launch of Salga at the end of 1996.

The launch was preceded by a two-day workshop during which women spoke about their experiences and their feelings of inadequacy in engaging with their new roles and with the administrations. Many who had only basic literacy skills and spoke very simple English had never before had to speak at formal meetings and found the experience intimidating, especially when faced with patriarchal, patronising attitudes from their own colleagues. They were forced to engage with predominantly old-guard officials who had to reconcile their own prejudiced views of people (in terms of race, gender and language) with the situation that faced them. The women felt hopeless, and discussions often heaved with a sense of despair.

At the first meeting of the newly constituted Gender Working Group, the terms of reference initially framed by the interim group were reviewed and adopted as Salga terms of reference. The overarching aim was to represent, promote and protect the interests of women in local government in relation to national and provincial gender machinery, initiatives, policies, and programmes. This would require the development of training and capacity-building programmes. Gender policies were to be developed for application at all levels of local government, accompanied by the establishment of monitoring guidelines that could be translated into mechanisms. It was further agreed to form gender working groups with supportive administrative machinery. Open channels of communication and consultation between local, provincial and national gender working groups were seen as vital, as was the need for the Gender Working Group to network with provincial and national government, the non-governmental (NGO) sector, and business. In tandem with negotiations at national level, provincial gender working groups were formed, with one representative from each province nominated to serve on the national working group. Where provincial working groups were still in the process of being formed, the provincial executive nominated a representative.

At the first strategic planning session of representatives of the Salga Gender Working Group in October 1997 in Johannesburg, three priority areas emerged. Firstly, the ability to intervene in council budgets was of crucial importance in order to influence the way council resources were allocated. Councils needed to be transformed internally to make them more women friendly, and women needed to be trained in leadership skills. Underpinning these priorities was the commitment to establishing gender structures in the local authorities and the drawing up of guidelines for their establishment (Salga 1997).

Because of the lack of resources and capacity at provincial level, Salga's Gender Working Group took the lead in implementing the priorities by embarking on a national programme of workshops throughout 1998. These were conducted in three phases and aimed to enable some 4 000 women and men councillors and officials to understand gender considerations and incorporate them into integrated development planning and budgeting.

At the same time capacity-building programmes were run by the Women's Development Foundation, serving five provinces (Eastern and

Northern Cape; Northern Province; Mpumalanga and the North West Province. GAP operated in the Western Cape and provided similar advocacy work to strengthen links between women councillors and community activists. Despite a lack of national co-ordination between these NGOs and Salga at a training level, the same broad objectives were pursued. This cohesion can be attributed to the informal networks that had been cultivated among these groups as well as to the similarity of their experiences as women involved in building a democracy.

The formation of gender working groups in local councils, one of the key outcomes of the training – and a Salga resolution – was undertaken by the provincial working groups, with varying degrees of success. The attempt by Salga to set up a new form of organisation nationally was plagued by problems. While some provinces had sufficient resources (both human and financial) to set up provincial structures others either had no idea of how to do so and/or had too few resources. There also appeared to be a lack of political will within individual councils to support this new network.

From its inception to the end of 1999 the Salga Gender Working Group was serviced in an ad hoc capacity by an official from one of the councils. This made follow-through difficult, limiting the group's ability to implement programmes and coordinate with provincial working groups. As a result the working group was seen as failing to deliver. This situation was aggravated by understaffed and under-resourced provincial local government associations, which made communication and coordination between Salga, the provincial associations, and Salga's representatives extremely difficult. In most cases provincial associations were unable to provide regular administrative support to working groups, which affected attendance at meetings and workshops, the implementation of working group resolutions, and the circulation of documents requiring comment and feedback. As most councillors worked part time and had their own duties to perform, without administrative and technical support they did not have the capacity to implement programmes at provincial level or follow up decisions taken at national level (Naidoo 1997). This situation was compounded by a lack of leadership skills. The inability to engage in strategic planning was identified by councillors as hampering the operation of their working groups and their relationship with the Gender Working Group (Salga 1997).

The wider problem of the absence of an effective communications mechanism for sharing information over vast geographic areas was intensified with respect to the gender working groups because of the negative attitudes towards gender of the provincial directors and officials in individual councils. This coloured their responses to their responsibility to forward information to gender representatives. Added to organisational difficulties was the fact that large distances separated councillors, and, unlike their colleagues in provincial or national government, many did not have access to a telephone or transport. This led to inconsistent consultations between provincial representatives and their individual members. It further impacted negatively on the level of debate within the Salga Gender Working Group, and limited its ability to play a meaningful role in policy development. Each provincial working group thus operated largely in isolation.

Instead of the intended bottom-up approach where local municipal priorities would inform provincial issues, which in turn should have informed Salga's national programmes and approaches, the mode of operation worked in reverse. Programmes were initiated at national level and even driven nationally. The shortcomings of this approach manifested in an ad hoc response from women and men in local councils to training programmes. More importantly, there were difficulties in forming gender structures at local council level. Dissension in the provinces challenged the legitimacy of those heading provincial gender working groups.

The resistance to forming gender structures at local level arose out of a number of factors. One was the lack of sufficient funding. Financial constraints meant that gender was low on the list of priorities. A second factor stemmed from the lack of a common understanding of gender and its integral role in transformation. Many councillors, mostly men, were inclined to see gender as a women's issue or as affirmative action, and not as fundamental to every aspect of a council's culture and delivery. This approach meant that gender equality was not seen as a priority and consequently there was a reluctance to fund gender structures or to make staff available. Nor was there clarity, in spite of the development of terms of reference by Salga, on the role of council gender structures. At the root of these problems lay the continuing, and often unrecognised effect of the unequal power relations between men and women in local government politics and administration.

Since 1996 local government has been subject to restructuring to provide a more balanced distribution of resources and to promote efficiency. In this process, gender structures were not prioritised.

The hard lesson that has been learnt at all levels is that ad hoc approaches and programmes do not work, and that setting up gender structures without the necessary budget or technical support is an exercise in futility. The only way to achieve sustainable change would be to deal systematically with gender issues through the creation of resourced structures which take responsibility for the integration of a gender perspective internally with respect to council functions and administration, and externally with regard to the development and delivery of local government services.

THE REPRESENTATION OF WOMEN IN LOCAL GOVERNMENT

When, in 1995, local government elections were held throughout the country except in parts of the Western Cape and in KwaZulu-Natal, research conducted by Idasa's Local Government Information Centre (Logic) found that 19.4 per cent of all councillors elected were women. Although this meant that more women were present in local councils than at any other time, the figure was substantially below the 30 per cent critical mass considered necessary to shift gender balances in organisations.

The figure of 19.4 per cent was further broken down into PR seats and ward seats. Forty per cent of candidates for each council were elected via the PR list while 60 per cent came from wards or, in the case of metropolitan councils, were nominated from the primary local authorities. The percentage of women rose to 28.2 per cent (852 of 3 024) for the PR seats, but dropped to 10.87 per cent (368 of 3 3845) of ward seats. This election of women to PR seats was seen as consistent with international trends. The reverse is true, by implication, for ward seats where women are regarded as 'risky' candidates. The *White Paper* appealed to political parties to ensure that at least half the candidates on party lists for the next three municipal elections would be women (*White Paper* 1998).

Other factors that limited women's representation were political party bias towards male candidates, the influence of traditional leaders in rural communities, and popularly held stereotypes about who could participate in politics, linked to the shortage of women willing to stand, and public service practices which excluded women (Chan 1996).

The experience of local government in highlighting the disparity between women's representation via PR as opposed to ward seats prompted gender activists (including the Gender Reference Group of EISA) to agree to argue for the retention of PR seats at national and provincial level when the election laws came under review. There were also efforts by such organisations as GAP to ensure gender representivity in the selection of officials for the second election. By 2002 these efforts were being linked to a broader international campaign to increase the representation of women to 50 per cent.

Of elected councillors nominated to executive committees after the first local government election, 14.4 per cent (360 of a reported 2 502) were women. Most of these held mayoral or deputy mayoral positions which, under the system in existence at the time, were mainly ceremonial and were less influential than the positions of chairperson or deputy chairperson of the executive committee. Although party caucuses influenced, to a large extent, the way decisions were taken, and advised the executive committee accordingly, members of the executive committee wielded the most power. Mayors, however, had little influence on executive committee decisions. This situation changed after 2000, when a new local government system came into effect that gave power to elected executive mayors chosen by the political parties. Few women were selected as executive mayors in 2000. Before this, in many cases, political party caucuses supported women candidates as mayor because to do so was a means of acknowledging their responsibility to promote gender equity without necessarily relinquishing power. Parties dominated by male leadership benefited from these appointments by giving the impression of supporting the empowerment of women while in fact, in most cases, simply being politically expedient.

This view is supported by a second Idasa Logic Report produced in 1997 that found that in 73 of the 75 councils surveyed in KwaZulu-Natal, women were elected to 16.2 per cent of local government seats and occupied 15.69 per cent of seats on the executive committee (62 of the reported 395 seats) and in the Western Cape women were elected to 15.8 per cent of all local government seats in the province (272 of 1 717 seats) and occupied

12.98 per cent of executive committee seats. The report drew attention to the predominance of men in decision-making in metropolitan and regional councils, where policy and implementation decisions were made for local government. However, the 30 per cent critical mass was reached in urban KwaZulu-Natal, where women had close to 35 per cent representation on the metropolitan local councils in Durban, probably because of the ANC majorities on the councils and the party's compliance with its internal quota. The highest representation appears to have been achieved by women in the Cape Town area where they made up 25 per cent of the smaller local councils in the Cape Metro, and up to 45 per cent of the metropolitan council itself. At one stage both the chairperson of the executive committee and the mayor were women.

What these figures do not show is that women were not equally spread throughout local government, their presence varied from council to council. In some bodies, such as the Cape Metropolitan Council, it was as high as 45 per cent, while in others there was one woman, or, in rural councils, no women at all.

With the second local government elections in 2000 the issue of representation and quotas once again came to the fore, although this time women were able to use some important legislative provisions to lobby and mobilise. The political systems mooted for the new Unicity Councils in the 2000 elections created a new set of factors. The ANC supported the introduction of executive rather than ceremonial mayors. Executive mayors would wield a great deal more decision-making power than even executive committees and would not be obliged to take advice from their executive committees. It is significant that after this change was made very few women were elected to mayoral positions in 2000.

The Municipal Structures Act (1998) contained two important provisions relating to the elections. The first divided the number of PR and ward seats equally so more seats were available on a ward basis. The second 'encouraged', but did not oblige, parties to adopt a 50 per cent quota for their PR lists, and to alternate men and women. At the time this signalled an important victory for the work done by gender activists. Numerous submissions had been made about this issue by GAP, the CGE and Salga at the public hearings in Parliament. Advocacy organisations like GAP predicted that if parties adhered to these provisions the number of women represented at local government level would rise to 30 per cent. However Mirjam van Donk of GAP contended in August 1999 that unless civil society organisations and women within political parties exerted pressure on parties, the parties would ignore provisions calling for a quota. The situation did not in fact change significantly in the 2000 elections – the ANC retained its 30 per cent quota, while other parties did not introduce quotas at all.

While representation appears to be key, the struggle by gender activists within local government and NGOs extended beyond it to the issue of effective participation. This was clearly the consensus view at the Conference 'Entrenching Democracy and Good Governance through Women's Empowerment' organised in November 1998 by the Women's Development Foundation (WDF), CGE, the Women's Empowerment Unit, Salga, the Office on the Status of Women, and the Women's National Coalition. For the first time women from national, provincial, and local government, and from all political parties, discussed medium- to long-term strategies to increase women's participation in decision-making, institutional transformation, and capacity building.

Among the proposals was a creative media strategy to engage political parties about their commitment to the quota system for women. Lobbying for increased representivity and supporting the development of a uniform, non-partisan manifesto was also mooted, as was more strategic participation of women in voter education beyond the 1999-2000 elections. There was, further, a commitment to ensuring gender sensitive transformation processes within all institutions. and the development and co-ordination of training programmes for women in all spheres of government.

THE ROLE OF ORGANISED LOCAL GOVERNMENT IN ADVANCING GENDER EQUALITY

Although gender activitists and women politicians used the creation of access to political power as an important strategy it nevertheless has some serious limitations in practice. Thenjiwe Mtintso, former chairperson of the Commission on Gender Equality (CGE), and now ANC deputy secretary general, argued that while access is a quantitative leap towards transforming gender relations (in Parliament) it is not sufficient to achieve the qualitative changes that can produce gender equality (Mtintso 1999).

Although she was speaking about Parliament, the same observation is true of local government. Local government councils and their administrations are patriarchal both in structure and in operating culture. Most local government administrations have remained virtually 'unchanged' by the broader institutional transformation on which national and provincial government embarked. The nature of the responsibilities made it imperative that there be no break in the provision of services. It would not have served governance to have brought in a whole range of 'new' people with very little real experience of service provision at local government level. This obstacle to institutional transformation meant that in most councils it was business as usual. Newly elected councillors, without knowledge or experience, had to learn about processes and procedures while 'on the job', with little institutional support.

Councillors, both men and women, initially experienced a sense of powerlessness as agendas, meeting times, reports, and plans were drawn up by experienced officials. Tensions were inevitable when the new political dispensation found itself served by an administration with a very different culture. The desire for fundamental change led to clashes with old guard officials. As a result of feelings of inadequacy and mistrust ANC caucuses began to place the issue of the transformation of local municipalities firmly on the table. Gender activists, councillors, and, to an extent, officials who had their roots within the ANC began to think carefully about how best to challenge the status quo. The fundamental issue identified was that unless the structures and systems were transformed and operated differently, local councillors would remain at a serious disadvantage.

At a deeper, more intangible level, women councillors, 'progressive' officials, gender NGOs, and other community gender activists saw women being absorbed into the male workings of council if they were unable to challenge gendered assumptions about the systems. While working as a council official one of the authors experienced isolation from senior management team decisions, even though she was employed as an affirmative action officer. A council decision requiring her participation at all senior management meetings relating to transformation was often ignored or was implemented inconsistently. Challenges to the male status quo within management resulted in her being immobilised and frustrated so that even the most basic tasks were extremely difficult to carry out. An independent audit of this council also highlighted an extremely high degree of frustration and dissatisfaction among many staff members, in particular female staff, with the authoritative management style of most senior managers (audit report conducted by Simeka management consultants 1999).

SUCCESSES OF THE GENDER INITIATIVE

In spite of the frustrations experienced by women in local government, a review of the period 1996-2000 shows that an important foundation was laid for achieving gender equality in that sphere. It is still too early to determine whether this will lead to significant gains for women in terms of the delivery of services to improve their quality of life.

When the pre-interim structures of local government were set up in November 1994, gender equality was not even on the agenda of either local councils or associations of organised local government. In discussions about the model for national machinery, there was consensus that the 'National Machinery should be made up of an integrated package of structures, like three legs of a stool supporting the ideal of gender equality' (*Handbook* 1996). The three legs would be government (national departments), the legislatures (national and provincial), and independent bodies which 'rest on a platform of civil society structures'. Nowhere was there mention of local government in either the government or the legislative components, despite the fact that it is constitutionally regarded as a distinct sphere of government.

By the end of their first term, women in local government had raised awareness of the need for gender equality, significantly contributing to the creation of a political climate and framework which promoted gender issues in local government. The full impact of women in local government has yet to be assessed. However, trends suggest that their struggles have contributed in some visible ways. Among these is the fact that women are increasingly represented on decision-making structures. The appointment of a gender officer within Salga's administration after a four-year struggle is another indicator. Many more councils accepted the need for a gender officer or a gender focal point, and approached the national office for assistance in setting this up. Almost all municipalities participate in commemorative events on National Women's Day (9 August), and many metropolitan councils ensure gender representivity on selection and recruitment panels. Salga engaged in the development of a gender policy for all councils, and in Gauteng the provincial working group has developed a policy and process to deal with sexual harassment.

The effectiveness of gender policies and of gender transformation, however, depends on the continued commitment and mobilisation of gender activists at local government level. This requires gender activists to continue to enter local government, both as representatives and as officials.

POSTSCRIPT

David Pottie

As this chapter has indicated, the representation of women is one crucial aspect of women's participation in local government. This issue has assumed increasing importance as local government has begun to articulate the developmental responsibilities proposed for it in the Local Government *White Paper*.

South Africa held its second democratic local government elections in December 2000. This postscript provides a brief update of women's representation in local government following these elections and thus hopes to serve as a statistical point of reference to indicate some patterns of women's success as candidates in these elections.

After the 2000 elections the overall representation of women as elected councillors improved dramatically, with women comprising 28.2 per cent of all councillors. A total of 2 271 women were elected out of 8 044 seats.

This improvement was influenced, in part, by the mixed system used for municipal elections. Thus, while women won 28.2 per cent of local government seats overall, they were more successful on the party lists, where they achieved an average share of 38.1 per cent of seats, whereas they won only 16.9 per cent of ward seats nationwide.

In terms of political party representation 69.3 per cent of women ward councillors represent the ANC and 19.5 per cent represent the DA.

However, there were some important variations in provincial patterns of support for women by various political parties. For example, in several provinces, including Mpumalanga, Northern Cape, Northern Province, Eastern Cape and Free State, there were more women councillors from the ANC than from all other parties. By contrast, ANC and DA women achieved relative parity in Gauteng, with 46 and 40 ward seats respectively. DA women claimed 40 of the 68 ward seats won by women in the Western Cape, with ANC women winning the balance. In KwaZulu-Natal IFP women won 61 of the 96 ward seats that went to women, followed by the ANC with 23 and the DA with 12. UDM, UCDP and PAC elected marginal numbers of women as ward representatives.

Overall, these figures correspond to the general pattern of party support across the country, suggesting that while South Africans are willing to elect women as ward councillors, their choices remain primarily determined by party preference.

In the December 2000 elections, South Africans voted for three basic types of municipal councils: metropolitan, local, and district. Women comprised 18.4 per cent of ward councillors with Cape Town electing the highest number – 6 from the ANC and 19 from the DA – a total of 25 in 100 wards (25%). Johannesburg followed closely with 10 ANC women and 15 DA women (22.9%). Tshwane (formerly Pretoria) returned 15.7 per cent and Durban 12 per cent, with Nelson Mandela (formerly Port Elizabeth) returning only 11 per cent. None of the three women metropolitan mayoral candidates was successful.

Some provinces also revealed interesting patterns of distribution of women ward candidates between urban and rural areas. For example, in KwaZulu-Natal, 96 women won ward seats, of which 12 were in metro Durban (the ANC won 5, the DA 7). ANC women won an additional 19 ward seats throughout the province. By contrast, IFP women won all 61 of their ward seats outside metro Durban and all of the DA women who won ward seats did so in metro Durban

In other parties, these patterns of urban and rural support varied. For example, in the Eastern Cape, a total of 95 (15.8%) women won ward seats (ANC 82, DA 7, PAC 1, and UDM 5). But in Nelson Mandela, the only metro council in the province, women won only 6 ward seats (DA 4, ANC 2). Thus, ANC women won the overwhelming majority of their ward seats in local councils, and the UDM and PAC were frozen out of the metro council, while DA women won more than half their share of provincial ward seats in the metro.

Women ward candidates performed least well in Northern Province and KwaZulu-Natal and did best in North West (23.6%) and Northern Cape (23.1%) but over all there was an improvement on the previous national average of 11 per cent women ward councillors.

With women comprising nearly 30 per cent of local councillors, local government now matches the levels of national government. One can largely credit this achievement to the ANC's internal quota. In fact, the representation of women on the ANC party list exceeded the agreed 30 per cent, reaching 45 per cent. AZAPO, IFP and UCDP PR lists also included more than 30 per cent of women – a notable improvement over the figures in the 1999 national elections.

Women typically performed twice as well as party list candidates than as ward candidates and in both KwaZulu-Natal and Northern Province, they did three times better.

Both the party list quota of 50 per cent encouraged by the Municipal Structures Act, and the ANC's internal party quota provide possible models for the future improvement of women's representation in local government. Further reflection by South Africa's other political parties on their internal processes of candidate selection may create additional opportunities.

For the moment, South Africa's achievement of nearly 30 per cent women local councillors places the country on a firm footing for additional steps towards building a more equitable record of gender representation in its spheres of government.

APPENDIX

CHECK LIST FOR ENSURING GENDER EQUALITY IN THE CONTEXT OF FREE AND FAIR ELECTIONS

This list, although not exhaustive, is intended to serve as a mechanism for enhancing the free and fair aspects of an election[1], taking gender equality into account. Once this objective is attained, South Africa will be considerably closer to achieving genuinely free and fair elections.

The following conditions must be met:

Citizenship

- a definition and understanding of citizenship that has inherent in it a commitment to substantive equality with regard to gender.

Conduct of elections

- the structure managing elections must be committed to the concept of gender equality;
- in accordance with this commitment, the structure managing elections must employ women at all levels of its operation;
- all policy formulated and legislation promulgated which is relevant to the conduct of elections must give effect to substantive equality with regard to gender;
- all policy and legislation must be implemented to give effect to substantive equality; and
- the criteria for demarcating voting districts or constituencies (where applicable) must not affect women adversely. For example, a particular voting district must not be established so that it comprises areas in which women are particularly susceptible to violence or harm. In rural areas voting districts

must be established so that access to the voting station does not constitute any (further) impediment to the right of rural women to vote.

Registration of voters

- the right of women citizens to an effective, impartial and non-discriminatory procedure for registration of voters;
- the stipulation of clear criteria for the registration of voters: *inter alia* age, identification, and citizenship. Citizenship as a criterion must guarantee the right of men and women to vote in the same way; and
- the right of women citizens to easy access to registration stations.

The vote

- the right of women citizens to vote on a non-discriminatory basis in elections of legislative bodies;
- the right to vote for a political party with a record of addressing issues which affect women;
- the right to vote for a political party which has women in leadership positions;
- the right of every citizen to be eligible as a voter, subject only to disqualification in accordance with criteria established by law that are objectively verifiable and not subject to arbitrary decisions based on sex or gender;
- the right of women citizens to have equal and easy access to a polling station in order to exercise their right to vote; and
- the right of woman citizens to vote without fear of violence or intimidation.

Public office

- the right of women citizens to present themselves as candidates for election to public office;
- an express commitment to gender equality on the part of political parties;

- the inclusion of women in the structures that formulate party lists and choose election candidates; and
- the inclusion of women in decision-making in relation to the composition of party lists and choice of election candidates;
- an electoral system which facilitates the electoral success of women on party lists or as candidates;
- a mechanism inherent in the electoral system which facilitates the electoral success of women, for example, internal party committee quotas, voluntary party list quotas, mandated party list quotas, and double-member constituencies (where appropriate).

Voter education

- the state must ensure, through national programmes of civic and voter education, that the electorate becomes familiar with gender equality as central to electoral issues and procedures;
- civic and voter education programmes must entrench gender equality as a central feature of democratic citizenship;
- voter education programmes must develop an understanding of substantive equality with regard to gender;
- voter education programmes must be aimed specifically at women;
- voter education programmes must explain complex electoral processes in a manner which will be understood by illiterate voters (the majority of whom, in South Africa, are women);
- voter education workshops must take place at times suitable to accommodate the domestic and economic roles performed by women;
- voter education workshops must take place in venues accessible to women (these venues must be chosen to accommodate children who may have to accompany their mothers to workshops); and
- voter education workshops must take place in an environment in which women feel confident that they can express themselves without fear of disruption and ridicule.

Political opinions

- the right of women citizens to express political opinions without interference other than that permitted by law.

Access to information

- the right of women citizens to seek, receive, and impart information and to make an informed electoral choice.

Freedom of association, assembly, and movement

- the right of women to join, or together with others to establish, a political party for purposes of competing in an election; and
- the right of women party members and candidates to move freely within the country in order to campaign for election.

Campaigning

- the right of women party members, candidates, and voters to campaign on an equal basis with their male counterparts;
- the right of women party members to campaign on issues that are of particular concern to women, for example, domestic violence;
- the right of women party members, candidates, and voters to security with respect to their lives and property during campaigns (and throughout the electoral process);
- the content of campaign messages must be directed at men and women so that stereotypes are not entrenched;
- campaign messages must be formulated so that they express a commitment to substantive equality with regard to gender issues;
- the right of women party members and candidates to access to the media in order to put forward political views on an equal basis with their male counterparts;
- the provision and regulation of funding to political parties and electoral campaigns in order to ensure the promotion of

equality of opportunity between women and men candidates;
- the right of parties and of women and men candidates to equal access to government-controlled media for purposes of campaigning;
- the media must recognise the importance of gender equality as an important aspect of democracy and report on it in relation to an election; and
- the media must report on all women candidates as often as it reports on their male counterparts.

Secrecy of the ballot

- the unrestricted right of women citizens to vote in secret;
- women must be assured of respect for the integrity of their choice; and
- secrecy of the ballot must be explained to both men and women during voter education workshops.

Review of electoral procedures or decisions

- where the right of women citizens to vote or to be registered, or any other political right is negatively affected by an action or omission of the state, its organs, or officials, there must be access to a procedure which permits the review of such actions promptly and effectively before an independent tribunal or court.

NOTE:

1. See Guy S. Goodwin Gill *Free and Fair Elections: International Law and Practice* (1994) on suggested international standards for free and fair elections.

CONSOLIDATED BIBLIOGRAPHY

African National Congress. 1993. ANC Adopted List Process for National Elections.

Ahikire, J. 2000. 'Gender Equality and Local Democracy in Contemporary Uganda: Addressing the Challenge of Women's Political Effectiveness in Local Government'. Unpublished paper presented to a Conference on Local Government, Centre for Basic Research, Jinja, Uganda.

Albertyn, C. 1994. 'Women and the Transition to Democracy in South Africa'. In C. Murray (ed). *Gender and the New South African Legal Order*. Kenwyn: Juta & Co.

——— and B. Goldblatt. 1998. 'Facing the Challenge of Transformation: Difficulties in the Development of an Indigenous Jurisprudence of Equality'. *South African Journal on Human Rights* 14, 248.

———, B.Goldblatt, S. Hassim, L. Mbatha, and S. Meintjes. 1999. *Engendering the Political Agenda: A Case Study of South Africa.* New York: United Nations Institute for Research and Training for the Advancement of Women.

———, S. Hassim, and S.Meintjes. 1998. *Women's Participation in Electoral Processes: South Africa in Global Perspective*. Unpublished paper.

Alex-Assensoh, Y. and K. Stanford. 1997. 'Gender, Participation, and the Black Urban Underclass'. In C. Cohen, K.B. Jones and J.C. Tronto (eds). *Women Transforming Politics: An Alternative Reader.* New York: New York University Press.

Badat, S. 1995. 'Women Better Equipped'. *Democracy in Action*. Idasa.

Baden, S., S. Hassim, and S. Meintjes. 1998. *Country Gender Profile: South Africa.* Pretoria: Swedish International Development Co-operation Agency (SIDA).

———, S. Hassim, and S. Meintjes.1998. *Women's Participation in Electoral Processes: South Africa in Global Perspective.* Unpublished paper.

Ballington, J. 1998. 'Women's Parliamentary Representation: The Effects of List PR'. *Politikon* 25(2).

———. 1999. 'Gender and Elections: What Are the Issues?' *Election Update* 11. Johannesburg: Electoral Institute of Southern Africa (EISA).

———. 1999a. *The Participation of Women in South Africa's First Democratic Elections: Lessons from the Past and Recommendations for the Future.* Unpublished paper. Johannesburg: EISA.

———. 1999b. 'Political Parties and Gender Equality: What Do the Manifestos Say?' *Election Update* 14. Johannesburg: EISA.

———. 1999c. *National and Provincial Election Results, South African Elections, June 1999*. Johannesburg: EISA.

——— and G. Fick. 1999. 'Educating all Voters in Support of Multiracial Democracy'. In *Youth Voter Participation: Involving Today's Young in Tomorrow's Democracy*. Stockholm: International IDEA.

Bam, B. 2000. 'Forewords'. In J. de Visser, N. Steytler, and J. Mettler. *Electing Councillors: A Guide to Municipal Elections*. Cape Town: Community Law Centre.

Barrett, M. and A. Phillips (eds). 1998. *Destabilising Theory: Contemporary Feminist Debates*. Cambridge: Polity Press.

Britton, H. 1997. *Preliminary Report on Participation: Challenges and Strategies*. Unpublished mimeograph. Syracuse University.

Brown, W. 1998. 'Wounded Attachments'. In Joan B. Laudes. *Feminism, the Public and the Private*. Oxford: Oxford University Press.

Budlender, D. 1997. *Gender Issues at the Local Government Level*. Researched for the Commission on Gender Equality and Salga.

———. 1998. *Women and Men in South Africa: Report based on data from the 1995 October household survey* (the detailed statistical tables from that survey are available as 'October household survey', CSS statistical release PO317 (South Africa as a whole) and PO317.1 to PO317.9 (nine provinces). Directorate of Analysis and Statistical Consulting, Central Statistical Services.

——— et al. 1999. 'Synthesis Report on the Participation of Women in Parliament'. Researched for the European Union. Johannesburg: CASE.

Camay, P. and A. Gordon. 1996. *There will be Elections … An Evaluation of the Local Government Elections in South Africa*. Johannesburg: Co-operative for Research and Education (CORE).

Caul, M. 1999. 'Women's Representation in Parliament'. *Party Politics* 5(1).

Centre for Applied Legal Studies (University of the Witwatersrand) and the Commonwealth Secretariat.

Centre for Human Rights. 1994. *Human Rights and Elections: A Handbook on the Legal, Technical and Human Rights Aspects of Elections*. Geneva: United Nations.

Chan, H. 1996. *Women at the Periphery of Power: A Brief Look at Why Women are*

Under-represented in South Africa's Premier Democratic Local Elections. IDASA Logic.

Clarke, P. B. (ed). 1994. *Citizenship*. London & Boulder: Pluto Press.

Cock, J. 1997. 'Women in South Africa's Transition to Democracy'. In J. Scott, C. Kaplan, and D. Keates (eds). *Transitions, Environments, Translations: Feminism in International Politics*. New York: Routledge

—— and A. Bernstein. 1998. 'Diversity and Disadvantage: Feminist Perspectives from the USA and South Africa'. *Politikon* 25 (2), 17.

Coetzee, A. 1996. *The Experience of Women in Local Government in South Africa*. Paper prepared for the Commonwealth Local Government Forum and Major Urban Areas Association (MUAA), Johannesburg, 7-10 May.

——. 1998. *The Salga Experience of Gender Advancement in Local Government*. Paper prepared for Women in Local Government Forum organised by Municipal Development Programme (MDP), Harare, Zimbabwe, 12-14 May.

——. 1998. *The Role of Salga with regard to Gender Transformation in Local Government*. Paper for the Conference 'Entrenching Democracy and Good Governance through Women's Empowerment', Eskom, Johannesburg.

——. 1999. 'Harnessing the Power of Partnership for Gender Equality'. In A. Coetzee (ed). *The Election Bulletin* 2. Women'sNet and Commission for Gender Equality (CGE).

Commission on Gender Equality (CGE). 1998. *Gender Dialogue: Women, Politics and the Election*. Johannesburg: CGE.

Conover, P. J. 1988. 'Feminists and the Gender Gap'. *Journal of Politics* 50(4).

——. 1999. *Review of the 1999 General Elections: A Gender Perspective*. Johannesburg: CGE.

Convention on the Elimination of All Forms of Discrimination Against Women (CEDAW). *Report* Part II, Article 7, see www.un.org/womenwatch/daw/cedaw

CORE. 1994. *The People Shall Govern: A Dream Realised*. Johannesburg.

Council of Europe. 1997. *Final Report of the Group of Specialists on Equality and Democracy (EG-S-ED)*. Strasbourg.

Crow, Barbara A. 1997. 'Relative Privilege? Reconsidering White Women's Participation in Municipal Politics'. In C. Cohen, K.B. Jones and J.C. Tronto (eds). *Women Transforming Politics: An Alternative Reader*. New York: New York University Press.

Cullinan, K. 1993. 'Giving the vote meaning'. *Work in Progress* 90, 23.

Dahlerup, D. 1998. 'Using Quotas to Increase Women's Political Representation'. In A. Karam (ed). *Women in Parliament: Beyond Numbers*. Stockholm: International IDEA.

Dalton, R. J. 1988. *Citizen Politics in Western Democracies*. New Jersey: Chatham House.

Daniels, G. 1992. 'Frene on Feminism'. *Work in Progress* 82, 21–22.

De Kock, C. and D. Ehlers. 1994. 'Realising Voter Expectations'. In L. Schlemmer and I. Hirscheld (eds). *Founding Democracy and the New South African Voter*. Pretoria: HSRC.

De Ville, J. and N. Steytler. 1999. 'Introduction'. In J. de Ville and N. Steytler (eds). *Voting in 1999: Choosing an Electoral System*. Durban: Butterworths.

De Waal, J., I. Currie, and G. Erasmus. 1999. *The Bill of Rights Handbook* 2 ed. Cape Town: Juta.

Dietz, M. 1985. 'Citizenship with a Feminist Face: The Problem with Maternal Thinking'. *Political Theory* 13 (1).

———. 1992. 'Context is All: Feminism and Theories of Citizenship'. In Chantal Mouffe (ed) *Dimensions of Radical Democracy: Pluralism, Citizenship, Community*. London: Verso.

Dubow, S. 2000. *The African National Congress*. Johannesburg: Jonathan Ball Publishers.

Dundas, K.1996. *Let's Talk About Elections: The Theme*. London: Commonwealth Secretariat.

Education and Training Unit (ETU). 1998. *Gender and Development: Handbook for Councillors and Officials*. South African Local Government Association (Salga).

Edwards, M. 1991. 'Towards a Third Way: Women's Politics and Welfare Policies in Sweden'. *Social Research* 58(3), 677-705.

Electoral Institute of Southern Africa (EISA). 1999. *South African Observer Mission Report: The 1999 National Assembly and Provincial Elections in South Africa*. Johannesburg: EISA.

Enslin, P. 1995. 'Encounter with a Straw Man: A Rejoinder to Cross and Leroke'. *Perspectives in Education* 16, 329.

Fester, G. 1997. 'Women's Organisations in the Western Cape: Vehicles for Gender Struggle or Instruments of Subordination?'. *Agenda* 34.

Friedman, S. and L. Stack. 1994. 'The Magic Moment: The 1994 Election'. In S. Friedman and D. Atkinson (eds). *The SMALL Miracle: South Africa's Negotiated Settlement*, Johannesburg: Ravan Press.

Funk-Bridgman, M. 1994. 'Breaking the Silence'. *Sash*, January.

GAP and CGE. 1998. *Towards a Gender Sensitive Sphere of Local Government: Reflecting on the White Paper on Local Government*. Report of a seminar.

Gasa, N. 1998. 'National Machinery for Gender Equality'. In Harris and Reilly (eds). *Democracy and Deep-Rooted Conflict: Options for Negotiators*. International IDEA Handbook Series, 320.

Gear, S. 1999. 'The Hidden Costs of Housing'. *The Election Bulletin* 1(4). Women'sNet and CGE.

Geisler, G. 1998. *Parliament in Another Struggle of Terrain: Women, Men and Politics in South Africa*. Unpublished paper. Bergen: Chr. Michelsen Institute.

Gevisser, M. 1994. 'Crossing the Line'. *Work in Progress Supplement*, April/May.

Gilder, B. 1994. 'Voter Education: Democracy's First Challenge'. In L. Schlemmer and I. Hirscheld. *Founding democracy and the New South African Voter*. Pretoria: HSRC.

Giliomee, H., L. Schlemmer, and S. Hauptfleisch (eds). 1994. *The Bold Experiment: South Africa's New Democracy*. Johannesburg: Southern Book Publishers.

Goetz, A.M. 1998. *Getting Institutions Right for Women in Development*. London: Zed Press.

Goodwin-Gill, G. S. 1994. *Free and Fair Elections: International Law and Practice*. Geneva: Inter-Parliamentary Union.

Gouws, A. 1999. 'The Gender Dimension of the Election'. In A. Reynolds. *Election '99*. Cape Town: David Philip.

Govender, P. 1998. 'Foreword'. In D. Budlender (ed). *The Third Women's Budget*. Cape Town: IDASA.

Haffejee, F. 1999. 'Interview' with Sheila Camerer. In *Redefining Politics: South African Women and Democracy*. Johannesburg: Commission for Gender Equality.

Hassim, S. 1999. 'Gendering Parliament'. *Southern Africa Report* 14(3).

———. 1999. 'Consolidating Representation: Post-election Challenges'. *The Election Bulletin* (August). Women'sNet and CGE.

——— and A. Gouws. 1998. 'Redefining Public Space: Women's Organisations, Gender Consciousness and Civil Society in South Africa'. *Politikon* 25 (2).

Heater, D. *Citizenship: The Civic Ideal in World History, Politics and Education*. 1990. London: Longman.

Herrman, L. 1974. 'Solomon, Bertha'. In *Standard Encyclopedia of Southern Africa Vol 10*. Nasou Limited.

Hirst, P. 1990. *Representative Democracy and its Limits*. Polity Press.

Holcomb, D and L. Ndlela. 1997. 'Women Councillors in Local Government Western Cape and KwaZulu Natal'. Idasa Logic.

Horn, P. 1991. 'ANC Women's Quota: The Debate Continues'. *Work in Progress* 77, 37.

———. 1994. 'Women at the Crossroads'. *Work in Progress Supplement*, April/May.

HSRC. 1999. *Public Opinion on National Priority Issues – Election '99*. Pretoria: HSRC.

Independent Electoral Commission. 1994. *Report of the Independent Electoral Commission: The South African Elections of April 1994*. Pretoria: IEC.

Independent Mediation Service of South Africa (IMSSA). 1994. *Report on IMSSA's Voter Education Training Programme*. Johannesburg: IMSSA, August/September.

International Union of Local Authorities. 1998. 'IULA Worldwide Declaration on Women in Local Government'. Signed in Harare.

Inter-Parliamentary Union. 1997. *Democracy Still in the Making: Men and Women in Politics*. Geneva: IPU.

———. 1997. *Women: What the IPU is Doing*. Geneva: IPU.

Website. See http://www.ipu.org/wmn-e/world.htm

Jacobson, R. nd. *Gender and Democratisation: The Mozambican Election of 1994*. Unpublished paper. University of Bradford.

Johnson, R. W. and L. Schlemmer. 1996. 'National Issues and National Opinion'. In R.W. Johnson and Lawrence Schlemmer (eds). *Launching Democracy in South Africa*. London: Yale University Press.

Jones, B. and J. Ballington. 1999. *South African Elections June 1999: National and Provincial Results*. Johannesburg: EISA.

———. 1999. *South African Handbook of Electoral Laws and Regulations*. Johannesburg: EISA.

Karam, A. (ed). 1998. *Women in Parliament: Beyond Numbers*. Stockholm: International Institute for Democracy and Electoral Assistance (IDEA).

Kathree, F. 1995. 'Convention on the Elimination of All Forms of Discrimination Against Women'. *South African Journal on Human Rights* 11, 421.

Kaufmann, K. M. and J. R. Petrocik. 1999. 'The Changing Politics of American Men: Understanding the Sources of the Gender Gap'. *American Journal of Political Science* 43(3).

Kelley, M. 1992. *Choosing an Electoral System: Structural and Contextual Factors in Women's Political Participation*. Unpublished paper. Johannesburg: Centre for Applied Legal Studies.

Klaren, J. 1998. 'Legal Culture and Transformative Consitutionalism'. *South African Journal of Human Rights* 14.

Klingeman, H-D. and D. Fuchs. 1998. *Citizens and the State*. Oxford: Oxford University Press.

Kooma, S. 1994. 'NP's Bad News for Women'. *Sowetan*, 24 March.

Krennerich, M. 1996. 'Electoral Systems: A Global Overview'. In J. De Ville and N. Steytler (eds). *Voting in 1999: Choosing an Electoral System*. Durban: Butterworths.

Lang, S. 1997. 'The Ngoization of Feminism: Institutionalization and Institution Building Within the German Women's Movements'. In J. W. Scott, C. Kaplan, D. Keates (eds). *Transitions, Environments, Translations, Feminisms in International Politics*. New York: Routledge.

Levy, M. 1993. 'Women and Democracy'. *Die Suid-Afrikaan*, February/March.

Liebenberg, S. 1999. 'Social citizenship: Precondition for Meaningful Democracy'. *Agenda* 40, 59.

Lodge, T. 1999. *Electoral Information Digest: South Africa*. Unpublished paper. Johannesburg: EISA.

Lovenduski, J. 1986. *Women and European Politics: Contemporary Feminism and Public Policy*. Brighton: Wheatsheaf

—— and A. Karam. 1998. 'Women in Parliament: Making a Difference'. In A. Karam (ed) *Women in Parliament: Beyond Numbers*. Stockholm: International IDEA, 125-157.

Lowe-Morna, C. 1996. 'Strategies for Increasing Women's Participation in Politics'. Paper prepared for the Commonwealth Secretariat, November.

——. 1999. 'Overview'. In *Redefining Politics: South African Women and Democracy*. Johannesburg: CGE.

——. 2000. 'Women's Political Participation in SADC'. Presented at the conference on 'Towards Sustainable Democratic Institutions in Southern Africa, International IDEA, Botswana, May.

Madlala, N. 1994. 'Building a Women's Movement'. *Work in Progress Supplement*, April/May.

Mbere, N. 1999. 'Gender Analysis of Voter Education Material'. In S. Motara. *Women Voters March to the Polls*. Johannesburg: CGE.

Mandela, N. 1994. 'State of the Nation Address'. *Hansard*, 24 May.

Mansbridge, J. 1999. 'An Anti-essentialist Argument for the Descriptive Political Representation of Gender, Race and Sexuality'. Paper presented at the

Conference on 'Politics, Rights and Representation', University of Chicago, October 14-17.

Marshall, T. H. 1950. *Citizenship and Social Class and Other Essays*. Cambridge: Cambridge University Press.

Mathye, M. and S. Motara. 1999. 'Observations on Election Day 2 June 1999'. *Review of the 1999 General Elections: A Gender Perspective*. Johannesburg: CGE, 67.

Matland, R.E. 1998. 'Enhancing Women's Political Participation: Legislative Recruitment and Electoral Systems'. In A. Karam (ed). *Women in Parliament: Beyond Numbers*. Stockholm: IDEA.

Mbere, N. 1999. 'Gender Analysis of Voter Education'. *Review of the 1999 General Elections: A Gender Perspective*. Johannesburg: CGE, 35.

McLaughlin, T. H. 1992. 'Citizenship, Diversity and Education: A Philosophical Perspective'. *Journal of Moral Education* 21 (3), 235.

Media Monitoring Project, The. 1999. 'Media Coverage of Women During the 1999 Elections'. *Review of the 1999 General Elections: A Gender Perspective*. Johannesburg: CGE.

Meintjes, S. 1990. 'Looking for the Women's League? Leave a message…'. *Work in Progress* 70/71, November/December, 15-16.

——— 1992. 'Dilemmas of difference: The Women's National Coalition'. *Work in Progress* 81, 17.

———. 1993. 'Chartering Women's Future'. *Southern Africa Report*, November.

———. 1998. 'Gender, Nationalism and Transformation: Difference and Commonality in South Africa's Past and Present'. In R. Wilford and R. L. Miller (eds). *Women, Ethnicity and Nationalism: The Politics of Transition*. London: Routledge.

Mendus, S. 1996. 'Losing Faith: Feminism and Democracy'. In R. M. Stewart (ed). *Readings in Social and Political Philosophy* 2 ed. New York & Oxford: Oxford University Press.

Merton, M. 1994. 'Women's Votes Said to be in Jeopardy'. *Business Day* 9 March.

Minkoff, D.C. 1997. 'Organizational Mobilizations, Institutional Access, and Institutional Change'. In C. Cohen, K. B. Jones and J. C. Tronto (eds). *Women Transforming Politics: An Alternative Reader*. New York: New York University Press.

Ministry for Provincial Affairs and Constitutional Development. 1998. *The White Paper on Local Government*.

Mojola, P. 1994. 'Women Chary of Using their Power'. *Sowetan*, 8 February.

Moller, V. and T. Hanf. 1995. *Learning to Vote: Voter education in South Africa's 1994 elections*. Durban: Indicator Press.

Moon, J. and I. Fountain. 1997. 'Keeping the Gates? Women as Ministers in Australia, 1970-96'. *Australian Journal of Political Science* 32(3).

Morrell, R. 2001. *Changing Men in Southern Africa*. London: Zed Books.

Motara, S. 1999. 'Women's Participation in Voter Registration'. In *Review of the 1999 General Election: A Gender Perspective*. Johannesburg: CGE.

Mtintso, T. E. 1999. 'The Contribution of Women Parliamentarians to Gender Equality'. Unpublished Masters Dissertation, University of the Witwatersrand.

———. 1999. 'Women in Politics: A Conceptual Framework'. In *Redefining Politics: South African Women and Democracy*. Johannesburg: CGE.

Naidoo, S. 1997. 'Salga Gender Working Group: An Assessment: what we have achieved/way forward'. Report tabled at the Salga Gender Working Group meeting in December.

———. 1999a. 'Gender and Integrated Development Planning'. Unpublished research paper.

———. 1999b. 'Gender Equality High Priority on Salga Agenda'. *Salga Voice*, 4 June.

Negotiation News 13, 15 December 1993.

New National Party. 1999. *New National Party Women's Policy Document*.

Niemi, R. G. and H. F. Weisberg. 1984. *Controversies in Voting Behaviour*. Washington: CQ Press.

Norris, P. 1996. 'Legislative Recruitment'. In LeDuc et al (eds). *Comparing Democracies*. California: Sage.

Parliament of South Africa. 1998-1999. *Annual Report of the Joint Standing Committee on the Improvement of the Quality of Life and Status of Women*.

Okin, S. 1979. *Women in Western Political Thought*. Princeton, N. J: Princeton University Press.

———.1989. *Justice, Gender and the Family*. New York: Basic Books.

Oliver, A. 1994. 'Status of Women is Central in South African Election'. *National Catholic Reporter* 30 (25), April.

Oyegun, J. 1995. 'Challenging the Given: Women and Local Government'. *Beijing Agenda*, 18 July.

Phillips, A. 1989. *Engendering Democracy*. Pennsylvania: University of Pennsylvania Press.

———. 1991. *Engendering Democracy*. Cambridge: Polity Press.

——. 1993. *Democracy and Difference*. Pennsylvania: University of Pennsylvania Press.

Pottie, D. 1999. 'History'. See http://www.localelections.org.za/history/history.htm

——. 2000. 'Women and Local Government: By the Numbers'. In *Local Government Elections, Update No. 9*. Johannesburg: EISA.

Rai, S. 1996. 'Gender and Democratization: Ambiguity and Opportunity'. In R. Luckham and G. White (eds). *Democratization in the South: The Jagged Wave*. Manchester: Manchester University Press.

Randall, V. 1987. *Women and Politics: An International Perspective*. London: Macmillan and Chicago: University of Chicago Press.

Rantete, J. 1998. *The African National Congress and the Negotiated Settlement in South Africa*. Pretoria: Van Schaik.

Rebehn, M. 1999. *Learning to Trust Democracy*. Berlin: ABI.

Republic of South Africa. Constitution, Act 200 of 1993.

Reynolds, A. and B. Reilly. 1997. *The International IDEA Handbook of Election System Design*. Stockholm: International IDEA.

Reynolds, A. 1999a. *Election '99*. Cape Town: David Philip.

—— 1999b. *Women in African Legislatures and Executives: The Slow Climb to Power*. Johannesburg: EISA.

Rule, S. 2000. *Electoral Territoriality in Southern Africa*. Aldershot: Ashgate.

Rule, W. 1994. 'Parliaments of, by and for the People: Except for women?'. In W. Rule and J. Zimmerman (eds). *Electoral Systems in Comparative Perspective*. London: Greenwood Press.

—— and J. Zimmerman. 1994. *Electoral Systems in Comparative Perspective*. London: Greenwood Press.

Sapiro, V. and P. J. Conover. 1997. 'The Variable Gender Basis of Electoral Politics: Gender and Context in the 1992 US Election'. *British Journal of Political Science*, 27.

Schefer, R. 1992, 'Women talk votes and power'. *Democracy in Action* 6(7).

Seady, S. (ed). 1999. *Post-Election Focus 1999*. Johannesburg: Human Rights Committee.

Seekings, J. 2000. *The UDF: A History of the United Democratic Front in South Africa 1983-1991*. Cape Town: David Philip.

Serote, P., N. January-Bardill, S. Liebenberg, and J. Nolte. 1995. 'What the SA Parliament has done to improve the quality of life and status of women'. Report prepared for Parliament, Cape Town.

Shapiro, R.Y. and H. Mahajan. 1986. 'Gender Differences in Policy Preferences: A Summary of Trends from the 1960s to the 1980s'. *Public Opinion Quarterly* 50.

Shvedova, N. 1988. 'Obstacles to Women's Participation in Parliament'. In *Women in Parliament: Beyond Numbers*. Stockholm: International IDEA.

Sinclair, J. 1975. 'Women'. In *Standard Encyclopedia of Southern Africa Vol 11*. Nasou Limited.

Singh, M. 1990. 'Malibongwe Conference' Briefing. *Agenda* 6, 23-25.

Singh, R. 1996. *Designing and Implementing Electoral Education in South Africa: Reflections on an Action Research Project conducted by VEETU*. Johannesburg: University of the Witwatersrand.

Smith, S. 1997. 'Voter Information: Materials and Objectives, Public Awareness Programmes and the Gender Dimension'. In C. Dundas (ed). *Discussion of Election Issues in Commonwealth Africa*. London: Commonwealth Secretariat.

South African Local Government Association (Salga). 1997. 'Report on the Salga Gender Workshop', 10/11 October 1997 in Johannesburg.

——. 1996. Constitution of the South African Local Government Association (Salga) adopted at the inaugural meeting of the Association in Durban, 20 November.

Speak. 1994. 'Party Promises'. *Speak Election Supplement*, May.

Suzman, H. 1993. *In No Uncertain Terms*. Johannesburg: Jonathan Ball Publishers.

Tip, I. 1997. 'Creating Resources to Promote and Enhance Democracy and Free and Fair Election in the Southern African Region: Civic, Human Rights and Voter Education'. Paper presented at *NGO Roundtable: Strengthening Democracy through Civil Society*, Gaborone. Johannesburg: EISA.

Tremblay, M. 2000. 'Women, Citizenship, and Representation: An Introduction'. *International Political Science Review* 21(4), 339-344.

Turok, M. 1990. 'The Women's Quota Debate: Building Non-Sexism'. *Work in Progress* 76, 9.

Van Donk, M. 1998. *Women in Local Government in South Africa: From Marginalisation to Empowerment*. Research paper prepared for Women In Local Government Forum organised by Municipal Development Programme (MDP), Harare, Zimbabwe, 12-14 May.

——. 1999. 'Work starts NOW for Local Government Elections'. *The Election Bulletin* 1(6). Women'sNet and CGE.

——. 2000. 'Key Challenges for Gender Equity Presented by the Local Government

Elections'. Presented at *Challenging Gender Politics at the Local Level*. Cape Town: Gender Advocacy Programme (GAP), 31 May – 2 June.

Vincent, L. 1997. *Mother of Invention: Gender, Class and the Ideology of the* Volksmoeder *in the Making of Afrikaner Nationalism, 1918 to 1938*. Doctoral Thesis, Oxford University.

Vutela, Z. 1994. 'A Female Voice for New Parliament'. *City Press*, 20 February.

Walby, S. 1994. 'Is Citizenship Gendered?'. *Sociology* 28 (2), 379.

Walker, C. 1982. *Women and Resistance in South Africa*. London: Onyx.

Watson, B. 2000. *Educating Women Voters and Candidates for Gender Equality*. Occasional paper. Johannesburg: EISA.

WDF. 1998. Report on the 'Symposium on Entrenching Democracy and Good Governance through Women's Empowerment' convened by the WDF, CGE, OSW, WEU, NWC and Salga, November.

Wells, J. 1993. *We Now Demand!: The History of Women's Resistance to Pass Laws in South Africa*. Johannesburg: Witwatersrand University Press.

Wessels, E. 1993. 'Insight into Multi-Party Talks'. *Women's National Coalition News*, July-August.

Westcott, S. 1990. 'Not a great day for women'. *Democracy in Action*, July/August.

Williams, M. 1998, *Voice, Trust, and Memory: Marginalized Groups and the Failings of Liberal Representation*. Princeton: Princeton University Press.

Wixley, S. 1994. 'Out of Sight'. *Work in Progress Supplement*, April/May.

Women's Empowerment Unit. 1998. 'Needs Assessment of Women in Parliament'. MBM Change Agents.

Young, I. M. 1989. 'Polity and Group Difference: A Critique of the Ideal of Universal Citizenship'. *Ethics* 99(2), 251-272.

——. 1990. *Justice and the Politics of Difference*. Princeton: Princeton University Press.

Zondo, N. 1994. 'Women and the vote'. *Agenda* 20, 57.

——. 1995. 'Rural Women Pessimistic'. *Agenda* 26.

INDEX